11.11 STE

PRODIGAL DAUGHTERS

PRODIGAL DAUGHTERS

Catholic Women Come Home to the Church

Edited by
Donna Steichen

IGNATIUS PRESS   SAN FRANCISCO

Cover art: *Feast in the House of Simon*
by Philippe de Champaigne, c. 1656
Musée des Beaux-Arts, Nantes, France

Cover design by Riz Boncan Marsella

© 1999 Ignatius Press, San Francisco,
All rights reserved
ISBN 0–89870–732–3
Library of Congress catalogue number 99–73010
Printed in the United States of America ∞

For the contributors, who bared their private anguish and joy in hope that their experiences will help other wanderers to find the way home.

For all the prodigal daughters and sons in my heart and my prayers, that they too may soon return to their Father's house.

CONTENTS

INTRODUCTION

From unrequited love, it is said, we learn how God must feel. The truth in that remark is that God is not abstract love, but a Lover, whose love is astonishingly singular; He offers it not only corporately, to His people, but individually, to each heart, as ardently as if He had never created another in the entire universe to love. All the stories in this book are recollections of His courtship.

In times when the Catholic world is healthy, God woos most of us through the institutional channels of family, Church, and culture. But even today, when the family is fractured and the Church in turmoil, when little survives of traditional Catholic culture and the object of His love is apt to spurn Him for worldly pleasures, still His quest continues, until either He wins the heart of His beloved or death intervenes. When His courtship is successful and His love returned, He forgives past neglect and pours out His grace unstintingly; repentant sinners are as likely as anyone else to become saints. Blessed Josemaría Escrivá, founder of Opus Dei, urging his followers to welcome a penitent, once advised, "Remember that he may yet become an Augustine, while you remain mere mediocrities."

The second Person of the triune God demonstrated the depth of His love for us when He became incarnate as the man Jesus. The Church's Morning Prayer for Christmas Day says of His origin: "Your eternal Word leaped down from

heaven in the silent watches of the night." [1] Almighty though
He was, He did not come as an imperious king, or as some
kind of angelic sorcerer, to stun the world with His power.
Instead, He came as an ordinary mortal, subject to the pains
and risks of the human condition. Surrendering all majesty
and sovereignty, He entrusted His vulnerable infant body
to human compassion, appealing for love first with His
helplessness.

It was not only to teach us by example how to live that
Jesus became man. He came as the Messiah, the long-prom-
ised Savior, to suffer and die in order that the scales of onto-
logical order could perfectly balance mercy and justice in
judging men. No merely human person could reconcile God's
justice with His mercy, only Christ the Son, because He both
embraces and surpasses all mankind. [2]

Some people are troubled to learn that God's perfection
demands justice. They want to enjoy His mercy while denying His justice, because they think justice is cruel. In fact, as
Caryll Houselander wrote, justice is compassion:

> Justice is a supreme example of His love . . . Justice is the de-
> fense of the defenseless. It protects the weak, and restores to
> little ones those things of which they have been robbed by
> force. [3]

In so giving His life, Jesus revealed what kind of being God
is: a Creator of perfect compassion, whose perfection requires
justice but who so loves the persons He made that He sent
His only Son to ransom them from the insuperable penalties

[1] From Wis 18:14: "For while gentle silence enveloped all things, and the
night in its swift course was not half gone, thy all-powerful word leaped from
heaven, from the royal throne" (RSV).

[2] *Catechism of the Catholic Church* (CCC), 616.

[3] Caryll Houselander, *Wood of the Cradle, Wood of the Cross* (Sophia Institute
Press, 1966), 123.

due in justice for their sins. And He offers us this salvation by inviting each unique soul, individually, to live with Him forever in Heaven.

Christ's Resurrection is both a sign of fulfillment and a promise that even the repentant may attain it, a sign that His love has brought humanity into God's glory,[4] and a promise that all who live in faithfulness to His covenant can one day share that glory.[5]

Jesus describes the purpose of His life in three related parables about the relationship between God and sinners. In the first, He compares God to a devoted shepherd who leaves the main body of His flock to search out a single lost sheep. In the second, He compares Him to a tenacious housewife who stops all other activities to search for one lost coin. Finally, in the third, He compares Him to a desolate father who watches without ceasing for the return of a wastrel son.[6]

This story of the Prodigal Son is the most fully developed of the parables. In it, He incorporates three familiar models of human behavior: the needy remorse of the bankrupt spendthrift, the jealous, unforgiving rectitude of the elder brother, and the endlessly faithful love of the father, solicitous not for himself but for his beloved lost child. Despite the title, the central character in the story is neither the prodigal son nor his sanctimonious brother, but the father with God's heart, who watches and yearns for the absent sinner with selfless love. When the son, hungry and humiliated, turns homeward at last, his father rejoices without recrimination.

So poignantly does Jesus portray him that this father is universally recognized as an icon of God's tenderness toward the

[4] CCC, 656.
[5] CCC, 655, 658.
[6] Lk 15.

sinner. Even people whose perspective is otherwise entirely
secular respond to the theme of pure mercy and forgiveness
in this parable. If we live our faith well, we hope eventually to
come to reflect the Father. In the meantime, whether sons or
daughters, most of us can see ourselves in the different characters of this parable at different times in our lives.

When we hear about prodigal sinners, however, we ordinarily expect them to be sons, like the figure in the parable.
Throughout history, human societies have expected daughters to be more pious than sons, more constant in fulfilling
the duties of their faith. Four hundred fifty years before the
daughters of Jerusalem wept and prayed along the way of the
Cross, Sophocles' Antigone witnessed to the same expectation among pagan Greeks. Around the world and down the
centuries, women have filled most of the pews at pre-dawn
Masses, at Vespers, at Compline, at Rosaries and novenas.

During the past three decades, however, it became impossible to take feminine fidelity for granted. The 1960s were
years of worldwide cultural revolution, and women, culture-
bearers to the family, were significant both as instigators and
as targets. In China, Mao's Red Guard tried to crush all traces
of tradition and redefine female roles along communist party
lines. Among the young in the United States, anti-war activism fused with sexual permissiveness and drug experimentation in an antinomian "peace movement" that was often
contradictorily violent. Those upheavals in society, followed
by the ascent of feminism and postconciliar disorders in the
Church, combined to draw women into rebellion as never
before in history.

Mutiny has raged like a typhoon through American Catholicism since the mid-1960s, as theological dissenters have
tried to tear down the traditional, hierarchical Church and
install in her place a bureaucracy shaped and dominated by

the spirit of the age. The rebellion began in Rome, during the Second Vatican Council, when manipulative clerical change agents, their theology rooted in the nineteenth-century Modernist heresy, put political "spin-doctoring" to ecclesiastical use. Citing ambiguous phrases from conciliar documents, they easily persuaded like-minded reporters that the Council Fathers were replacing the Church's ancient teachings with a sensational and permissive "new theology".

Exposure to this procedure radicalized observers from the relatively unsophisticated United States, especially when they saw the spinners' spurious opinions embraced by the world's media as "the Spirit of Vatican II". As president of the Congregation of Major Superiors of Women (soon to evolve into the Leadership Conference of Women Religious), Sr. Mary Luke Tobin, S.L., audited the Council's final session. On returning to North America, she was one of the enthusiasts of change who helped weave that "new theology" into a deliberate rebellion against traditional Catholicism. In 1987, Sr. Tobin reminded an audience of Women-Church extremists how important strategic language had been to the campaign for change.

" 'The Church Is Changing!' Wow, did we use that!" Tobin chuckled. "People didn't know how to respond! They didn't ask why it was changing, or who was changing it. So we ran with the ball while we had it. You run with the ball while you have it, too, around the end or straight down the middle." [7]

Sr. Tobin and other ideologues of change, in collaboration with avant-garde "feminist theologians" and strategists like Rosemary Radford Ruether, Elisabeth Schussler Fiorenza, Sr. Theresa Kane, R.S.M., Sr. Marjorie Tuite, O.P., Mary Jo Weaver, and Sr. Joan Chittister, O.S.B., targeted women in a

[7] Donna Steichen, *Ungodly Rage: The Hidden Face of Catholic Feminism* (San Francisco: Ignatius Press, 1991), 174.

public relations campaign designed to foment rebellion against Church authority.

Among those swept off their feet by its wake were most of the women whose histories are included here. Propaganda slogans—such as "The People Are the Church", "If It Feels Good, Do It", "A Woman's Right to Choose", and "It's All Relative"—moved some Catholic lay women to enlist in the mutiny because it seemed to promise liberation, autonomy, and empowerment.

One of the writers in this book, Constance Buck, tells of becoming an early member of the National Organization for Women, a thoroughly secular feminist, who for years looked to her consciousness-raising group as a substitute spiritual director. Juli Loesch Wiley describes how she lost her faith to the anti-war movement and found it again, ironically, in a religious community that was deteriorating into religious feminism.

Most of the other writers were affected by the prevailing climate of rebellion as well, though overt feminism was seldom the principal cause of their defections. Instead, the movement of these women away from the Church most often began in unexamined conformity to society's attitudes. For example, accepting her peers' opinion that relativism is the only absolute truth, Rosemary Hugo Fielding drifted across the globe with the currents of transient spiritual fashion. Referred by her insurance company to a center for "pain control" training, Moira Noonan became an adept in the occult arts of gnostic New Age spiritualism. Kathleen Howley scorned religion as a crutch, until she recognized that she herself was depending on a chemical crutch to "feel good". An unexpectedly large percentage were made religious refugees by their parents' loss of certitude, including Julie Baker Maguire, Maureen Cassidy Quackenbush, and Deborah Beauman Harvey,

Liturgical change is a common ingredient in the accounts of apostasy. Contraception is another. One writer, Marcella Trujillo Melendez, found her immature faith inadequate to sustain her through her mother's early death and its tragic aftermath. Concluding that the God who allowed such suffering must be cruel, she shut Him out of her life for years. And as Leila Habra Miller indignantly reports, simple ignorance of Church doctrine has been a major contributing factor in the phenomenon of defection. Like the largest part of her generation, she was a victim of purportedly Catholic institutions that had shifted aim without notice.

Few of the writers recognized, at first, the revolutionary agenda and manipulative strategy of the mutineers. Like most women of the time, Zoe Romanowsky and Allyson Smith were unaware that what was underway was a culture war; they thought their lives were unfolding naturally. But all of them were wounded, and for various reasons, at various times, all stopped practicing the Catholic faith.

Their stories make it plain that when they left the barque of Peter, the authors were uprooted, scattered, disoriented. Most wandered into a desert, to vanish into the box canyons of social modernism or the alkali-flats of heterodox spirituality. A few, like Mary Epcke Kaiser, retreated to enclaves of the religious right; many allied themselves with the Pelagian idealism of the left. Debby Beauman Harvey and Diane Yelenosky Spinelli joined a flood of Catholics seeking reassurance in Christianity without the sacraments. Others, like Zoe Romanowsky, looked for ultimate meaning in nature, as Mary Partridge Pease did in the arts, Moira Noonan in New Age occultism, and Constance Buck in academic and professional achievement. But wherever they went, whether they wore laurels or scarlet letters, their Father never stopped seeking them.

Within their hearts, He continued to whisper and tug, and so they remained unsatisfied. Some of the narrators are among countless fortunate Catholics who recovered their bearings when they heard the prophets God has sent to the present age. A surprising number of the writers report that God reached out to them in extraordinary spiritual experiences. Others were led by His grace to the intellectual light that allowed them to recognize changeless truth.

All of these writers heard God murmur in the hollow of their hearts where He had once lived, and so they continued to hunger for almost forgotten meaning. He followed them, setting traps, catching their attention with whispers and echoes of memory, with sudden, powerful waves of longing, with prophetic voices, until at last He caught them in snares of grace. Now, they are all at home again in the Catholic Church, grateful witnesses to His mercy, eager to tell about their encounter with the Love that raised them back to life.

These women are representative of a vital movement in the Catholic Church today, a current running counter to the flood of contemporary corruption. A vigorous and growing stream of humble believers is seeking to join the Body of Christ in its fullness, despite shocking scandals, casual betrayals, and self-serving deceptions committed by some who should have been her heralds. Many prodigals are coming home, so many that they have been tagged with a categorical label as "reverts".

So unexpected is this phenomenon that it makes God's initiative in their return indisputably evident. He appears to be filling up His wedding banquet with humble sinners who admit their sinfulness and praise the riches of His merciful love. Now, as mothers or in other apostolic work, they are engaged in restoring the Church from her foundations.

The repatriation of these prodigal daughters is a bitter disappointment to the graying insurgents. Their hope for an ecclesial coup d'état has hinged on selling a new feminist religious paradigm to Catholic women. Over and over, they insist they have done so, though anyone attending weekday Masses, from 1965 up to this morning, knows that women still predominate among worshippers.

"Women are leaving the Church in droves", the rebels declare, averting their gaze from the reverts and pointing instead to a recent Lilly Endowment study that claims young Catholics are not returning to traditional Catholicism in large numbers. Given the state of society and the prevalence of doctrinal illiteracy, we should not be surprised if "reverts" do not yet constitute a majority of the younger generation. Yet the writers in this book, and others like them, constitute a vital remnant, a yeast in the measure of flour that can eventually leaven the whole of society.

Here are their stories.

Donna Steichen

When Good Things Happen
to Bad People

(or How I Learned to Stop Sneering and Love the Lord)

Mary Lou Partridge Pease

Immersed as we are in a self-revelatory culture, one is loath to add to the blather. Only the desire to recount some of the lavish gifts of our Lord, the very gracious Christ, persuades me to tell this story—which is a comedy, I hasten to assure you.

In a nutshell, it's the tale of a willful little girl who ripened into an arrogant, intellectual young miss (and, eventually, Mrs.), then ultimately got her desserts through that same intellectualism. Her folly revealed, she was compelled to turn 180 degrees around, providing the audience with a fitting chuckle. A comedy, I say, produced by the boundless generosity of God.

First among the gifts God gave me were good and kindly parents, who, though not demonstratively pious, were conscientious in bringing their children up in the sacraments and providing them a Catholic education through grade eight. Second, He gave me a quick, bright mind that easily assimilated the truths of the catechism I was faithfully taught by dedicated Sisters of St. Joseph of Carondelet. Without that indoctrination in the faith, I would not be writing this today.

At least through 1962, when I was in their charge, those nuns were wonderful, faith-filled teachers. Let us take a moment to thank God for them, and for the many other holy men and women who gave us that knowledge by which we could all find our way home if we were lost in later years.

Pride and a different kind of obtuseness sometimes go with above-average intellect; at least they did in me. I reckoned many people not up to my caliber, including some of my teachers. Everything put in front of me I handled with ease, and often with boredom. Soon I grew impatient. Where was the good stuff, the challenging, exciting stuff? I found it at last, in philosophy, in literature, in art.

By age seventeen I was a complete atheist—not out of re-bellion, not out of hatred for the Church or for some per-ceived wrong, not even because she had rules that might interfere with one's pursuit of sexual fulfillment (though one can never totally discount that in one's motives). No, I had been given all the gifts, and I had read all the right books—just up to the point where I was certain organized religion was a collection of comforting, or cautionary, fairy tales, con-ceived as a crutch for simpler folk than me. I truly thought it a fact that God did not exist. Period. And how could I be mistaken? I, the honor student, the award recipient, the win-ner of scholarships, the valedictorian in a class of almost eight hundred? The dogged pursuer of truth, the vestal of reason?

(Understand that I concede there was some good in this sentiment, that I know the love of truth is a very high and good object, and that I really was, for the most part, honest in holding my error at the time. But what a cliché it is, isn't it? The foolish intellectual!)

Returning to the graciousness of our Lord, it was at about this time that I met my dear husband, who, after my faith, remains the greatest gift of my entire life. Another fallen-away Catholic, he was several years older than I was, very, very bright (even up to my exacting caliber!), and an admirable and attractive man to boot. He swept me off my feet; we got married when I was eighteen and he twenty-one, to the horror, chagrin, and dire predictions of nearly everyone. Of course we did not get married in the Church, because that would have been hypocritical, as neither of us believed in her. Besides, we had hopelessly antagonized the parish priest by coming in and smugly telling him our plans for a simple, non-Catholic, Catholic ceremony. He was not amused and refused to marry us unless we did it with the works, meaning a full nuptial Mass. We grandly refused, and he grandly ushered us out. Period, again.

How absurdly generous God is with His goodness. Why should insufferable, thoughtless kids such as we were be given the gift of each other, a determination never to part, and succeeding years of ever-increasing love? Others surely deserved it much more than we did. I pray every couple may be given the same amazing providential grace that has been granted to us.

Meanwhile, our early married years were marked by frenetic activity. We were both in theater and music; we were involved in the art scene to an extent. Lots of parties—lots of dash—the university—*la vie bohème* about describes it.

Now note the wiliness, the subtlety of a loving God. What to do with a proud little twit who fancies herself a bravely independent thinker and big-time intellect? Why, appeal to that pride, naturally. This He did by putting in front of me an essay (by whom I do not recall, but thank you, whoever you were) that stated that most people who fancy themselves independent thinkers are in fact only parroting lines fed them by writers of editorials and magazine essays.

I was stung, I'll tell you. For some reason, I took this as a direct challenge. In our front yard at that time I had a lawn sign for a Democratic candidate for a local office. All right: Why? *It was there because I was a Democrat, naturally.* And why was I a Democrat? *Well, because we were all Democrats, weren't we?—oops. No, because we were all liberals, and the Democrats were the liberals, weren't they?* Well, why was I a liberal? *Because we are all liberals—oops again!* Could I be one of those people who act on dull prejudice, not on personal conviction? Perish the thought! So I felt compelled to undertake a review of liberal and conservative, the better to understand why I was the one and not the other.

You can probably see where this was tending; a very dangerous line of investigation indeed. But this intellectual attack on my self-satisfaction didn't come unaccompanied. In and around this time I was given the other of my greatest gifts, my children. When I got to the "liberal" dilemma, I had two precious daughters. Those readers with children will no doubt concur that they wonderfully change one's whole perception of the world and its meaning.

Our good God has given us women a very concrete, elemental connection to the reality of creation. Thus I was led profoundly out of myself and into an awe of the mystical presence of Something by my joy in new life, by the desire to sacrifice for my little ones, by a fierce maternal love that told me this couldn't be all accidental, that the non-being of these children would not have been just the same as their being. By the time my second daughter was eighteen months old, her big sister was five and ready to start school. The liberalism project was not looking so attractive by then. Strange, is it not, that when it comes to our own children, most of us abandon the disinterested stand on theory and get really choosy? To wit: Wait a minute, that's my child you want to take and mold, and I find that I have extremely definite views on the subject.

Also, by that time I had all but completed my study of liberalism and conservatism and had found to my embarrassment that I was in fact a conservative, at least on many issues. Only conservatives, it seemed, cared about getting it right more than about having benign intentions. It was they, it seemed, who really valued the contributions of those sages of the past whom I had read, liberals preferring the wisdom just around the corner, or whatever was new, which apparently amounted to the same thing.

All this put my atheism in a compromised position, for as I extended my reading list, I bumped into authors insinuated there by the good and artful Lord. Let me quickly drop names as various and, for me, salubrious as St. Augustine, John Donne, Samuel Johnson, and Blaise Pascal. Crashing into the mountains of their genius, I simply couldn't ignore the fact that these giants were immeasurably beyond me in every respect, yet somehow were Christians. Nor was their faith separable from their genius: it was absolutely central.

Matters developed rather more quickly then. There were the new acquaintances, the first in my experience with people whom I greatly admired and respected, who "happened" to be Christians. Talented, learned people. People, as my eyes were now open wide enough to see, who were my betters in practically everything, yet somehow were believers. Could there be something to this religion business?

I was given a period to think it over. Now I was in a position to see that faith was attractive, and beneficial, and perhaps even true. It might be good, I thought, to join these folks who seemed so much happier and more settled in their approach to life than I was. The existential position of having to create one's own reality, one's own good and evil, I was finding to be a very tiring, hapless task. Truth be told, I really didn't believe any more that the world works that way. But now I wanted faith and found I didn't have it: I didn't think the story was true. One cannot simply order up faith on demand. It must be granted by God Himself, and He was going to make sure I was serious about accepting it before making any offers.

After allowing me to stew for a few months, maybe half a year, God set me to thinking about the Bible, that recounting of salvation history. I knew that it was a collection of wisdom sayings and legends and that it had been put together by clever scribes and priests who wanted to buttress their own construction of reality. Manufactured myth, in other words. This in spite of the fact that I had not myself actually ever read the Bible, anyway not more than tiny snips or paraphrased stories.

One unforgettable day, when my older daughter was at school and the younger was safely down for a nap, a small, proud voice inside taunted me: *How do you know the Bible is all fairy tales?*

Well, everyone knows that, I said to myself. *How could the men in religious power structures keep their power if they didn't have a book of myths to validate them?*

Everyone? How do you know it isn't true?

Well, one can see they've made up a bunch of stuff in the New Testament to make it look like the ambiguous sayings of the Old have come true. They jury-rigged it. And it's filled with miracles, things that are completely against reason and science. (This although in fact I knew very well that miracles are not really *against* science at all, but rather *above* it.)

Such an independent thinker! the voice sneered. *You haven't even addressed the text, have you?*

I don't need to!

What are you afraid of? If it's as transparent as all that, a smart person like you should be able to dismiss it in ten minutes.

I would, but I don't know where I'd get one. Money's tight, I can't just go out and buy one.

There's a Bible that used to belong to your brother-in-law in the bookshelf behind the couch, down on the lower shelf. Go on, take a look, see for yourself. The voice did not actually add, *I dare you.* It didn't need to. And I have never heard it again.

I went to the bookshelf, bent down, and saw the book immediately. With trembling hands and a dry mouth, I took it up. After twenty-two years, I can still recall the light in the room, the arrangement of the furniture, just where the book was on the shelf, and my physical reactions. I was physically unsettled. Sitting on the couch, I opened it to Genesis and began to read the fables that are called the Old Testament. I was confronted by episodes such as God calling to Abraham: "Abraham!"

"Ready, Lord."

I still shiver thinking about those words. Anyone who has read much—or even a little—of the literature of antiquity will know that this is unprecedented stuff. It wasn't so much the content, with which I was somewhat familiar through childhood Bible stories and a high school literature class that had used the Bible as a source. It was much more that I was alive to the unique nature of both the claims and the mode of presentation. Anyway, by hit or miss, guided, naturally, by the hand of the gracious Lord (why would He go to the trouble with me? I still marvel), I dipped in here and there. The prophecies of Isaiah, the strangeness of Job and Jonah, the facticity of Kings, and the overriding consistency of the claim that God was directing all this were the things that most impressed me, who had just done a large college project on the historical-critical tradition of Homer's works.

How much time passed I cannot say. Line after immortal line, unlike any other literature in the world, reeled away under my scanning glance. Lower and lower sank my heart. More and more rocklike grew the mountain of testimony in front of me.

Finally flipping to the end, I took a deep breath and tried to reassure myself: *that's only the Old Testament.* The damning part, the really fraudulent part, must be in the New Testament. *Oh, yes, there's still the whole New Testament; I could still possibly be right!* I didn't murmur this to myself with much conviction, however.

A good thing, too, because three minutes into the Gospel of Mark, the hair on the back of my neck began to stand on end. Speeding along now, I saw that it was all over. What was before me was of course the crowning glory. What on earth! It was not possible as a text unless it were true. Men simply do not construct such things, at least not in this universe. I knew very well that this had nothing to do with any other categories of first-century literature or philosophy. There were enough familiar words to make it intelligible Greco-Roman human language, but the import was absolutely astounding. What was in the New Testament was completely different from what was in the Old, yet it obviously fulfilled that which had come much earlier, and in surprising, unpredictable, unaccountable ways. People who think they know it don't read it with fresh eyes. Someone who came here from Mars and read it in light of the Old Testament would see what a blindingly remarkable corpus it is.

What was my reaction? Finally, I closed the book in my lap and sputtered a curse. I had been wrong! Completely wrong. Everything I had dismissed, so wittily and so often, was true.

My friends, this ought to be a laughing matter. And as the climax of a comedy, no doubt it was. It did not feel very amusing or pleasant at that moment, however, because I understood what the implications were.

While it might have been a suitable subject for a Restoration theater piece called "The Matron's Comeuppance", being wrong about this was not so light a matter as just any old intellectual error. To be wrong about the very ground of Being, about First Principles, about the fealty owed a Creator, has rather darker consequences than to have erred about the flatness of the earth, say, or the identity of the sea peoples. To be wrong in this way is to mistake what is good and what evil. To live according to the doctrine that God doesn't exist necessarily affects one's behavior, one's thoughts, one's goals and desires. They won't be His behavior, His thoughts, His goals and desires.

In short, in the light of His reality, they will be sin. That's what we are talking about. And sin is not ever funny. Sin is ugly. When it is recognized, it disgusts everyone who hears of it, not least the sinner. Sin hurts others. Sin wrecks much. Sin is bleak and an affront to God and man. And I saw that I was indeed a sinner. A bitter recognition, then, and this day still. God forgive me.

Of course, it was also a defining moment, and another of the tremendous gifts of our Lord. When my daughter Anna went down for her nap, I had been a dissatisfied atheist. When she woke up, her mama was a Christian. Not a good one, nor a practicing one, but a Christian all the same, and sure in the conviction that had been graciously bestowed on her that whatever was required of her she would do, as far as she was able. And thus began the road back to the Catholic Church, through repentance, recollection, reading, and prayer, the road so faithfully prepared back in grade school by those good nuns. The road led to the home I now love so deeply, the

Mystical Body of Christ. Where, I wish to say, my beloved husband joined me a few years later, where today we abide as a family, along with our children, now six in number, and dear children-in-law.

Truly, all's well that ends well. Truly, it's a divine comedy.

૨૾

A lifelong resident of Minneapolis, Minnesota, Mary Lou Partridge Pease began voice studies at fifteen, married Greg Pease at eighteen, and spent the next four years playing leading roles in local musical comedy, while completing her B.A. degree at the University of Minnesota. After her conversion and the birth of her third child, in 1978, she gave up professional singing to raise her children. In her spare time, she says, "I play the violin badly (took it up at age thirty-eight), but I love it so much that I wish I had gotten this instrument when I was three, like a sensible person." A grandmother of three, she currently works with her husband designing and managing websites for small to medium-sized companies.

My Bumpy Road Home

Juli Loesch Wiley

I was a cradle Catholic, but I left the Church when I was eighteen years old. A few years later, I started back, but my road home was bumpy and indirect. The problem in explaining it is that there wasn't one identifiable moment when I left the terra firma of the faith, and another when I climbed out of the swamp water and came back. For a while when I was still in, I was on the way out; and for a while when I was out, I was drifting back in.

In the early 1970s, when I was in my early twenties, I was a syncretist feminist-pagan-Christian. Other confused women are evidently in that same place today. I know how it feels, because I've been there. With the help of God's grace, I'll never be there again.

I believed then that restructuring Catholicism along non-patriarchal lines would be a spiritual work of mercy, useful to global progress. I thought it would be rather a hoot, too, since the enemy was ridiculous and already tottering, and the victory of Uppity Women assured. So I signed up as a lay associate with congenial Benedictine Sisters who seemed to be traveling on the same road.

Over the next decade, though, I found myself reevaluating my itinerary, cautiously applying the brakes, then doing a U-turn and coming about in the opposite direction. It is hard for me to explain, even now, why I changed. Of course, I can

29

say, "It's all grace." But *how?* And *when?* And *why?* In some senses, it still isn't clear to me.

It does connect in my mind, however, to a spiritual crisis I had suffered years earlier. Such experiences are not uncommon, I'm told; maybe such crises converge with the emotional bewilderment that often accompanies changing bodies and fluctuating moods in adolescence. It may have to do with hormones. It also has to do with faith. My grip on my faith—and my reason—loosened once when I was thirteen. I almost willed myself dead. When I came back to my right faith, I was in my right mind.

My mother and father were steady, gentle, domestic folk. All through my childhood, my father did unskilled labor at a laundry. He never made a penny more than the minimum wage. He walked home every afternoon sweat-soaked and weary, occasionally with red burns on his arms from touching a steam pipe. But he didn't seem to mind if my brother and I climbed all over him. His life consisted of work, his wife, his two kids, reading (philosophy and botany), and his garden.

My mother was a housewife. Life with her included going to Mass on Sunday. My father didn't go, except at Easter Vigil and Christmas Midnight Mass. He thought the choir director, Mr. Allard, had a perfect voice for Gregorian chant. When that was discontinued, he didn't go at all.

Even in grade school, I used to get into my father's books, skimming rapidly what I couldn't understand and reading avidly what I could. So it was that I came on a series of tracts against religion: the Little Blue Books, published by E. Haldeman-Julius and featuring essays by Julian Huxley, Bertrand Russell, and Clarence Darrow. They strove to demonstrate that the Bible was a collection of superstitious tales, that the Church (especially the Roman Catholic Church) was an institution gummed together with the blood of historic crimes, and that the religious impulse itself was a failure of nerve in people unable to face reality without flinching.

My father doesn't talk much. So, very gingerly, I brought a few questions to my mother. Is it true, I asked, that Middle Eastern people all have creation and deluge tales, which Jewish tribes copied, putting in their tribal god, Yahweh, to satisfy local chauvinism? Is it true that many pagans had gods with virgin mothers, gods who died and came to life again?

She had no idea. She hadn't even read the Bible, let alone E. Haldeman-Julius. When I realized that she would worry about it, and me, without having any means to resolve the problem, I stopped asking. But misery grew in me. I wrote a long philosophical poem, with illustrations. In one, a throng of people were walking, eating, writing at desks. Unaware, each was poised above a trapdoor, and one poor fellow was already falling through into nothingness. So would they all. This was the meaning of Life. Another illustration showed a line of figures, from worms through apes and Cro-Magnons to an American type, all walking up a hill that ended at a cliff, right at the tip of the American's shoes. Beyond the cliff yawned vast nothingness. This was the meaning of History.

I remember walking out in the night, in pouring rain, tears streaming down my face. Wailing aloud, I trudged a couple of miles, grateful for the concealing darkness and the thunder of passing trucks that meant no one would see or hear me losing my mind. Finally I turned and went home.

"It's late!" my mother fretted. "And you're soaked! Where were you?"

"I'm O.K.", I said, but I knew I was going to die. I changed my muddy clothes and went to bed. Whether in sleep or in a waking dream, I had a sense of falling through starless space. Hundreds of other people were falling, too, but each was alone. I could have reached out and touched them but didn't. It didn't matter.

Then I saw that my father was falling, too. No! No! I didn't want *his* life to be futile, his self-sacrifice to be meaningless. I would be a bad daughter if I let him fall. But what could I do? Suddenly I thought that if I grabbed hold of Jesus with one hand, I could save my father with the other. And so I did. The next morning I felt a whole lot better. I was, as I said, thirteen years old.

The next time I began to lose my faith the Vietnam war had made me into a primitive-Christian anarcho-pacifist. I was fourteen, and watching the war on television every night at suppertime had begun to shape my conscience. My parents had voted against Barry Goldwater, I knew, because my father had taped to the refrigerator a news story saying Goldwater would use tactical nuclear weapons to defoliate the jungles of Vietnam. Goldwater must be out of his mind, my father said.

But President Johnson didn't seem much better. On television one night I saw a stack of bodies, with elbows and knees bent at strange angles and heads hanging. My father's big, work-worn hand went down SLAM! on the table. I was shocked; he was rarely angry, and I knew it was because of what was on the television screen.

When the Mass was translated into English, I was excited to notice how the prayers repeat "Peace", over and over again, like a heartbeat. I perked up my ears at the Gospels, too, and Matthew 5, 6, and 7 won my heart. It seemed so simple! We are to pray for our enemies and give them food and kindness. That is what our Lord wants us to do, even if they kill us. After all, are we better than our Master? Surely, in a couple of weeks, once everyone caught on, the war would be over.

But the war dragged on, and I was baffled. Nobody I knew spoke out against it; even bishops and cardinals seemed to bless it. My tenth-grade history teacher, Sr. Mary George, suggested I look into the politics of the thing. Zeal is fine, she said, but don't be ignorant. So I went to the public library and checked out *Two Vietnams* by French historian Bernard Fall, and *The Law of Love and the Law of Violence*, by Leo Tolstoy. It was there I learned the name for what I was: a Tolstoyan. It was reassuring to know, yet it gave me little comfort. There I was, obsessed with the war, isolated from my classmates, sick that the Church seemed in league with French colonialism, just as those nineteenth-century atheists had said she was. Without moral authority, Church and State seemed to be collapsing; thousands of people were making their exodus. Anything to escape this house of arsonists, of Great Men in High Places who had already napalmed Vietnam and might yet nuke our planet itself. Pale, bookish, overweight, lonely schoolgirl that I was, I wanted desperately to affiliate. I ached to belong to my generation, to which I had never belonged before. Whither they went, I would go.

The impulse that drove many countercultural radicals was something like the passion that drove the Psalmist to vow he would "never eat at the table of evil-doers". America, the Church, Western civilization itself, looked to us like a huge table groaning with rich fare that it would be moral death to eat. We antiwarriors wanted to strip ourselves of anything that would contribute to the deathward rush. Why stay in school, preparing for a career with corporate criminals under the wing of the American eagle? Why stay with this fawning Church, this wholly owned subsidiary of the warfare state, holding up the Gospel book with death, like rings, on all its fingers?

So we didn't believe anything handed down to us. We had to invent everything anew. Nothing was valid unless we knew it from experience. We found it hard to acknowledge any truths we ourselves didn't originate. That attitude makes for a noteworthy limitation: your truths can never be bigger than your hat size.

I blasted out of Villa Maria Academy and twelve years of Catholic schooling with maximum glory, arrogantly delighted that I was the valedictorian whom they wouldn't let speak for fear of what I might say. Afterward, I did three big months at Antioch College. But I didn't want college. I wanted life. Experience. Some kind of raw material to think upon firsthand, never mind those philosophers who lived before the turning point of history, which, back then, was *now*.

I worked for the United Farm Workers and lived with a remarkable, hard-working Chicano family. That was sweat, struggle, and salsa. That was real enough. I worked for the antiwar movement and for a feminist publishing collective in Pittsburgh. I wrote three tiny books with poems and pictures, the texts thick with hot concepts and goddesses, sparkling with sophomoric pizzazz and anguish.

I saw some action in the sexual revolution, but no pregnancies or abortions, thank God. This was supposed to be a nonviolent revolution, but I could still get a Purple Heart for injuries sustained and, I suppose, inflicted. The political lesbian movement, which also arose at that time, was, I suspect, spurred by the realization that something was going very wrong with heterosexuality under prevailing conditions. A learn-by-doing relationship with a man could have positive values and satisfactions, but like a parachute with a hole in it, if you relied on it for long, somebody ended up hurt, or dead.

Some of my friends said, "Feminism is the theory; lesbianism is the practice." As they recommended it, lesbianism provided the solidarity and sharing of sexual love without the anxieties and tragedies of contraception and abortion or the endless hassles with men. But surveying lesbian relationships around me, I was troubled by ambiguity. Where was it going? What did it mean? I didn't want to wake up someday and find I'd spent a whole lifetime harming people unknowingly. My contemporaries expressed impatience with anyone who "craved security". That was considered the mark of a dependent personality. People with *healthy* personalities were supposed to be free, to "be open and take risks". To risk being hurt.

But to risk hurting others? I couldn't imagine us tolerating that kind of moral argument from, say, the nuclear industry. ("Hey, loosen up! Risk is what life's all about!") We'd be indignant if a pharmaceutical company took a trial-and-error approach to mass marketing a powerful drug. ("What's all this clamor for safety? There are no certainties in life, you know.") I wasn't sure what possible bad effect it could have, the wholesale demolition of the sexual mores of an entire culture. But I thought my own sexual gifts, and others' too, must have some significance too deep to squander on trial and error.

So, in 1972, twenty years old, several years a wanderer, newly celibate, still agnostic, still grappling with multiform goddesses and shifty radical paradigms, but humbled and tentative, I came to the Benedictines. Some Sisters of St. Benedict in my hometown were starting a peace and justice center. I was attracted. Peace, after all, was a calling still close to my heart, however sidetracked during my years awandering. As to the Catholic part, well, if the Catholic Church had produced *Malleus Maleficarum* and burned poor women healers as witches, she had also produced Dorothy Day and the Catholic Worker Movement. I brought equal measures of skepticism and hopefulness with me into the Pax Center.

Sr. Mary Lou Kownacki, founder of Pax, calls me "co-founder" or "a founding member". Actually, I was just one of the first disciples. I thought that I would be monastic if I didn't have to be Catholic. I was in orbit around Catholicism, but in no hurry to come in for a landing. Sometimes I went to Mass, and sometimes I didn't. I received Communion sometimes, but I wasn't sure what I was receiving. I remember praying, "Jesus, if this is You, please come in and excuse the mess . . ."

I think the Sisters regarded me fondly as a bright, eccentric, earthy young person. I was like a child with a can of spray paint, seeing no reason why I shouldn't scrawl witty slogans on the walls of the cathedral, confident that the Sisters were pillars who would continue to hold up the roof.

From 1972 to 1983, I was a lay associate of the Benedictine Sisters of Erie, Pennsylvania. During most of those years, I supported myself by working at "outside" jobs—elevator operator, hamburger patty packer, plastic molder, grocery clerk—while living at the Pax Center, a small, inner-city Benedictine community, including Sisters, laywomen, and a few laymen, involved in a variety of peace and justice ministries. We had great fun at Pax, formed genuine friendships, shared laughter and silence and seriousness, shared, too, the intensely personal work of the women's shelter. Every day there were runaway teenage girls, retarded, manic-depressive, or otherwise needy homeless women living with us and requiring extensive attention.

In 1979, after living and working with the Pax community for seven years and evolving in ways I can't trace, I started a new organization I called "Prolifers for Survival". Its purpose was to build a bridge between the peace movement and the pro-life movement. I knew abortion was wrong because I knew abortion pictures looked like Auschwitz pictures, which no one can bear to look at. Once you've seen one murder, you've seen them all.

In the beginning the people at Pax Center supported Prolifers for Survival. At one time it was listed as an "associated ministry" of the center and given free office space and copying services. I myself was given free rent. Once when I asked Sr. Mary Lou what she could contribute to PS, she said wryly, "I've already contributed my co-founder." And when Sr. Carolyn Kopkowski was going through great pain in her life, she offered up her prayers and sufferings for my work and for *me*. Like so much that the Benedictines did, this was a matter of great personal loyalty. *Lateral* loyalty. They would have supported me, Juli, whether my project was pro-life or gay rights or Jung or eco-anarchy or creation-spirituality or anything, I think, except felony or popery. And felony could be excused. But I also know that if Pax Center had to list its top twenty-five concerns, abortion would be somewhere between twenty-six and infinity.

Between 1979, when PS was founded, and 1983, the year I departed from Pax, I was becoming more and more Catholic while the Sisters were becoming more and more—what? Post-Catholic? Ex-Catholic? Anti-Catholic? Even now, looking back, it's hard to name it. Anyway, we were traveling in opposite directions, relentlessly picking up speed, and at some point we careered past each other and found ourselves on different sides of a chasm, looking at each other with incomprehension and wounded love.

My journal entries from those years reveal how I was changing better than I knew when I wrote them. I was "on the road" a great deal then, speaking against abortion and nuclear weapons for Prolifers for Survival. My pro-life associations let me hear what more conservative Catholics were saying, and I was beginning to question some feminist dogmas.

September 1, 1979

Went to Buffalo with Mark Walko, another young Pax worker, for the Holly Near No-Nukes Concert. We were all giddy and up for a good time. The concert hall was packed with lesbians and lefties, women outnumbering men four to one; my kind of people, and yet . . .

When I saw the abortion rights literature table in the lobby, my heart sank. I love Holly Near for trying to make No Nukes a feminist issue, but that ends up linking it, crazily, with the pro-abortion cause, too. One moment I'm a comrade, the next, an alien.

The concert was a splendid entertainment. Everybody was pro-everybody: the deaf, the fat, the wheelchair people; we were "nurturant" and "open to life". After the concert, the abortion rights leaflets blossomed everywhere, with no apparent sense of contradiction. Crazy; the concert was, in its way, pro-freedom and pro-life, and here I was afraid to exercise *my* freedom by handing out my pro-life leaflets!

I ran into Sr. Rosalie Bertell, key scientific researcher, nuclear critic, and member of the Grey Nuns of the Sacred Heart. "Hi!" I said. "I've got my shoulder bag full of PS leaflets, and I'm too chicken to hand them out!"

"Oh, come on. Sure you're going to hand out your leaflets", she said. Nothing more than that. But suddenly I was even more afraid—to be a coward in front of *her.*

Dread: legs shaking, mouth already dry. "Here, take a leaflet, *here* you go." People didn't jump me. It got easier. A few people handed them back, but that didn't faze me.

Steve Vitoff, a dear, hairy, secular Jewish leftaroo, turned when I called his name. "You know," he reflected with a smile, "sometimes when I'm in an antinuke march and they start talking about the radiation threat to 'the unborn', I think, 'Hey, we're out here defending those little globules the same as you.'"

"That's right, Steve."

"I learned that from you." He took a leaflet. Easy.

Now comes a familiar looking group—oh, yeah, Sisters of St. Joseph from a Catholic peace and justice center in upstate New York. I had to smile at their graying boy-cuts, blue jeans, Guatemalan vests, female-symbol earrings, and not a cross in sight. I'm not saying they're lesbians, but they'd sure pass for wanna-bes.

"Hi, there!"

"Hey, Juli!"

"Take a leaflet!"

I'm proud of this leaflet, well written—if I say so myself—in fluent left-feminese, designed to introduce my fellow peaceniks to the pro-life cause. They scan it quickly.

"Here, we don't need this junk."

The air seems to turn cold. The Sister drops the leaflet. It flutters to the floor. In explanation, she spits out the words, "Pro-life junk." Quickly they scurry away from me.

Ten seconds later, one of her companions runs back, picks up the leaflet, and puts it back in my hand. "Sorry."

Sorry? Sorry for what? Sorry for the babies? Sorry for me? Sorry for littering? I was in tears. I thought, "You sorry Sisters."

September 22, 1979 (Burke)

It amazes me. Everybody in this Pax house has as many responsibilities as I have, or more. The Sisters with obligations to the high school, to the Mount,[1] to committees and boards, to the Sisters' Council and Pax Christi. To the soup kitchen! The women's shelter! Jail ministry! I don't know how they do it.

---

[1] Mount St. Benedict Priory.

Old Calvin Johnson is dying. He's poor, and black, and has no family; he's a special friend of ours. Sr. Carolyn and I sat with him at the hospital until 1 A.M. yesterday. Carolyn stroked his brow, held his hand, said loving things. She is a true witness of the passage through death to life.

At table today, everybody is buzzing about the Pope's visit to the U.S. and his resistance to the priestly participation of women, his incessant harping on *Humanae Vitae*.

October 3, 1979 (1 day)

Every day I get up at six, get to bed at eleven, just work all day and sleep all night. Maybe I should take more time to think, to dream . . .

Pax board meeting today. Sr. Marlene Berthe, a talented, earnest import from the Covington (Kentucky) Benedictines, feels guilty (and thinks we all should) for not personally working at the soup kitchen every day. My God, we did it for years; then we recruited a bazillion volunteers; it's being done. Why flagellate ourselves?

Odd thought today: I have a number of prejudices against priests in this diocese—Fr. Levis, for instance—who the Sisters say are sexists. I don't even know the guys. I should make an effort to actually meet them. (Mary Drumm knows them, I'm sure, because of the pro-life thing. Yes! There's my connection! And *be fair!*)

Something else: over the years I've seen fit to criticize *Humanae Vitae* to make a point about being anti-abortion but pro-contraception—and I've never even read it. If I'm going to have an opinion on the thing, I ought to scan it through *once*, shouldn't I? Do I have time? Hell, I don't have time for anything. But if I *don't* read it, I'm operating on prejudice, right? I'm a bigot, right?

October 5, 1979 (2 days)

Srs. Mary Lou, Marlene, Carolyn, and Rosanne Hynes—our four Gospel pillars—are going to D.C. to raise their voices for women in the Church at the Pope-in-America extravaganza.

October 7, 1979 (2 days)

It was enough to break your heart. Here's Karol Wojtyla on the steps of the Shrine of the Immaculate Conception, beaming with happiness, joking with thousands of students from Catholic U.

"Long live the Pope! We-love-YOU!" they roared, and he would seize a microphone and chant back, "John Paul TWO! I-love-YOU!" Laughter, kiss the babies, throw away the script. He was in his glory. Finally: "Vell, I haf to go! The Pope geeves you hees blessink! Goot bye! Goot bye!"

He turns and goes into the massive basilica, and his face changes perceptibly, as if a shadow had passed over the sun. He's going to talk to the Sisters.

The head of LCWR,[2] Sr. Theresa Kane, gives an introduction that sounds loving and loyal but unflinching in its reference to the pain of women in the Church. The Pope's face becomes grim; he drops his head in his hands.

Afterward, she kneels for his blessing. He responds woodenly, then gives his address. He speaks for forty minutes. He recommends Mary as a model for Sisters: meek, self-effacing. He praises Sisters in two ministries only: teachers and contemplatives. The entire speech is read from a prepared text, which he holds before his face the whole time, not once seeking eye contact with his audience. Meanwhile, in blue arm bands, some sixty of the women, including my four gospel

---

[2] Leadership Conference of Women Religious, the liaison organization between women's religious orders and the hierarchy.

pillars, stand silently in their places while the other five thousand sit.

After the speech, John Paul was again surrounded by men:
cardinals, bishops, priests. Though he had just finished talking to a basilica jammed with women religious, there was no
distinguished woman at his right hand, no prioress or Sister-
President at his elbow to comment, to question, to offer feed-
back. No, his milieu is obviously male only.

Later, at the Mass on the mall, I was again charmed—as
everybody is—by Karol, the scholar, poet, big, huggable man.
So where are the women?

October 21, 1979

*(With Sr. Mary Lou, Caroline Kopkowski, and Bob Skwaryk at the
Pax Christi National Assembly in Atchison, Kansas)*

I fell in happily with a raucous caucus of Catholic feminists
for beers and song. I taught the whole gang our splendid,
wickedly satirical song in favor of women's ordination, and
we all laughed ourselves sick. Then we wrote up a great resolution promoting feminism in Pax Christi, the Church, and
the world. I made sure there was no abortion language in it.
There was consensus support. Yahoo!

Afterward a venerable-looking nun came in and asked,
"How did reproductive rights come to be left out?" Things
got quiet. Some probably agreed with her, some disagreed,
but none had the heart to oppose her openly. Her question
hung in the air. But "quod scripsit, scripsit." The resolution
stayed as written.

Later I had to ask myself, "How *did* I manage to keep reproductive rights—which everybody knows means abortion—out of the resolution?" I know the answer: I had
charmed everybody by going along with the women's ordi-

nation, lesbian rights stuff, so they saw me as "O.K", "not a right-winger", and my anti-abortion perspective seemed at least plausible to them.

Plausible. Is that enough? I want people to accept pro-life because it's true. Because abortion is wrong. Because life is sacred. Because Pax Christi stands for non-violence. I feel disturbed.

After that there was a *gorgeous* liturgy. Women's insistence on participation in the Mass, coupled with the hierarchy's refusal actually to ordain women, has led to this proliferation of paraliturgical rites and roles for women: incensors and holy water sprinklers, singers, readers, dancers, musicians, gift bearers and commentators, Communion ministers and more. It makes for a colorful, *crowded* altar and a jolly good show.

Once the Pax Christi crowd hit the road, I was on my own. I decided to go to Evening Prayer with the Atchison Benedictines. This is a large motherhouse, about four hundred Sisters under its jurisdiction. I saw dozens in the cumbersome medieval habit, many in the simpler reformed habit, more in plain dark jumpers and veils. The large majority—even those in street clothes—wear the veil. Only a few wear no distinctive garb, just a ring or medallion as our Pax Sisters do.

Evening Prayer could have been in a European cloister. Massive, ornately carved wooden prie dieux face each other in two great choirs. Polished benches with dividers that sequester each Sister in her individual carrel with its uncushioned wooden kneeler and small collection of prayer books: antique Gregorian Latin as well as English plainsong chants. The stately beauty of a hundred female voices chanting in lunar, unaccented tones. It made me quiet inside.

Odd thought. If the Pax liturgy people are right, these women are all wrong—and have been for fifteen hundred years. They haven't been updated; they've been repudiated.

October 22, 1979

A dozen people from the college community came to my PS rap. To my surprise, what they questioned me about was not the moral significance of nuclear war or abortion—the Big Questions I can usually take a mighty swing at and knock right out of the park—but very subtle, technical points: the relationship between probability and risk, the exact definitions of causality and intentionality and responsibility. I felt as if I had come with baseball equipment, and suddenly the other team wants to play ping-pong. Well, I never evade a question. If I can't answer it, I store it up in my overcrowded brainbox.

October 23, 1979

On the way to the bus station I was informed that half the Benedictine philosophy faculty was in my audience last night—and were favorably impressed. Whew. I know I was out of my league. An elderly Sister came up and gave me a copy of *Humanae Vitae*, asking me to read it "prayerfully" and "with openness to the wisdom of the Church". Then she said, "You know, I really think a lot of the problem is with capitalism, dear."

"You think so, Sister?"

"Yes. Capitalism concentrates wealth in the hands of the few, at the expense of the many. And it deliberately cultivates envy and covetousness in hundreds of millions of people, and you know, dear, these are sins. That's what produces this awful pressure toward war and abortion. Don't you see, dear?"

"Well, Sister, you may have a point there!"

October 24, 1979

Traveling by Greyhound bus, mile after weary mile, I spent about 190 miles furrowing my brow over *Humanae Vitae*. I must say the style is unattractive; it reads like a treatise on flying written by a punctilious hippo. It couldn't inspire a married man or woman with confidence that the authors knew *in the flesh* what they were talking about. But the content raises all kinds of questions about what it means to be a human being. That's important. It *raises* these questions; I don't say it answers them. I wrote four pages of questions. Who *could* answer them? I mean who that's credible? Who knows about "Human Life" from *life;* who knows what it is to be hungry for love, to be breathless and juicy and weak in the knees.

Not somebody who memorized the catechism and thinks *that's* life.

October 26, 1979

It's my twenty-eighth birthday. A good time to look at myself. I spend weeks on the road talking to all kinds of people—right wing, left wing, and middle-of-the-bird—about the consistent ethic, the Ban-the-Bomb-Not-the-Baby thing. I love it, it's stimulating, but it just wears me out. Then I get home, and I'm crushed under the work that's piled up waiting for me.

I finished Bernard Nathanson's *Aborting America* at a grubby bus station that smelled of Cheez-Puffs, vinyl, and urine. How did Nathanson manage to ignore the moral reality of what he was doing for so long?

1. He was very busy; no time for evaluation.

2. He saw opponents and critics as either:
   a. fools, to be ignored, or
   b. "the other side", to be refuted.

3. He'd had little experience with perinatology: the unborn as *patient*.

It concerns me that I might be blind to my own moral situation, too, in small respects (or even in big ones) because *I'm* too busy to think things through; because of my tendency to dismiss people as jerks; or because my personal experience is narrow. Nathanson had a conversion to truth. This is what I need. God grant me continuous conversion. «

To communicate the message of Prolifers for Survival, I was writing not only in such Christian-left publications as *America*, *Sojourners*, and *The Other Side*, but also a regular column in the quite orthodox *National Catholic Register*. The major rift between me and the Pax household, though, was started by a piece I did for *New Oxford Review*, where I was a contributing editor. *NOR* was, all at the same time, ecumenical, near-pacifist, religiously orthodox, and politically leftish on economic, foreign, and military policy. "In Defense of the Male Priesthood" was my first published attempt to use "feminist" arguments to explain and affirm traditional Catholic doctrine on the priesthood. Jesus gives us, in the priesthood, a subversive redefinition of manhood, I said: one of sacrifice, not domination; chastity, not sexual prowess. Jesus instituted priesthood "just for the men", because it is a "school of humility" that requires them to put aside "self-assertion, will-to-power, and treating others as objects", sins to which men in patriarchal cultures are typically tempted—but to which women in such cultures are not. In my journal, I wrote about the genesis of those ideas.

December 31, 1982

I've been running a lot of my ideas past fellow NOR contributors Stu Gudowitz and Christopher Derrick, to get the straight-ahead papist view of things. I trust them to be Catholics—not just right-wingers—because they're antinuke. If conservative Catholics can't say "Bombing Hiroshima was murder", then I have a pretty good hunch their political conservatism has mugged their Catholicism and stolen its clothes. The same thing goes for liberal Catholics and abortion. If they can't say, "Abortion is murder", they may be liberal *somethings*, but liberal *Catholics* they ain't.

It was Stu Gudowitz' challenge that resulted in my writing the "Male Priesthood" article.[3] Even in *thinking* it. I was pestering him for reasons why women are "excluded" from the priesthood (asking that way makes an assumption, as in "Are you still beating your wife?"). Anyway, rather than answering my every objection point by point, he simply said, "Why don't you try something different? Consider it possible that the Church is right about this. Then you can use your feminist sensibilities to find reasons why the 'male priesthood' is defensible, even necessary, from a *feminist* point of view!"

Assume the *Church* is right? What an unheard of . . . Isn't it intellectually disreputable to start with an assumption and then work backward to find reasons for it? Isn't that rationalizing? Craven? Treason?

But if, on the other hand, I assume that feminist demands are always right and the Church wrong, isn't that also starting with an assumption and working backward? Because of a reflexive notion that feminist demands always represent justice for women? And if they don't, then which is more important: "feminism", or *justice for women?*

I could just shift my default position, I suppose, and assume the Church is innocent until proven guilty. That seems only fair. And it would put the burden of proof on the Church's critics, instead.

Well, this was kind of a stunning idea. Leave it to Stu, a

---

[3] "In Defense of the Male Priesthood" appeared in *New Oxford Review* in December 1982.

Jew, a convert, to tell me I could give the Church the benefit
of the doubt. It was like the day I realized that an idea could
be true, could even be cool, though it was—how embarrassing!—my mother's idea.

January 1, 1983

The kind Roseboroughs had me for dinner. They're pro-life
peacenik friends with two half-grown daughters and lots of
radiant family love. During the evening, Barb and Virgil asked
why the Pax people never show up for pro-life events. Not
very confidently, I said, "Invite them! Invite Pax and Benedictines for Peace to the Erie March for Life. I think they may
respond. Nudge them."

Incrementally, like the persistent love that cures the autis-
tic, the comatose, the incorrigible, that may someday cure
me. Keep nudging.

January 2, 1983

Because I assert that God is our *Father*, my housemates look
at me as if I were sneaking around the meditation room
painting phalluses on the seraphim. It's hard even to defend
the Nicene Creed without being entered in the Torquemada
Look-Alike Sweepstakes. In the midst of a Benedictine New
Year's party, somebody said, "Let's sing *We Thank You,
Father.*"

"We thank you WHO???" came the instant, mocking
query. Laughter all around.

"Father", I said. Quietly, I thought. The laughter stopped.
Started again.

"Yessss! I am from ze Spanish Inquisition. Scourge zese heretics!" I could feel my face burning. How supersensitive I am;
all this because, for one careening moment, the laughter
stopped.

January 5, 1983

In a spurt of chutzpah, I sent copies of "In Defense of the Male Priesthood" to Erie's Bishop Michael Murphy and to Sr. Joan Chittister yesterday. I have to act quickly, before an impulse goes wimp—and quick as usual, Joan responded today with a note. "Sexist", she said.

I was not surprised that Joan wasn't sold on my thesis, but I was a little shocked by her tone, which had an edge of viciousness. She didn't critique the article; she merely insulted it. (*Sexist* is not an analysis, it's an epithet.)

"Your article will thrill women who hate men and care nothing for theology", she said. So not only must she insult it, she must insult anyone who likes it, call them psychosexually sick and impious.

Christopher Derrick wrote, too, to say he *liked* the article. But he said the feminist-priesthood people "hate sex", and those who hate hierarchy "hate heaven". So in an exactly parallel spirit, he feels obliged to call his opponents on this subject psychosexually sick and impious!

Sr. Joan, Mr. Derrick, love one another.

February 12, 1983

One of the Sisters was down with a cold. I stopped by her room last night with a cup of tea. Her college-age friend, a "professed" lesbian known to me only as Chris, was with her, reading to her from *Beyond God the Father*, by Mary Daly. My heart froze. They noticed my stricken look.

"Oh, the post-Christian", I said. "Myself, I'm a post—", and I didn't know how to finish the sentence.

March 10, 1983

Women's History Week. I went out to the Mount to hear Arlene Swidler.

"I'm almost embarrassed to tell you, Juli, but—I can't say that I'm even *interested* in all this," said Barb Roseborough, sheepishly. "When something is advertised as a 'women's' something or other, I get the feeling they don't mean me." Then laughing, quoting Sojourner Truth: "And ain't I a woman?"

"I know what you mean", I smiled. "But let's just go to see if she has anything to say about women's right to you-know-what."

Swidler, a historian, a true academic, looks the part: thin intellectual face, severe hairstyle, Mother Hubbard shoes. She told a few stories of American Catholic women—foundresses, apostates, saints—in a dry, witty style that implied a great deal: "Of course, for her basic good sense she was accused of heresy", she'd say of some nineteenth-century foundress, putting two-fingered quotes in the air around "heresy". Thirty women rolled their eyes.

"The Ho-oly Fa-ather," she'd say, elongating the vowels, raising an eyebrow, and laughter would ripple across the room. Skillful.

Afterward, I led off the questions by asking if stories of *pro-life* women were part of our "usable history". She would not answer. She literally declined to say.

At my nudging, Barb asked whether Catholic feminists were not under pressure to *prove* their feminism by approving abortion. Swidler evaded this, too. It amazed me, her refusal to take a stand.

Chris again—I note with half a smile her entwined female-symbol earrings—raised some basic points from atheology: "Why continue any longer with this Christian patriarchal myth that first sells us the problem—original sin—and then sells us the solution—redemption, sacraments, Church—when we could be liberated from the whole oppressive structure simply by disregarding the debilitating myth of original sin?"

How did I get to be spokeswoman for orthodoxy around here? I *alone* raise my voice to speak what is apparently now unspeakable: that I *am* born alienated from God, that *I need* a Savior, that the sacraments have power unto salvation—sacramental power; you couldn't prove it by me: I who, with my daily Mass and Rosary, don't even have the power to fast from lunchtime to suppertime—I defended Christian doctrine, and forty Sisters of Saint Benedict sat silent.

But CJ is easy to argue with. She doesn't try to maintain a pose that she is still in the Church. She's outright. Outspoken. Out. But Swidler, amusing as she is, is slippery, frustrating, not quite with "the Church as we know it".

But the Church is the only part of the Nicene Creed we can see. If you don't believe in the Church you *can* see, how can you ever believe in the wildly improbable rest of it, which you *can't* see? Believe it or don't. I wish Swidler would find her on/off switch. But, no; she uses a rheostat.

March 22, 1983 (12 da—

Read Christopher Derrick's *Sex and Sacredness*. Very interested in his idea of sacredness as illuminating sex and sacraments; the baptized-pagan world view. Irritated, though, by his sexist details: his use of "man and girl", asymmetrically; his use of collective words as male-biased ("the Egyptians and their women"); his use of absurd constructions making women passive ("the late Victorians dressed their women along lines that seem sexually suggestive." Come now, surely Victorian women dressed *themselves*). And his disturbing use of coercive overtones regarding heterosexuality ("the explosive spearing . . . the microscopic rape that begins us all" to describe sexual penetration and the merging of sperm and egg, as if violent imagery made it more robust).

March 25, 1983

Annunciation; the beginning of the Holy Year. Nobody took any notice of it at Pax, but I wanted to. So I went to the Blue Army of Fatima observance at St. Ann's, the only Holy Year observance in Erie. The church was well-filled, about 90 percent older women, along with some young women and children. In the front, though, it was 100 percent men: two priests, two Knights of Columbus in plumed hats, capes, and swords, boy cross-bearers, book-bearers, candle-bearers, incense-bearers, and four men carrying the Virgin on a litter. Colorful in their plumage they were, those brocaded males. I'd had no idea such a thing could occur in Erie, in 1983.

Odd thought: if it weren't for the assigned roles of those dozen men in front, there'd be practically no men here at all. It would be a rite "of the women, by the women, for the women". Anthropologically, men's rites and women's rites are fairly common; what's uncommon in human experience is a religion that includes both. I suppose if women were priests, Catholicism would be all women; there would be no men in it at all.

But then, in procession, came the Blue Army Cadets: kids—both boys and girls—with blue sashes and scapulars. Then the Blue Army Choir: about sixty women in blue robes, and one or two men. Then the Divine Spirit nuns, ascetical, all in blue habits. Then the statue of Mary with tender features and a slender neck, her head topped by a crown so huge it seemed it must bend her down. So where are the landed gentry? Yet these aren't aristocratic dames; I see the check-out clerk from the Blue Ribbon Market and the cafeteria lady from the school, and the woman who makes bridal gowns in that tiny shop on Parade Street. That is why I trust them, *whatever* it is they're up to. What *are* they up to?

First the Stations, then the Rosary, then, knees aching, the

Litany of the Sacred Heart, then St. Louis de Montfort's Act of Consecration. Then an altar call for individual consecrations; I was not expecting this, and I decided, impulsively, to do it. I went up and said to Mary, silently, "Well, Queen of Peace, are you God's secret weapon for disarmament? Look at all these people! What an organizer you are! Can you conquer the bomb? Wouldn't God be delighted to give you that panache! Well, go for it, Little Mother! I'll be on your team, if that's any use." I am mildly astonished by this blue wave that has picked me up like a cork and carries me along, bemused.

All this was followed by Benediction, with fragrant wafts of Latin I can't translate except for a phrase or two. *Sensuum defectui.*

Palm Sunday, 1983

At Mass at the Mount, Sr. Christine Vladimiroff proclaimed a kind of introduction to the Paschal Mysteries. The gist of it:

"Only a person with a very positive self-image could have done what Jesus did. Jesus could confront the structures of injustice because He believed in Himself. His strong self-concept carried Him through when Church and State, Caiphas and Herod, turned on Him. His positive self-image gave Him the strength to engage in the struggle against oppression even unto death, and through death to Resurrection—for ultimately the forces of liberation must prevail."

I felt like standing up and shouting, "Rubbish, Chris! Jesus did not rise from the dead because He 'believed in Himself', He rose because He was obedient to His Almighty Father, because He *emptied Himself out*!"

So I can go to the Blue Army and get what looks like nostalgia for the Portuguese monarchy, or I can go to the Mount and get marxist baby talk, this mishmash of Friedrich Engels and Phil Donahue. Show me your face, O Lord.

April 15, 1983

Went to Mary Drumm's house last Sunday so she could give me some clothes. Mary was the first actual pro-lifer and outright whole-cloth Catholic ever to befriend me, when I was a lonesome lefty nosing into the pro-life movement a half-dozen years ago.

My impulses are divided. On the one hand, I want Mary to understand the Pax people, to love them as I do. I still think of Mary Lou, Carolyn, Marlene, and Rose as the four Gospel pillars. They pray. They do so much good. They surpass me a hundred times over in every virtue; anyone who really knew us would see that.

On the other hand, Mary and Chuck both said they felt cold, arms-length alienation from Pax people; bitterness and rejection from Deni Howley—young, skeptical, smart, the newest affiliate (they used to call them postulants) at the Mount. We cried over the future of the Church.

So yesterday, who should come into Pax, to lunch, in tears? Deni. Why? Because *she* felt such coldness from Bishop Murphy, felt rejected. She cried, was angry, but more hurt. I cried too, for all of us.

April 16, 1983

To Warwick, New York, for the Religious Democratic Socialists meeting. John Cort invited me to hold up the pro-life end. I said, "John, I ain't no socialist."

"Can you still talk Left-feminese?"

"Fluently."

"Good, then. Come. I need you."

What a crowd. Up-front Jews and closet Catholics. The Jews all had yarmulkes, the Catholic clergy not even a cross. There were a dozen priests and nuns I knew personally, none with any identifying garb or title. Jewish speakers used and explained Hebrew and Yiddish words: *mitzvah, midrash, l'chaim, baruch*. The Catholics were actually ashamed of their Catholicism. Whispered, from one to another undercover priest, "We're having Mass Sunday morning in Room 103. Don't worry; no vestments, no big deal."

But, in casual conversation, John Cort, Peter and Peggy Steinfels, Joe Holland, and the others were fun. After some poking, I actually persuaded them to wear the "Pro-Life, Pro-Peace, Proletarian" buttons I had hand-painted. And nobody tried to throw us out after all.

There *was* a blatantly pro-abort speaker on the Socialist Morality panel: Howard Moody of Judson Church. I raised my hand and asked him straight out how he could try to convince *this audience* that life and the means of life are not "entitlements".

He said, "We all have the right to the means of life, but not to life itself."

He must have known how lame that sounded; because immediately, he said, "Does anybody *else* have any questions?"

Nobody did. So I piped up. "I have another one." There were a few soft moans from the audience, but I went on: "If we approve legal abortion, aren't we saying the State has the right to create two different classes of people, one class with rights and another without?"

"It's not a question of State action, it's a question of individual action", he said with an air of exasperation.

"You mean we each *individually* have a right to decide some human beings don't have rights?"

"That's ridiculous", he snapped. "Doesn't *anybody* have another question?"

Silence. I counted to ten. Then I ventured, "I have one more."

Some people were nettled. "That's enough!" "Tell her to sit down." "Shut up, you've had your say."

"I want to ask if he thinks the young are the private property of their parents . . ."

The moderator rushed to the mike. "Well, that about winds it up. Fifteen-minute break, then lunch."

"Great questions!" Joe Holland beamed at me. A sweet guy, he thinks John Paul II is "a post-modern intellectual giant". He's even against contraception, and capable of explaining his position in a kind of bright, rapid-fire leftaroo-language that drives right-wing types crazy but is actually quite orthodox.

"Yeah, but why didn't *you* say anything?"

"I'm in the process of getting something in writing, in a bigger context. The global population control agenda as critiqued by anti-imperialist forces at the Bucharest conference, the post-modern realization that we *are* nature and can't re-engineer our natures—this includes re-engineering our sexuality—without, in effect, aggressing against all who come after us. And that involves reevaluation of voluntarist and positivist thought going back to the eighteenth century."

The bigger context, footnoted. Joe gets things all worked out, in pages, chapters, books, before he's ready to say anything. Me, I have to stick my neck out and start talking when I don't even have the next word lined up. I hate always having to fly by the seat of my pants.

June 20, 1983

Deni Howley wrote an article in the diocesan paper proposing Mary Agnes Mansour[4] as a "model" for religious who wish to "serve the poor in the world". Not one word about

[4] Mansour was a Religious Sister of Mercy in Detroit. She had been appointed by the governor to head the state Department of Human Services, a position involving administrative responsibility for Medicaid abortions. After media hoopla over her defense of Medicaid abortions and eventual Vatican intervention, she was forced to leave the R.S.M.s.

the fact that this Sister is administering, among other things, a massive Medicaid abortion program for the State of Michigan. I wrote Deni a letter asking whether the "model" religious service to the poor was to help them kill their children.

Today Sr. Mary Lou and I got into it a bit. She says abortion is *not* the issue; religious-in-political office is *not* the issue. *The* issue is the hierarchy's "putting down" American women religious by projecting authority from Rome, riding roughshod over intermediate structures, usurping the power of elected superiors, without dialogue or due process.

It blows my mind that taking a bureaucratic lead role in snuffing 13,300 babies in their mothers' wombs is deemed so small a matter as to be dwarfed by the ecclesiastical power struggle. It's as if Jesus is being crucified but the important "justice" issue is that the Romans won't let women pound in the nails.

I was willing to say that dialogue and due process are issues, vexedly intertwined and not trivial. But Mary Lou said, *No*, there's only *one issue*: the women vs. Rome.

Wednesday, June 22, 1983

A terrible thought at prayer. If a person without Love is somehow given the gift of Truth, she can become its enemy even as she propounds it. Because any message given by a person manifestly driven by ego, a person prone to meanness and pride, is bound to repel us. The loveless truth-teller makes the truth repulsive. So I am full of fear when I ask God to grant me the truth. Will I be granted it, only to discredit it by my sins, my weaknesses? Will I inoculate people with a bit of truth only to make them immune to it by my failings?

O God, first make me a good person, a virtuous person, a loving person.

Then give me the truth.

Sunday, July 10, 1983 3 w

Thinking of my own weakness, myself so dull, distracted, and diffuse, my head so obtuse and fickle, my will so wavering, my mind so cloudy, my strengths, such as they are, so intermittent, I am mourning the wet tinder of my soul, which even the Holy Spirit apparently can't ignite.

Yet, to tell the truth, I am not in despair. I am not even in imminent danger of despair, because I refuse to give first place to my (depressed) emotions or to my (skeptical, disillusioned) intellect, but I give—*try* to give—first place to faith in God. Jesus suffered in heart and mind and body, but He trusted in His Father. Dorothy Day saw every failing in the Church, but she believed in God. Thomas Merton knew all about skewed history and scarface psychology, but he believed in God. In a plague year, Julian of Norwich believed in God—good God. I will not abandon their company. Let me stand with them.

Wednesday, July 27, 1983 2 w

Got into a heated discussion about the Mansour affair with Sr. Anne McCarthy. She's an idealistic young woman and, by the way, a registered nurse, acquainted with delivering babies. It drives me wild that some people think hacking tiny babies to pieces is something we should help the poor participate in. I simply can't believe anyone could think this is right, or merciful, or just. The really maddening thing is that Anne is certainly not pro-abortion, nor even (that prissy phrase) "pro-choice." Nobody here at Pax is. They just don't think it's all that important.

The integrity of a pregnant woman, body and soul, is un-interesting. Fetuses are boring. One sentence spoken on the subject is one sentence too many. Two sentences are enough to provoke scowls. Worse, yawns.

At the same time there is intense interest over the minutiae of their liturgies: our Father–Mother God (why not "god-dess"?), our gracefully arranged altar, our flowers, our candles, our dancers, our schola, our braziers of incense, our symbolic water and clay and milk and honey, our flutes and handbells, all tuneful and in such good taste.

This anger of mine: Is there love in that?

Saturday, July 30, 1983

I congratulate myself that I did *not* argue about the Mansour case at the Pax picnic today, despite the fact that Bishop Gumbleton and my prioress both brought it up, glancingly, once or twice. I just swallowed my spit and kept to myself.

Joan Chittister was in top form. She'd just come from a fifteen-day diplomatic trip to Egypt and Israel, sponsored by some "Ecumenical Intercultural Women's Dialogue" group. She met with Menachem Begin and other leaders, asked (as usual) outrageously blunt questions, came back full of chutz-pah and hot stories.

The Benedictines—the Pax Sisters—are so good: brave, warm-hearted, justice-loving, prayerful, loyal. That's what makes conflict with them so difficult. I think, especially, of their tenderness toward their parents. So frequently, Mary Lou will speak of her deceased mother, Mary, and her father, Ed, with words of deep respect and affection. Marlene honors her father and mother, as does Carolyn, and Sister Mary Ellen Plumb—all of them. And their parents, as far as I can tell, are really good people. Hardworking. Brave. Devoted to their chil-dren. Genuine. Catholic-with-a-capital-C. And the Sisters see their parents as friends of God and bulwarks of their lives.

They serve them, too, with kindness, often putting them-selves out to go home and cook and clean for them, run errands, help them in many ways. (This honor of their par-ents may be their salvation.)

The Benedictines are in fact much better than I am. (This is no false humility, it's—hah!—*true* humility, since anybody who observed me in action could see what a poor specimen I am, compared with them.) That's why it's so difficult to reprove them. Especially on this subject, which *nobody* wants to hear.

Sunday, July 31, 1983

Today when Tom Gumbleton celebrated Mass, I had an experience of being filled with a petition. Tom had said repeatedly in his homily, "We must take a resolute stand against many of the axioms of our day . . .", so I was swept with the desire to say, "That we may take a resolute stand against abortion: its alienation as a private choice, its brutality as a public policy, let us pray to the Lord."

But there was no chance to do so. Prearranged petitions (against the arms race, the oppression of women, and the abuse of power in the Church) were sung by a cantor. There was no opening for congregational participation. Shaking slightly, I prayed God would give me the chance to say this, since He had given me the thought.

So after Mass I sat next to Bishop Gumbleton and Joan Chittister at breakfast. I did not initiate the subject. Tom was talking about how Franz Jaegerstatter[5] is not widely recognized as a *resister saint*, and I mentioned, quietly, that he is not widely recognized as an *anti-abortion* saint, either, though his opposition to abortion was very much part of his resistance.

That was that: fifteen words, in context. Two hours later, Sr. Marlene came flying into my room. "*Why* are you always talking about abortion? We are *sick* of the subject of abortion!"

[5] Franz Jaegerstatter (1910–1942) was the only known Catholic in Austria openly to refuse induction into the Nazi army. He was beheaded in Berlin on August 9, 1942

I rarely talk to people in this house about abortion—may God forgive my cowardly silence. But when I *do* speak, it is because nobody else talks about it—that is, nobody else ever *objects* to abortion.

But Deni Howley *initiated* the subject by writing a whole column in the diocesan paper describing Mansour as a "model for ministry" (though some babies get *ministered to death*). Srs. Joan and Mary Lou *initiated* the subject by saying we ought to observe Tisha b'Av to commemorate the injustices done *to women like Mansour.*

Tisha b'Av in the Jewish tradition mourns the destruction of the First and Second Temples. What desecrates the Temple of the child's body, if not abortion? What destroys the Temple of the Church, if not organized defiance of the Church's too-infrequent attempts to guard her moral integrity? These Benedictines are true daughters of those who destroyed the Temples—not those who mourn them.

No, I didn't say all this to Sr. Marlene. But at least I didn't just burst into tears as usual. This time, I showed my anger. For once! For once! Marlene reddened in the face, and walked out.

This will get worse.

Monday, August 1, 1983

When I get angry, I say things that may be exaggerated or even false.

For instance, I know that abortion clinic operators have publicly claimed Mansour as an ally, and to the best of my knowledge she has not repudiated their support, but I *don't* know that it was a Riker Clinic person specifically. I should have said, "It's *as if* a Riker Clinic person were to . . ."

So I'm ashamed of that. If Marlene fabricated a bit herself ("Several people have said they noticed how argumentative you are." Who?), it's only because she's a lot like me. Here we are, two angry women—two Christians, one flesh in the Lord.

Marlene stopped me in the kitchen to say, "I'm sorry. I didn't mean to make you so upset."

I said, "I was about to say the same to you."

She hugged me. "I love you, Juli."

"I love you, too, Marlene. This is going to go on being difficult, but I love you anyway."

Thursday, August 3, 1983

I was in charge of prayers today. The morning text, Matthew 16:13-23, I read as feelingly as I could: Simon Bar Jonah's prophetic acclamation of Jesus as Messiah, and Jesus' mighty approval: *You are the Rock!* Followed instantly by Peter's stumble and Jesus' rebuke: *Get out of my sight, you satan!*

As I was proclaiming the first part of the Gospel, I could see Marlene shifting in her seat and scowling. "My gosh," I thought, "she's actually angry that Jesus gave him the power of the keys." But when I read, "Get out of my sight, you satan!" the darkness of her face gave way to a broad grin. Peter is a satan. Hot dog!

Friday, August 4, 1983

Two days ago, I slipped a letter into Mary Lou's mailbox about that ever-festering Mansour affair. Today, just as I'm leaving on a five-day speaking trip, she hands me a reply. "It's harsh", she remarked shortly.

"Yours or mine?" I asked.

"Mine", she said.

I read it on the Greyhound bus, prepared for the worst. But it was not so bad. She showed her exasperation, which is honest, but she was *not* harsh. She did not deal with any of the points I raised, but she did say, "We'll talk about all this."

It's like seeing the Star in the east: we're on the way toward
the Way.

Sunday, August 7, 1983, Detroit

Don Yanovich, who has been teaching philosophy at Mercy
College for twenty years, knows Agnes Mansour well (she
was president of Mercy College before launching off into
"political ministry") and likes her as a person who wants to
be kind and just. Yet he says she is clearly wrong in her dispute with Archbishop Szoka and is confused not only about
abortion but about due process, which here means Canon
Law.

I think there are two issues Mansour could justly have complained of:

1. The Church has rarely criticized an American religious
   publicly for participating in an unjust government
   structure, in relation to abortion or unjust war or racism or any form of oppression. Louisiana politician
   Leander Perez was excommunicated for defiance of
   his bishop in opposing the desegregation of Catholic
   schools, and Jesuit Robert Drinan was forced to resign
   from Congress, but in neither case did the Church
   publicly teach *why* the person was being disciplined.
   So the flaming publicity of Mansour's case creates the
   appearance that she has been singled out arbitrarily, and
   this raises questions of motives.

2. Szoka waffled. At least he initially *appeared* to approve
   her appointment and was quoted in the *Detroit News* as
   saying, "She has to obey the law as it stands": the law
   appropriating money for ten thousand abortions! He
   was as confused as she was. It could be said he encouraged her to go out on a limb, then sawed it off.

On both points, the bishops and the Vatican can be criti-cized *for not exercising their authority enough, frequently* enough, *clearly* enough, *strongly* enough.

Monday, August 8, 1983

In Erie, "peace" means Benedictines. "Feed the poor" means Benedictines, too. Srs. Augusta Hamel and Lynn Weissert power the food bank: fork lifts, refrigerated warehouses, tons of buns; Sr. Agnes is the food pantry's generalissimo; Pax started the soup kitchen nine years ago, and Mary Miller, who runs it now, so lovingly, with such respect for the sad, sodden, pocked, flawed, sour-smelling, appealing, scheming people who come there—Mary is becoming a Benedictine. The Mount has no lack of novices. The Erie O.S.B.s attract those who love those whom Jesus loved most.

So, peace and the poor. Sound priorities. And pro-life? Lord, these good nuns are so overworked I don't expect them to *do* anything for pro-life, really. A nod, a few rhetorical crumbs. They'd be amazed how little it would take. Just the widow's mite—if their hearts were in it.

If they would just refrain from siding with the enemy.

Wednesday, August 17, 1983

Last night Mary Lou and I sat in my workroom, in dim light, and for a choking half hour, "had at it" about the Mansour case, abortion, Pax Christi, and the Benedictine radical femi-nist theology. It was a hard interview. I was in tears most of the time. Every once in a while, though, God and anger en-abled me to get a grip and *say* something.

Mary Lou is "of course" against abortion. Everyone "of course" is. But as an issue, she says she has not the slightest interest in addressing it. It is not on her agenda and *never will be*. She is emphatically *not* interested in "dialogue" with prolifers. She doesn't even want them in the peace movement, if they "come with all their baggage".

If Agnes Mansour had been a Benedictine, Mary Lou "would have fought against" her decision to accept a government post, on the grounds that *any* government job involves too many compromises. But at this point the *only* issue is Vatican "suppression" of women religious.

"Are you happy here at Pax?"

"Oh, I go back and forth between hope and . . ." I don't think I finished the sentence, just blew my nose and whimpered.

"I'm just worried that you're going to have a hard time staying at Pax," Mary Lou continued, "because of conflicts over prayer, the Eucharist, women's ordination, the feminist movement. You know, the Erie Benedictine Sisters just modified their corporate commitment to include the women's issue, so there'll be more experimental women's Eucharists, more woman-God language, and so forth." (She's worried that *I'll* have a hard time staying at Pax? *She's* going to have a hard time staying in the Catholic Church!)

"There's a lot of tension in the chapel on the days when it's your turn to lead prayer."

"You're tense, Mary Lou?"

"Yes. I'm furious when you pray. 'In the name of the *Father* and of the *Son*', when you pray '*Our Father*', 'I believe in God the *Father* . . .' We can't pray that way anymore."

The light was fading around us. The streetlight doesn't cast much light into my windows. We sat there in the dusk. "Mary Lou?"

"Yes?"

"Do you think Jesus misled us?"

Long pause. "I—I think He was limited. He learned a lot. He did as well as He could. He was human."

"Do you think His understanding of God was radically deficient?"

"Yes. I do."

"The Risen Christ told us to baptize all nations 'in the Name of the Father, and of the Son, and of the Holy Spirit'. Do you think the *Risen Christ's* understanding of God was radically deficient?"

Long pause. "Yes." Pause "And so is mine. But you can't *limit* God to Father."

"Mary Lou, Jesus said 'Father' because God *is* His Father. In heaven. His mother is Mary, down the street. In Nazareth. This 'limitation' you speak of: perhaps that's the scandal of the Incarnation?"

"This is exactly what makes me (want to puke,) Juli. You're so *dishonest*. So 'holier than thou'. You're so sure *you've* got the truth. I don't *pretend* to have the truth. I don't have the faintest idea who God is. It is just sickening to hear you spouting these smug little definitions."

I sobbed at that, thinking how true it is that my self-righteousness drives people away from the truth. But this little bit of truth I *do* have—how I'd like to let it go—but it *is* the truth. And Mary Lou will not make me ashamed of it. I *am* lousy with sin, self-absorbed and smug, dammit. But the truth is the truth.

"Mary Lou, it's not just 'Mother–Father God.' It's going to be everything. The other day Marlene did an on-the-spot revision that came out 'the Master, *she.*' Of course it will have to be 'the *Mistress*'. And Lord: the *Lady of Ladies*? The *Princess of Peace*? The *Queen* who beats down my foes and gives me their land for a heritage? You want that *Queen*?"

"That will all have to go", Mary Lou agreed. "The militarism, the nationalism, the aristocracy, the hierarchical language."

I wasn't sniffling anymore. "After the Great Revision, I suppose, we'll have a Bible the size of a pamphlet?"

"But we will have a truer understanding of the liberating God."

"But not a biblical God."

Mary Lou hesitated. "The biblical writers were honest and true to *their* concept of God. We can't do less. We must be true to *ours*."

I wonder how it will happen. I suppose the Pope will ask all the Sisters to return to the habit—some small but emotional symbol like that—and the Benedictines will refuse and declare themselves a secular institute, a pious union, beguines. Then, maybe, they will be even bolder about women's Eucharists, and the bishop will forbid them, and the Benedictines continue them.

And then? Will the bishop turn a blind eye? Put their house under interdict? Engage in fifteen years of "dialogue"? Excommunicate the prioress? They are "in" the Church in name only. *How long will they keep the name?*

When all the talk was over, I asked Mary Lou to give me a ride to my parents' home. Impulsively, when we were both on our feet, she pulled me toward her and hugged me, "There's still something in you I love, Juli."

I choked. "The two women I loved most in all the world, whom I respected above all others, were you and Joan."

"One of those is still a good choice", she said with a wry smile. I felt like dying.

At my parents' home I took a bath and crawled into my old bed and had a prayer-seizure till four in the morning. I prayed our Lady would appear to Mary Lou and show her the right way. I prayed that above all, Jesus would not allow me to lead others in the wrong way. "If I'm about to cause serious scandal, to lead somebody else toward serious sin, Lord, just send me a heart attack." I prayed that if my death would contribute to truth, unity, and peace at Pax Center, that God would kill me and make peace through my death.

When I got up in the morning, I opened my Bible at random, and the first words I saw were the beginning of John 14:

> Let not your heart be troubled.
> Have faith in God and faith in Me. . . .
> I am the Way, and the Truth, and the Life:
> No one comes to the Father but through Me. . . .
> The word you hear is not Mine:
> It comes from the Father who sent Me. . . .
> Peace is My gift to you. . . .
> Do not be distressed or fearful. . . .
> Come then! Let us be on our way."

I cried again.

Friday, August 19, 1983

Mary Lou knows it would be hard for me to leave Pax but harder to stay under the regime of the Motherfather God. I have friends who could offer me sanctuary where I could rest, read, work. I could go back to being a dishwasher.

But what about the women who have been Sisters for fifteen, twenty-five, thirty-five years, or more? Surely they are not all worshippers of Motherfather? Surely some still believe in the One Jesus called "My Father and Your Father, My God and Your God"? What do *they* do? Where do *they* go?

Saturday, September 3, 1983

Pax House meeting—Board meeting. The first part was a relief, family-at-home, all smiles. Second part, Board meeting, nothing about PS or Mansour or abortion. But in the discussion of prayer—with Sister Carolyn!—I was blindsided.

First, she said that when it was my turn to lead prayer, she became so angry she would almost have to leave chapel, because I'd begin the *sung* "Our Father", and singing it *forced* them all to use a term they found offensive. (Stunned speechless, I thought, "What is this? The only *F*-word that must never be said in polite company?")

Another thing: Sr. Mary Ellen said they're taken aback by my lack of solidarity with the community. I choose not to attend paraliturgical substitute Eucharists, but Deni Howley used to attend our "regular Masses—for the sake of the community" despite the fact that she was "in absolute pain".

Here is a mystery. Why should Deni join a Roman Catholic religious order (she is in her novitiate year now at the Mount) if the Mass causes her to experience "absolute pain"? Does she think the Church is quickly going to capitulate to her detailed objections to all its sacraments? Or are the Benedictines going to drop the Mass altogether?

Sunday, September 4, 1983

Catching me by the arm at the Mount, Sr. Joan said she wanted to see me for five minutes. A remarkable conversation followed. Scarcely giving me leave to interject one word, she proclaimed with passion: *Number One! Abortion is a heinous thing! It is the last worst evil foisted on women by sexist men! Number Two! She, Joan, thanks God that Agnes Mansour was not an Erie Benedictine! Because if Some Benedictine* had wanted to take a *Government Job* administering abortion funds or collaborating with *a Nuclear Missile Scheme* or whatever, she would *immediately deny her permission!*

Number Three! But Good Causes can be used to a Bad End! Hitler rode on *Legitimate German Resentment* of the severe

World War One settlement, to establish *Fascism in Germany!*
So let's not forget the *"F" Factor!* Legitimate anti-abortionism
can be used by *Fascists in Church and Society!*

(Even in a small room, when Joan is all steamed up, she
seems to be speaking into a bank of microphones. Here she
was, orating before an awestruck audience of one.)

*And Number Four! We must become aware of the Issues Behind
the Issues!* (This came out in one strong hot stream, causing
me some joy and some concern. Attributing abortion to sexism and comparing it to nuclear missiles is using the strongest
terms in the Joan Chittister lexicon. On the other hand, what
does she mean by "Fascism in the Church"? *Canon Law?*)

Agnes Mansour wants to be a Sister of Mercy, Joan remarked.
*And she still is, in all except a legalistic technicality. Everyone still
calls her Sr. Agnes. She attends all R.S.M. community meetings. She's
still sending every penny of her $50,000 a year back to the convent. I
don't know what they're doing with it.*

"Maybe buying a Potter's Field?" I ventured.

"Yeah, well, Juli, you and I see eye to eye on these things." (She
clasped me in a strong hug, knocking off my glasses.) *"You're
such a gift to this community. You bring us such a strong sensitivity
about these things. Thank you. We're fortunate to have you."*

My head was spinning as I left. What a blessing! What a
Prioress!

Monday, September 5, 1983

Today I learned that Joan is still going ahead with her Tisha
b'Av project. What can she mean by that?

Tuesday, September 6, 1983

It was my turn to lead prayers again this morning, and I was
struck with chilling dread. What can I do about the Lord's
Prayer? If we sing "Our Father", I'll be guilty of provoking

Carolyn's anger. If I start with a spoken Our Father, everybody else will say "Our Father, Our Mother", and I'll either be three syllables off, or wait for the others to say "Our Mother", which makes me feel culpable. Skip the Lord's Prayer. I tried to choose a hymn. "Father, May They All Be One". No good. "A Mighty Fortress Is Our God." Militaristic. "A Mighty Goddess Is Our Forte?" Quick, scan all the lyrics, find one that just says "Yahweh". Nobody knows what that means.

Today's reading: Jesus selects the twelve Apostles. Why did I have to get this one? Will they think I'm trying to make some kind of point?

I couldn't lead prayer. I just walked out of the house, went down to the public dock, sat on the edge of a pier, and stared at the waves a while. Pulled out my Rosary. Couldn't keep my mind on it. Sorrowful Mysteries. Jesus suffering, bleeding, spat upon, kicked down, dying. Holy One. Your ways are not like our ways.

Missed Mass, too. Crept into the back of St. Pat's and looked up the readings in the missalette. Today's Epistle, Colossians 2, warns against being "seduced by an empty philosophy, based on worldly traditions, teaching a 'cosmic power' rather than Christ." That made me think of feminist theology, which rips to tatters Jesus' theology of the Father. And of the heretical mystical traditions, with their 'cosmic energy', 'inner force', 'waves', and 'vibes', and anything but a Person who knows who He is and what He wants from us. So I find my beliefs affirmed and my opponents rebuked by Scripture. So I'm right. Sometimes I'd rather live in peace at Pax. Sometimes I think I'd rather be wrong.

Wednesday, September 7, 1983

Visited Fr. Levis today and got a reading list of Catholic Classics: Dawson, Péguy, et cetera. I want to read what Dorothy

Day read, what Peter Maurin read. I want to read history through the lives of the saints. I'm excited. I'm going to dump Prolifers for Survival, blast out of Pax, settle myself somewhere, and read!

Friday, September 9, 1983 2 d

Made a list of places I could go when I leave Pax. A lot of friends would let me live with them (God bless the pro-life movement), and that might be OK for a while. But I want to have the time and energy to read, and with this recent flare-up of rheumatoid arthritis, I don't know if I can do light industrial work anymore. And I do not want a job that requires thinking. I don't want anything competing with the education I *have to* get.

Sunday, September 11, 1983 2 d

The prayer books are gone from chapel. Mary Lou says that the Morning and Evening Prayers, recently rewritten to eliminate male-biased nouns and pronouns for human referents, will be rewritten again, to eliminate male nouns and pronouns for God.

I read of a French priest of the last century who was embarrassed to read certain parts of the Gospel to his bourgeois congregation. He could not bring himself to preach on "Woe to you, you rich."

But today's Catholic feminists are worse than that cowardly priest. They will *rewrite* the Bible so they need never encounter a theology of the Father. Revising the texts, purging every word that does not fit with their phobias, they will make it impossible ever to be confronted by the Word of God.

Wednesday, September 14, 1983 3 d

I'm feeling terrible anxiety as it becomes clear that I *must* leave

Pax, *soon.* I am not in danger of losing my faith; I am in danger of losing my hope and charity. If I were to stay here, I would develop a very cranky kind of Catholicism, molded by irritation, nipped by crabbed Catholicism based on rebuttal. I want the gentle personalism of traditional Catholicism. I want someplace where I can just make the Sign of the Cross without starting a controversy.

I want some space left in my heart for love. Lord, You claimed me at Baptism. Now somehow You have reclaimed me. OK; You win. Get me outta here.

Monday, December 12, 1983

Spent the day burning papers and books. To tell the truth, I am sick of the written word. It was all I could do not to burn everything I own. Every time I'm tempted to keep some trifle, I think, "Will it fit in my backpack?" And out it goes.

Friday, December 30, 1983

I will go to Berkeley and work with *New Oxford Review* a while. Mary Lou gave me a check for one hundred dollars. "For the return trip", she smiled. Hugs all around, just like family even now. I didn't know what to say. May we all return. «

So that was how gratuitous grace led me home, to live at last among ordinary, struggling, faithful Catholics. Ahead of me, unsuspected, were Operation Rescue, marriage, and motherhood. The Holy Spirit is still working on me and, I pray, on all of us.

⁊☙

Juli Loesch Wiley was born and raised in Erie, Pennsylvania, where she spent eleven years as a Benedictine lay associate with the Pax Center, a ministry of Mount St. Benedict community. Long an organizer for a variety of causes, she was an antiwar activist, a United Farm Workers boycott organizer, an opponent of the nuclear arms race, and an active eco-feminist. She won the National Catholic Press Association Award for 1986 (first place, columnist) and has done a great deal of writing and speaking, especially in opposition to abortion and other forms of socially sanctioned killing. She now lives with her husband, Don, and two small sons in Johnson City, Tennessee, where she is leading a fairly retired life and learning how to bake a decent loaf of bread.

Real Magic

Maureen Cassidy Quackenbush

When I was a child, I was always interested in magic. Not stage tricks, but the kind of magic found in fantasy stories. My favorite books were about children who found magic rings or stones or ended up in magic lands that no one else knew about. This was in contrast to fairy tales, which didn't interest me because they didn't make the magic seem real enough. My brothers and I would make up rituals and magic rites and write books of spells and stories of wizards. I always knew it was all pretend, but I wished it were real.

I was born in St. Cloud, Minnesota. Until I was twelve, we lived in a log house my parents built, on a lake near Collegeville, the hamlet where St. John's University is located. I have two younger brothers, close to me in age. After their third child was born, my parents apparently felt a bit overwhelmed. My mother, in particular, was having a hard time handling us all. So, as Dad now describes it, he scaled back his original plan for two big rooms upstairs, "one for all the girls and one for all the boys". Instead, we had an extra playroom and no more siblings.

My parents tell me they moved to Minnesota when they married to be as far away as possible from their parents. Both of them had grown up in strong Catholic families, though my father's mother raised her four alone. But a variety of things caused my parents to leave the Church when I was very young. Even today, we don't discuss these things much, but I surmise from hints that the rhythm method didn't work and *Humanae Vitae* was an unexpected blow. They also had unresolved emotional conflicts with their parents, which became inextricably entangled with their understanding of the faith, and that understanding—which I suspect was not very mature or nuanced or firm—was further thrown into question by changes they saw in the Church after the Second Vatican Council.

My two brothers and I were baptized, and I recall going to Mass in the big cement church at St. John's Abbey with the little lights in the ceiling and the big wall made of thick chunks of glass. I remember a gaunt bronze statue of St. John the Baptist and the peculiar blended scent of beeswax and incense that lingers in Catholic churches. But of the content of the faith I don't remember learning a thing.

I must have absorbed something, however, because it took me years to overcome my inhibition about using the name of God without lowering my voice and feeling presumptuous. I remember asking my mother to teach me the prayers to say on the Rosary, too, and trying it out a few times before forgetting it. Her mother wrote to us regularly, letters filled with holy cards and prayers, but they didn't stay around the house. I don't think I noticed when we stopped going to Mass, or whether there was any unease about it on my parents' part. I do remember, though, finding my mother's birth control pills and, as she evaded the question, getting a bad feeling for even asking what they were.

From a priest friend of Dad's, my brothers and I heard the music from *Jesus Christ Superstar*, and for a while we could sing nothing else. We also loved a song we heard on the radio for a while, the Our Father sung by a nun, and that's how I finally learned the prayer for keeps.

In school I was the perennial oddball, always on the outside of games and the wrong side of politics and religion. I feigned indifference to teasing, which only attracted more, and I earned the reputation of being proud and cold. The public school we went to was across the street from the parochial school. Once a week all the kids in my class marched over there for catechism, except me—because my parents didn't want me to—and one Protestant girl, who became my friend. We were not in the least curious about what they were learning, but I felt awkward when they came back and said I was supposed to be over there, that an empty seat and an unclaimed name tag were reserved for me. I knew from somewhere that the Catholic Church was the original church and I remember explaining that to a classmate who thought otherwise.

Even in elementary school I admired the hippies, though most of what I knew about them was their long hair and interesting clothes. In fifth-grade poetry class we sat in a circle reading Peter, Paul, and Mary lyrics. I'll never forget my music teacher, who rode a motorcycle and had a wild red wig with pigtails that she would lift up to scratch her head.

The social unrest of the sixties was of intense interest to my parents. We watched Walter Cronkite unfold the Vietnam saga every night during dinner, until casualties came to seem pretty casual. As McGovern supporters, my parents were deeply concerned that Richard Nixon was running for president. All the kids at school positively gloated at me when he won, since it proved them right (winners were right) and me—the sole, lowly Democrat—wrong. This only confirmed my self image as an enlightened misfit.

When I turned twelve, we were forced to sell our property to the state to make room for a new highway. We moved to Vancouver Island in British Columbia, and I entered a seventh grade academically far advanced by comparison with my Minnesota sixth grade. I remember having my first brief philosophical discussion with my classmates, in the context of Greek mythology, about whether God was made in the image of man or vice versa. The former seemed obvious to me, and I was mystified that a friend maintained the opposite. Mostly I remember being intrigued by the question and having no idea of how to begin to think about it.

When I was thirteen, we returned to the United States and lived in Oregon, moving about a bit until we settled in Eugene. I first went to junior high in West Eugene, where, academically, we were back to learning how to spell and, socially, the big excitement for students each day was to find out which girls were going to fight behind the school at three o'clock. Feeling lonely and out of place, I was befriended by a zealous Baptist girl who took me to church and youth group meetings. They gave me a Bible, and I tried to read it many times, starting always from the very beginning, but I could never make any headway. We even went on a Baptist camping trip, where, after getting chummy and emotional enough, we had witnessing and testimonies around the campfire. The pressure to accept Christ was focused on me, the only non–Baptist. I did so, of course, not feeling quite as wholehearted about it as I wished, but reluctant to disappoint them. My parents had no objections to driving me to the Baptist church on Sundays, but I couldn't sustain my interest, especially since some of the Sunday School stuff was a downright insult to one's intelligence. One book we had "read" to us was made of blank pages, each of a different color. Gold, for example, was for the gold that paves the streets of heaven.

Sometime later, while still in junior high, I really wanted my parents to settle the question once for all: Is there a God, or not? The film *Jesus of Nazareth* had moved me, and I'd read a book about life-after-death accounts that convinced me we don't simply go out of existence when we die. I begged my parents to tell me what they believed. Mother's answer was "I don't know", and my father's was "God is love." These were not satisfying answers. Mom seemed sincerely uncertain, and "God is love" sounded empty to me, sort of like "Love makes the world go 'round." I had hoped for a Yes or No. I would have understood that their answer was based in belief, not knowledge, but because I had a very high opinion of their judgment, I would still have taken it as a strong indication of the truth of the matter. But their concern, as they explained a few times, was not to influence my private decision unduly. They seemed to think it would be unjust to form me in a belief system I had not voluntarily chosen, which would leave lasting "hang-ups", as they believed it had done to them.

They were afraid to reveal our fallen-away status to our relatives. I knew because, when I was ten and we made a rare visit to my grandparents in Kentucky, all of us went to Mass, received Holy Communion, and lied to my grandmother when she queried us about our First Communions. I don't specifically remember our parents instructing us to do so, but I know we thought we were supposed to pretend, and they didn't stop us. The effect of this duplicity on me was not simply a religious neutrality. Rather, I concluded that the question wasn't important. And if there was a God, the Catholic Church certainly wasn't the place to find out about Him. Or Her; my Dad really cracked up over the joke about going to Heaven and finding out there IS a God—"and she's black".

When we moved to East Eugene, the university side of town, I went to an "alternative" school with groovy teachers. It was refreshing, by comparison with the past. Still considering

myself a misfit, I tended to cling to the teachers I most admired, to soak up every word and world view. Judy, my para-
psychology teacher, also taught kundalini yoga. We students
all called her by her first name and considered her cool. From
her, I learned about the untapped powers of the mind, about
centering, relaxation, self-hypnosis, channeling energies of
various sorts, chakras (focal energy points in the body), and
the "bad vibes" one might encounter in processed white sugar
and meat. Judy taught us foot and hand massage, explaining
that many illnesses of the body can be cured through yoga
and massage. I took her yoga class and tried my utmost to be
the ultimately relaxed, flexible, and centered person I thought
she was. But hard as I tried to please this teacher, I could
never achieve those admirable goals. I could not hypnotize
myself and watch my subconscious do things; I could not enter the state of stillness and peace where you are at one with
the universe and can sense a "light" of some sort. This inadequacy seemed frustrating proof that I was too uptight and
needed to practice letting go of things. In particular, I practiced never being shocked by anything Judy said or did.

Judy used to come back from yoga workshops fervent about
new techniques she'd learned and with notable calm teach us
how to focus or strengthen our digestive, mental, or sexual
powers. Believing she had endorsed it, my brother and I went
to hear the kundalini evangelist, Yogi Bajhan. His talk was
entirely forgettable, but what I unfortunately can't forget is
the droning song he taught us, "Happy am I, healthy am I,
holy am I." We dutifully chanted it during his talk, and it
haunts me to this day. As the Yogi left the room, he touched
my brother on the forehead, which instantly cured his pound-
ing headache. Today, I wonder what gave him that headache.

In retrospect, it's curious to notice that, for all the talk about
"meditation" and "spiritual awakening", none of these expe-

riences was really concerned with the supernatural. Each was something one did by getting in the right frame of mind and getting one's body to cooperate. It seemed to be a very physical, natural, unmagical, and so, to me, finally uninspiring business.

It was during this time that J. R. R. Tolkien's *Lord of the Rings* came to the rescue. My brothers and I, with nine acquaintances who had similar interests, formed a club of Tolkien devotees, modestly titled the "White Council". It sustained us through many of the vicissitudes of junior high, high school, and some time after. We still meet once a year in Oregon, sometimes nearly all twelve of us at once.

Back in junior high, we had weekly club meetings and went on twice-yearly trips to the coast (with an adult chaperone, until we were older). We had twelve silver rings made, and each of us chose an identifying virtue in conjunction with accepting them. We selected an eight-pointed star and a silver flame for our banner. I cherished this group of friends so much that I used to "pray" for them, in a manner of speaking, by calling each face to mind every night and "sending them white light". When we first started the club we found a book (one of the many companions to the Tolkien trilogy) in which the author claimed he had inside knowledge that Tolkien's story was based on a book he'd found that recounted real events. I believed every word and for the first time had a little flash of hope that magic might really be real. In our excitement, we wrote a letter to the author asking for more information. It was not answered, and as time passed we tried to forget about our embarrassing little foray into gullibility.

We all got involved with *Dungeons and Dragons*, the fantasy board game where the dungeon master creates a world and takes characters on adventures through it, with the use of dice to determine the strengths and weaknesses of the characters as well as the outcome of events. A few of the boys became really good dungeon masters, and they all learned a lot about percentages and chance and stuff that I just couldn't grasp. I have since heard that some people who played the game regularly became obsessed by it. We were obsessed only in the sense that our games often continued into the night and were carried on for weeks. But they were very much like the pretend-adventure games my children play now, except that they had more structure and rules.

Finally, though, we did start down the dangerous avenue of the occult. It began as an innocent adventure, but soon we found that the Ouija board was working so well and speedily for us that we needed someone on hand just to write the words down before we forgot them. We could make a board with a piece of notepaper, a quickly scrawled alphabet, spots on the paper for yes and no, and a plastic container lid for a moving piece. We "spoke" to people out of faraway times and places, and all of them had something to tell us about a mysterious thing called "zoma" or "soma". The meanings were fascinating for us to try to unravel, though the descriptions were often enigmatic: "Soma is the flute in the maze" or "the stone on the fjord" (variations depended on what country the "spirit" hailed from).

Soon the messages started to change, however, and the tone of our gatherings got more ominous as the board began to flatter and finally to "instruct" us. We were described as "a great white light in the Willamette Valley" and then told to release the spirit of a notable tree on the University of Oregon campus. It was a Dawn Redwood, a kind of tree thought to be extinct until a grove was found in China in the 1940s. The one on the campus had been successfully grown from seed brought from China. But this "tree spirit" wanted to be freed. We were given specific details of the ceremony required to accomplish its release, including the time (night, of course), the placement of our club rings about the base of the tree, and what we were to do and say. The ceremony prescribed was itself so unremarkable that I hardly remember it. But I remember feeling guilty afterward, when the tree seemed to look less healthy than it had before.

About then, a strange man took to following one of the younger boys in the group, claiming to be able to read his mind. The boy believed him, so we did, too. This stranger was probably unbalanced, but a very convincing fellow to us. He carried around with him a folder full of the obituaries of his friends, which he showed to us as proof that "they" were after him, too, and it would be only a matter of time. When he said he had come in search of the "white light" in the Willamette Valley, our attention was captured, and I, at least, was tantalized for the second time by the possibility that the supernatural might be real.

Providentially, at this point in our adventures one club member, who had taken "healing" as her virtue, rescued us from the perils of occult infestation. The Healer (who later fulfilled her ambition by becoming a doctor in real life) said it was time to ditch this strange man and the Ouija board. If we didn't, she said, she was going to quit the club. So we did.

Our enthusiasm for the world of Tolkien's trilogy had kept us childlike in some ways, and our friendships had so far saved us from being drawn in and overwhelmed by the peer pressures and gloom of high school. Still, we were not to escape the drug scene. In fact, our interest in the 1960s and early 1970s, which we had all just "missed", made us rush to embrace it. The four older White Council members, my three girl friends and I, were all in high school, while the younger members, all boys, were still in junior high, so for a time we were traveling on separate tracks. In high school, everyone in our circle of friends tried to be countercultural. We mourned the end of the 1960s, admiring chiefly the music of the period and its broadening life-style. Regarding ourselves as outside the mainstream, we disdained sports and all official high school activities, except, of course, the recycling club. Yet we were conscientious about our academic responsibilities and, though we scorned that status, were all quite successful students. Despite feeling compelled to do my homework to the best of my ability, I was convinced that my success was meaningless and the school "system" perverse. I didn't have a reasoned critique of high school beyond the convictions I still hold, that the brightest students are not those who get the highest grades and that schools reward cleverness and obedience more than they teach love of learning, or even how to learn.

Like my family, my friends and I were intellectually rather elitist in our tastes. We didn't watch much television. Together, we disdained things like McDonalds, Republicans, new cars, current fashions in clothes and music, industrial and technological development, and progress. All my clothes came from the army surplus store or the men's section of the thrift shop. We smoked marijuana together, though I hated its oppressive, brain-disconnecting effect. Though we talked a lot about doing LSD, I didn't try it until I was out of high school. But as I was the oldest in the group, and enthusiastic about the experience when I did try it, I was doubtless one of the reasons the rest of our Council got involved with it.

What the "drug scene" meant for us was not merely a way to escape our troubles but a desperate hope that for those with eyes to see—which we maintained drugs would help one acquire—there might be more to the world than the television ads indicate, or so we desperately hoped. The joyfulness of children had been replaced by the mood-swings and general dullness of the teenager. Life was "depressing", we all agreed. I think now that it was because we were wasting twelve important years of our lives trapped in the artificial school environment.

After high school I went to a Youth Conservation Corps summer camp, whose leaders were exactly my type but just enough older to be real hippies. They were aficionados of the Grateful Dead, interested in preserving the environment and teaching us appreciation for nature, which of course included a religious reverence for Mother Earth and a distaste for humans and their abuse of the world. Such a position inevitably results either in a double standard ("we environmentalists are exempt from the general condemnation of mankind") or an oppressive sense of guilt and inadequacy (because our behavior fails to correspond perfectly to our sense of obligation to the needs of the earth).

Instead of going to college, as I had half-heartedly planned, I decided to join these new friends for the fall semester at their outdoor school, a kind of environmental education camp offered to sixth graders in the Tualatin school district. The program wasn't bad, and I found it a lot of fun to teach children who still had some sense of wonder about the world. But it was with these people that I first tried LSD. When I did, I thought I had found the ticket to beauty and intense, mystical friendships no longer separated by anything.

My first acid trip was spent walking up and down an Oregon beach through sunset and on into the starlit night, talking and looking at all the beauty with two other workers from the outdoor school. In the throes of drug intoxication, I believed we were all thinking the same thoughts together. Afterward, I realized that this was a delusion caused by the drug. One of the two girls, however, wrote and illustrated a brief description of the experience, and I was amazed that she remembered the same things and drew the same images that I had retained. Yet even so, I did not stay in touch with them later, a fact that should have been a clue that friendships are not made or kept magically. Subsequent LSD trips never equaled that first experience, and soon my enthusiasm for it wore off.

But I kept looking for an encounter with a greater reality, hoping that a perfect love would be part of it. The love I sought was some mixture of romance and ideal friendship. I had not yet realized, as eventually we all must, that complete intimacy, which many people think of as true romantic love, isn't possible between human beings. Our desire for it is in fact our longing for God.

There was a gap between the end of the outdoor school term and the beginning of spring semester at college. While I waited, I worked at a number of part-time jobs in Eugene. Thus I began a kind of dreary dream, the ugliest, most miserable months of my life. I turned to men, especially to being loved or sought after, as a way to find joy. I would think I'd fallen in love, long enough to lure someone into loving me, and then realize I didn't love him after all or that I hadn't really wanted love but some kind of admiration or glory. I tried to sustain the optimistic view that I was happy and all things are good (except, of course, capitalist monopolies and right-wing anti-environmentalists), while my behavior was proving otherwise. I turned from one relationship to another, my whims and desires spinning personal entanglements everywhere, with each new venture initiated primarily to escape the previous mess.

The classes I took at the Southern California college the next year—Creative Mythology, Environmental Psychology, East-

ern Religions and Anthropology—were bizarre, disconnected, and undemanding. The chaotic, alcohol- and cocaine-
ridden life of the student body disgusted me, which doesn't
mean that I shunned it. Though I joined in, I simultaneously
hated to think of the money I was wasting on a year-long
party with a lot of spoiled children. I resolved not to return
the following fall.

But when I arrived home without plans for the future, I
realized I had no idea even how to decide what to do next. I
felt incapable of acting and became increasingly depressed. At
last my parents offered suggestions, warning that if I didn't
get off my duff they would start charging me rent. So I vol-
unteered for a crisis hot line, worked part-time at a donut
shop, took T'ai Chi, even tried an absurd Gestalt Therapy
class. I might have gone on in this way indefinitely if my
parents hadn't intervened again. My mother proposed that I
look into a program for students who wanted to work abroad
for a summer, improving their foreign language skills while
earning both money and experience. So I applied to go to
West Germany and was accepted for a job working on a farm.

To prepare for it, I started working on a dairy farm outside
Eugene and took junior college classes in German. The dairy
farm, especially the dairy farmer, who couldn't keep his hands
to himself, became very unpleasant, and I began to look forward to Europe as an escape.

But in Europe, as in Eugene, I repeatedly got myself into
relationships (one with a burgermeister, no less) that started as
adventures but turned into embarrassing or even frightening
situations. I escaped the troubles in Germany with a trip to
England, where I met a man who was supposed to be a traveling partner but wanted to be much more. My subsequent
escape back to America was a terrific relief.

I look back on all this and can't quite explain the things I did except to say I felt trapped by my circumstances, as though I were watching myself in chains, but I did not see that it was all caused by own behavior. I remember looking at myself one night in the mirror—it was when I was in Germany, but had sneaked away from my host family—and thought to myself "she's dead"!

After my summer of work, travel, and escapes, I came to rest at last at Evergreen State College in Olympia, Washington. Evergreen is an "alternative" school, where classes are small and the curriculum is called "innovative" because it takes some account of the need for coherence. I was accepted for admission and even won a modest scholarship on the basis of an application essay that answered the question of what I wanted to do with my education. I wanted to become a witch, I said, and live on the moors, dispensing herbal cures and communing with nature. Apparently I fitted their idea of the educated woman.

Deeply relieved to have only studying and moderately interesting classes to think about, I liked Evergreen at first. The curriculum seemed less arbitrary than had been the case at my first college, and the students more motivated and interested in their studies. Yet even more than at my high school, the Evergreen students were bent on being countercultural, creative, and unique. Uniqueness was hard to achieve, as there was also a strong unspoken pressure to conform to a vegetarian, leather-free, antinuke, bisexual, consciousness-raised pro-Sandinista line. One day one of my housemates shaved off all her lovely chestnut tresses except for one tiny long braid at the back (the pile of hair lay in the yard for months, I remember). When I asked why she did it, she said it was an attempt not to be beautiful, a rejection of femininity and the world's standards of beauty. But in fact, a great many students were starting to wear their hair that way, and it actually looked quite attractive on her.

Because I couldn't push myself to do much for the causes I thought I cared about deeply—feminism, saving the whales, nuclear power, and disarmament—I felt guilty continually. The Sandinista/Contra situation in Nicaragua wasn't something I followed with close attention, but I knew which side I was supposed to be on. Once, I trudged reluctantly through the rain to a railway line where a train carrying a nuclear missile was scheduled to pass. It pulled up to where we stood watching, moving so slowly that the two big bouncers on board were able to lift off the brave souls lying on the tracks without anyone ever being endangered.

Meanwhile, I was studying chemistry and biology and trying to assimilate as many facts as possible, assuming that fact-absorption was all college was intended to provoke. Whenever I considered how much there was to read, and how many subjects and fields I would like to master, I got frantic with anxiety because I thought I had to learn it all, and since I never could, I would always be incomplete and inadequate. Compared to my later experience of a real intellectual life, the class discussions of books were sterile and tedious. We never wanted to offend one another or uncover fundamental differences of view because it was too unsettling. Since there could be no possibility of resolution, we talked only about how wonderful the imagery was—in *Moby Dick*, for instance—or, when we read of current social problems, about how important it was to change The System—joining it and undoing it from within was always the plan. As we saw things, American political traditions and economic systems and the whole oppressive, patriarchal, heterosexual, white world view were society's fundamental problems.

As long as I didn't think about what in the world I was doing, or what I ought to do, I was content enough. There was very little connection, though, between my thoughts and my actions. My thoughts were disjointed and unclear, and my behavior became entirely whim-driven. As I grew more and more indifferent, I slipped gradually into a state where it didn't matter what I thought, even about simple day-to-day matters. When it came to making decisions, I was enslaved by my whims and really did whatever I felt like doing, regardless of what I thought might be better. I experimented with strange diets, just to see what it would be like, for instance, to eat only apples for a week, and I continued to look for relationships with men that would be adventurous. My roommate was a lesbian, and for a while I considered the possibility of being one, because the lifestyle of a houseful of women I knew looked so happy and wholesome. They baked their own bread and had a big garden and made beautifully crafted pottery.

Assuming I was invincible, I took such poor care of my health that it eventually broke. After one too many nocturnal swims in Puget Sound, in combination with some kind of virus, I had my first asthma attack. I happened to be spending the night at the home of a young Filipina secretary from the school office where I worked, who had taken an interest in my welfare. As I labored to breathe, I stared at the bare walls of my room, where one solitary crucifix hung. It reminded me of my grandmother's house and, so, of all old people. Shivering at the sadness of being alone, sick, and unable to help myself, I spent a night in fear, with no idea of what was wrong with me. I think that was a kind of metaphorical taste of my true condition.

In those days, I was constantly stumbling into new friendships that I tried to make into something more significant than they were. People seemed to enjoy being with me, but I felt these relationships required of me a level of enthusiasm more intense than I could consistently maintain. In one characteristic episode, I went hiking with two friends on a lovely autumn day. The weather was exhilarating, and the scented air seemed to stir faint memories of some precious, lost moment in the past. All day I talked about how our friendship was beautiful and unique, even as something destined, "different, and yet more natural" than others. They visited me when I was sick with asthma, and yet, after I recovered, I never called them or met with them again.

Trying to create my own happiness, involved in progressively more confusing relationships, unable to shake the growing feeling that college was only a more expensive continuation of high school, wondering at one level why I was there at all, I finally realized I wasn't just having occasional episodes of gloom. Rather, I was deeply and completely unhappy. This was an admission of utter failure to one taught, as I had been, that we are always responsible for our own happiness and should live by slogans like "visualize yourself bathed in a golden pool of light", and "you are what you believe you are."

At last, I reached a boundary where I felt I could no longer take care of myself. Sitting by a pond in the woods behind my house, trying to write something deep and significant in my diary, I ended up sobbing instead, and "asking" for help from the universe at large, from something I didn't even know. The whole action was unreasonable, and uncharacteristic, too, as I didn't believe in God. But it was an important moment, because it was an admission of my own limitedness.

I think God answered me immediately. Very shortly after that, I met my husband-to-be. First he tried to arrange an introduction through some mutual friends at the school office where we both worked, but I shied away from that proposal as contrived and unnatural, like dates, which I abhorred. We met, finally, at a party, and within a few minutes he mentioned that he liked President Reagan. Never having met a person with such tastes before, I was first stunned and then intrigued. We went on to discuss the current political situation, about which I soon realized I had many prejudices and no information. He said he was going to switch to a small college in California named Thomas Aquinas College. He described it as offering an education rather like that prevailing in the Middle Ages.

"Oh, I'm interested in the Middle Ages", I said. But I couldn't imagine that anyone would want to leave Evergreen. Didn't everyone agree it was far superior to most standard, conventional colleges?

The next time we met, David had a little Gideon Bible in his pocket, and he said he was considering Christianity. I told him I knew from experience that one place you don't want to go for that is the Catholic Church.

His response was, "Really? Tell me more about this." So I tried and discovered once again that I knew nothing at all about it, except for the undeniable fact that my parents had fallen away. He, on the other hand, knew of various Catholic people he admired, and he had read a lot in authors like G. K. Chesterton and Russell Kirk, as well as the Anglican C. S. Lewis. During our third meeting, he said that if Christianity were not "true", then he'd like to go out with a bang. The image he invoked was of taking a tremendous amount of drugs and driving a motorcycle off a cliff at sunset.

What struck me most strongly about this rash approach to a matter of words and ideas was the odd concept of considering whether or not "Christianity were true." It seemed like saying "if Kennedy were true". A historical fact is not a matter of truth. Truth might relate to the contents of the Christian creed, but I had long ago stopped thinking of it that way. It would be like saying "Is the Iron Age true?" I realized it sounded strange to my ears because I wasn't used to employing the word "true" except in quizzes. And quizzes would never ask a question like "Christianity is: True False (circle one)."

"Truth", for me, had been a very limited notion, insofar as I had had a notion of it at all. Long before that time, I had accepted the principle that there is no truth, that all is relative in this world of mirrors. People who divide the world into the true and the false, I thought, fail to see all the gray areas—which are chiefly in the moral realm. I think this is the natural conclusion of a mind that hasn't learned to reason clearly, whenever the resolution of two conflicting views would mean that one reputable person's deeply held conviction must be wrong. Or, worse, that someone would have to change what he is doing.

But once I considered the possibility that things could be true or false—that there actually is a Truth—my whole world turned right side up. Fired with youthful hope for goodness, I was as excited as I had been when I thought that perhaps the Lord of the Rings had really happened. My habitual effort to look happy—or as happy as was consistent with the knowledge that the world in general is not going well—was replaced by actual hope and soaring joy. I realized how much despair I had been carrying around as a skeptic.

Now, clear as could be, I had before me again the question: *Is there a God, or not?* Having just come to see how glorious it was that there is truth, it was not hard to see *Truth* as a name for God. Or to accept what the authors I took to reading had to say about the alternatives: Either there *is* a God, or this world is not only meaningless but a cruel joke.

The first remedial work I read was C. S. Lewis' "The Weight of Glory", which was not written as an introduction to Christianity but was very beautiful. It served to demonstrate that there exist in the world intelligent people who can discuss Christianity without sounding like gullible idiots. Not that I had read any gullible idiots on the subject; I had just presumed it was that sort of religion.

Next I read Russell Kirk's discussion of the demise of higher education, which rang entirely true and made much sense of my experiences with college. Then I read Lewis' space trilogy, *Out of the Silent Planet*, *Perelandra*, and *That Hideous Strength*. They likewise rang true, and they were complete eye-openers as to what is really happening in the world. Lewis is also very good at bringing out the Magic of it all. And yes, to believe in God meant believing or, rather, knowing, that limitless Good, the very best kind of magic, is really real.

At David's urging, I also read the Thomas Aquinas College handbook and its statement of purpose, called the Blue Book. It struck me as possibly a bit narrow-minded, since the authors thought you could search for and find truth and be a Catholic at the same time, without these coming into conflict. But I was willing to be proved wrong. After weighing my fear that it wouldn't be as good as it sounded and my realization that I would no doubt be shocking my parents, I decided to apply. That meant starting college all over again.

At Thomas Aquinas College, I found actual higher education, completely new and yet what I had thought all along that college was supposed to be. Near Lent, in my freshman year, I entered the Church. Many of the students were influences in my conversion, but my roommate was especially pivotal. She knelt by her bed every morning and night to pray, never pried or pushed her religion on me, but always thought-fully answered my questions.

I also think my maternal grandmother had been a "prayer warrior" on my behalf. I didn't really know her and hadn't written her letters since I was a child, but when I converted, I wrote her a letter telling her about it. She died a few months later, and I was told this letter was very precious to her.

Once I accepted that there is a God, I had no problem with miracles or doctrinal things, since God can do anything, and He calls the shots. I did have habitual thought patterns to undo. It took me a long time to really see that abortion is wrong, even though I promptly accepted that this is the Church's teaching. I had to experience as a mother the pass-ing of time from morning sickness through to a baby in the arms to come to see that one. I also feared that an obligation to go to Mass every Sunday might be too hard to keep, as I'd never made such a long-term commitment before, and I'd had a good deal of experience at flaking out. But Thomas Aquinas College, offering constant food for thought and faith, was a good place to be a fledgling Catholic.

At the same time, of course, I discovered what a suffering Church she is and learned of the scandal and corruption that seem to be part and parcel of the human condition. In our country Catholics in general do not seem to be awake in their faith, and I think it's probably because we don't suffer enough. There sometimes appears to be a vast bureaucratic "take-over" by unbelievers who call themselves Catholic but actually have an agenda that sounds like destruction. And even where the motive is not malice but just bad judgment, the Church's compelling truth is often hidden. Today I often cringe at Masses where there are a lot of ridiculous demeaning antics at the altar. When a priest tries to "make the liturgy meaning-ful" by changing the words of the Mass, sapping it of its meaning, or fails to mention the eternal truths that could actually help his parishioners, I see how much we need good examples around us—and how much we need serious prayer, for our priests especially.

But I know that discouragement is a failure to hope and that with God all things are possible, so I am not willing to give in to the kind of bitterness I have seen in some fellow Catholics at the internal disorders that afflict her. These trials should elicit from us a clamor of prayer rather than bitterness or withdrawal. I know Christ's Church isn't going to fail. Her treasures are so great that even when we diminish or veil her beauty with watered-down liturgies or bad homilies, His living grace still turns people's lives around and makes them whole. So until God restores His Bride to perfect order, we who see the decay are the ones who get to suffer and thus share with our Lord in bringing the very great good He will bring out of these evils.

Now that I have seven children, I do worry about passing the faith along to them. The self-serving habits of a lifetime tempt me away from fully living the virtues I'd like my children to see in their mother. But I try to remember that God works through His weak servants to accomplish His will, and He doesn't ignore prayer. I don't know how I could have gone on living if God had not rescued me, and I'll never be done thanking Him!

❧

Maureen Cassidy Quackenbush was born in St. Cloud, Minnesota, and spent her teen years in Eugene, Oregon. She drifted through several colleges before attending Thomas Aquinas College in Santa Paula, California, where she returned to the Church. Now she and her husband, David, live in Oak View, California, where they are raising and educating seven of the next generation of Catholics.

From NOW to Eternity

Constance Buck

I left the Catholic Church at the age of twenty-two, and did not return until I was thirty-five. My journey took me from the catechism to consciousness raising, from Church doctrine to feminist dogma, from God to man. What I found in life without God was a desert of chaos and despair.

I was born on the East Side of New York City, in an Italian-Catholic family, and grew up in Brooklyn during the mythic 1950s. In Bay Ridge, Brooklyn, under the shadow of the Verrazano Bridge, I went to Our Lady of Angels Grammar School and then to Fontbonne Hall Academy. I came of age in the "Age of Aquarius" and, in my early twenties, returned to Manhattan to spend the next decade in the only part of New York that New Yorkers consider "The City".

At the age of twenty-two, I married my high school sweetheart. We were married in the Church, but we did not have a Nuptial Mass because the groom, though raised a Catholic, refused to receive Holy Communion. Because I was already involved in the feminist movement, I did not take his last name. When I was twenty-four, our marriage was civilly annulled. I was deeply disappointed by its failure and deeply confused about my own part in all of it. Rather than own up to any responsibility, I let myself believe I was the victim in the entire affair. I refused even to consider seeking a declaration of nullity from the Church, assuming the marriage tribunal would invade my privacy to wound me even more.

Thinking I was "out of the Church", I believed I could not go to confession and receive absolution. I convinced myself that the Church was simply another patriarchy, so submission to her annulment procedures would be counterproductive to my search for freedom. Consequently, I embraced the women's movement as a kinder, gentler, more understanding "god".

I had gone to a small women's college in Greenwich Village, and now I went uptown to Columbia University for my doctorate in Child Development. My résumé began to fill up with the tokens of a success shaped by the feminist agenda. For five years, I taught in the Psychology Department at Marymount Manhattan College, where my courses included the Psychology of Women, Human Sexuality, and Abnormal Psychology. I completed two postdoctoral fellowships. During the 1981-82 academic year, I was a Bush Fellow in Child Development and Social Policy at the University of Michigan in Ann Arbor. The following year I was awarded a Congressional Science Fellowship, sponsored jointly by the American Association for the Advancement of Science and the Society for Research in Child Development.

As to specifically feminist credentials, I was a founding member of the Brooklyn Chapter of the National Organization for Women. I have a chapter in the New York Women's Yellow Pages. For more than five years, I belonged to a consciousness-raising group. As a member of a women's health collective, I worked in Boston one summer on the early version of *Our Bodies, Our Selves*. At that time it was not the glossy, expensive magazine now found in mainstream bookstores but an amateur production printed on newsprint and sold only in the feminist underground. I was listed in *Who's Who among American Women*.

Those honors and accomplishments failed to bring me peace or contentment, however. No worldly achievement was enough. I struggled constantly to define myself and my situation. Who was I? What would become of me? I would look at bag ladies and wonder, *What happened to them? How did they spin so far out of control?* In my anxiety, I saw myself in them. How could I ensure that I would not become one of them, physically or spiritually? Just one slip, and there I would be, on the street. I could not rest or take pleasure in my accomplishments, because I could not find any meaning to life, any purpose to claim as my own. So I searched.

Spurred by the feminist assumption that I was entirely a product of my culture, I spent countless hours pondering the meaning of my life. Feminist ideology holds that the very notions of what it means to be a man or a woman are culturally derived. Because males have dominated Western civilization, while women were taught to be submissive, every cultural tenet must be re-examined in order that the culture can be reshaped. I was called to examine everything I had become, because it was from society that I had learned to be a woman and do what was expected of women. If societal expectations had limited my development or denied me freedom, then those expectations had to be changed. In the process, I had to determine who I was and what I believed about my purpose in life, my vocation, my life-style, and, finally, my faith.

To accomplish this re-examination, I needed a looking glass. I found it in the consciousness-raising (CR) group that became an important part of my life for more than five years. I joined the CR group while I was still married and stayed in it through most of my graduate-school years: CR participation was the embodiment of the feminist axiom that the "personal is political". The phrase meant that in order to change the political culture, I had to personalize the women's movement by viewing all the world through a feminist lens. By definition, the purpose of a CR group is to develop that feminist lens and to support members in the personal changes that need to be made in each one's life. There were five other women in the group, and we saw each other through all of our divorces, abortions, lesbian crushes, sexual affairs, family struggles, drug and alcohol addictions, and career changes. The group became my confessional.

I was determined to define myself in my own terms, not to live out a life that my parents wanted for me or that the Church required of me. The CR group, I thought, could help me find my own voice, distinct from any cultural expectations, and provide me with the freedom to identify my goals. To do it meant clarifying my spiritual and political beliefs, my emotional investments, and, finally, my way of life in the world. This was an exploration I had to conduct without a moral compass to frame my choices or guide my decisions, because I believed that the compass itself had to be recalibrated.

Freed of cultural handcuffs, I thought I could become all I had the potential to be. Like Nora in Ibsen's *Doll's House*, I would soar above all those women leading "unexamined lives", because I would be at the center of my own plan, unencumbered by husband, children, or aging parents. To include such people in my plan would be to assume responsibilities that would handicap me.

By the mid-1970s, Betty Friedan was already too mainstream for most New York feminists. In the absence of a compass, I looked to the feminist writings of Kate Millet, Robin Morgan, and Ti-Grace Atkinson for guidance. Their writings focused on "marriage and family constructs" as limitations on a woman's "human capacity". Because everything I knew about marriage and family constructs came from my family and my Church, it was easy to start seeing these two entities as antithetical to my goals. So I began purging my life of both God and family.

Purging God from one's life purges meaning from one's life. My effort to replace Him left me very lonely and vulnerable to all kinds of other influences. While still in graduate school, I carefully read Freud and Marx; I meditated and took drugs to transcend time and space; and I ate macrobiotically. My search for meaning was, for the most part, a solitary pursuit, so consuming that I became disconnected from the common rhythms of life marked by family meals, holiday gatherings, birthday celebrations, weddings, and funerals, I listened to a lot of pop music but found no happiness in living by the rule of Janis Joplin's song, "get it while you can", or by Frank Sinatra's boast, "I did it my way." I followed any impulse or proclivity until bored. The road was painful and dangerous; not a journey at all, but a dead end.

When I was at the University of Michigan, I rarely thought about God. If I did, I would remind myself that because I was no longer married I was "out of the Church". Since God had thrown me out, why should I even think about Him? As long as I was "doomed", why not get all I could out of the experience? Only through experience, I believed, could I learn about myself and construct my life plan.

Experience for its own sake became important to me. Systematically, I sought many different experiences, trying to tease out answers to my questions of identity. Who was I? What was I not? But all those experiences did not make me wiser or evoke any paradigm shift. I learned nothing. I gained no insight.

Of all the representatives of ideologies and movements I encountered while a postdoctoral fellow—vegetarians, Sufis, yogi meditationists, drug and alcohol addicts, lesbians, yippies, radical feminists—I never met a practicing Christian or an observant Jew. The people I knew all had their own personal schemes, but not one looked beyond himself to any divine plan. No one I knew believed in God. Now, I am astonished that I couldn't see, then, that I was embracing in Ann Arbor the very lock-step homogenization I was fleeing in Brooklyn.

After a year in Ann Arbor, I was awarded a Congressional Science Fellowship, which took me to Washington to work on Capitol Hill, in the United States House of Representatives. I had recently finished an "est" course, a weekend experience intended to transform participants' consciousness by making them aware that they possess the wisdom and power to change their circumstances by thought control. As a first step, the "trainers" tried, through intimidation and humiliation, to break down any denial that we needed transformation. One technique they used was to require that we return to our seats to the sound of music. If we weren't in our seats when the music stopped, we had to answer to the leader in front of the hundreds of people in the room. I was never late.

Despite the fact that the experience was highly emotional and intense, when the weekend was over I felt spiritually empty as well as physically exhausted. Later, when the "est" people kept calling me to continue my "training", I resisted. Planted in my consciousness was a seed of awareness that my search for meaning had to go beyond group therapy, group consciousness raising, and "personal esteem" movements.

Not long after the "est" experience, I went to Naples, Florida, to spend Easter weekend with my parents. It was more than a decade since I had left the Church, and so long since I had gone to Mass even as a guest that my parents did not ask me to attend with them. But some visiting cousins were going to Mass that Easter Sunday, and as a convenience I decided to go along. They all sat together in a pew, while I stood alone against the back wall of the crowded parish church.

For a time, I watched the congregation, musing, *This is what ordinary people do on Sundays.* They seemed happy. Suddenly swept with nostalgia, I wished I too had an ordinary life.

When the time came for Holy Communion, I watched the people all filing up the aisles, freshly conscious that I could not receive. I watched families, husbands and wives and children, receiving Communion together. I saw my cousins receiving Communion. *They are happily being nourished by a Bread they hold to be Life itself,* I thought. I wondered if they realized that they were receiving the Body and Blood of Jesus Christ, or whether they did it unexamined, simply because they ordinarily received Communion on Sundays.

The contemporary building had circular seating and a stained glass dome, through which the sun cast its light into the church. Colors poured down from the stained glass, and motes danced in the streams of light, making everything else look bleached and dimmed. As my attention centered on the worshippers at Holy Communion, I thought, *"Do This In Remembrance of Me." This is not an ordinary event. To receive Holy Communion is a very extraordinary event. To receive the Body and Blood of Jesus Christ is to drink the same Blood that was shed on the Cross so that we might live, to eat the same Body offered up for us so that we might enjoy eternal salvation.*

A tremendous longing surged through me. *Oh, if I could ever receive Holy Communion again, how much that would mean to me. How blessed and honored I would feel! It would never be routine to me. It would indeed be extraordinary. I would never take Him for granted. Once you have found what you had lost, it will always remain precious to you.*

O Lord, I am not worthy to receive You, but only say the word and I shall be healed, I prayed. *"What is the word, dear Lord?"*

Then all at once I saw my errors quite clearly. It struck me that I had never been thrown out of the Church. I had done it myself! I had removed *myself* from the Church. *"Only say the word and I shall be healed?" But it can't be that simple. Isn't that only a prayer? It is not that simple,* I thought. *Surely, it is not that simple.*

I felt puzzled, as though I were on the verge of knowing something but didn't know what it was. Could it really be true that if I believed the words, "Lord, I am not worthy to receive You, but only say the word and I shall be healed", that in fact I would be? *Healed? What does that mean? Healed?*

Grappling with these unfamiliar ideas, I pondered, *Of course I am ultimately responsible for my own actions. But can my actions alone bring me salvation? Is it by my actions alone that I "earn" Heaven or "deserve" Hell? Or is God's love so encompassing—like a mother's for her child, or a lover's for his beloved— that despite all I have done, I could ask for "the Word" and really be healed?* If I believed in Him, then I would be like the thief who died beside Jesus: the fact of my salvation or damnation would not rest with me but with Him. All I really had to do was to believe with all my heart and ask for forgiveness. *Just say the word, and I shall be healed.* I was still lost in these utterly unexpected thoughts as the congregation departed.

From that moment on, I knew very surely that the direction of my life had to change. But change did not come immediately. What I recognized that day was the possibility of change. I still had to make the change happen, and I didn't know how.

Back home, I began to look more closely at the lives of people I knew. On Capitol Hill, I worked with one woman who actually went to Mass every day and always seemed to have a song in her heart. She hummed a lot and was genuinely cheerful. Imagine!

As you might guess, I regarded cheerfulness as a quality suited to morons. Knowing about male violence, the loss of our precious environment, the trampling on human rights around the globe, not to mention the incalculable tally of sexual and racial discrimination in our own capitalist country, what intelligent person could be cheerful? Yet there she was, cheerful. At the time, neither of us was married or had children, or even prospects of either, yet she was apparently content with her life. What did she have that I didn't have? She seemed entirely unworried about her personal future, happy just to be a "handmaid of the Lord".

I couldn't believe it. In the whole feminist movement I had never met a woman who seemed as happy as this one. She was no pushover; she did not allow anyone to dismiss her ideas, but neither did she wave the feminist flag. Her ideas were her own, but they were always based on some God-given principle. Having no other gods kept her life simple and focused; she viewed all the world through the lens of the one true God. Now, I saw, *that* was freedom.

I began to envy her. Perhaps she had not been born that way, I thought. Maybe she worked at it. But how? Gradually, I recognized that God was the consuming center of her life.

Around this same time, several close friends contracted the HIV virus. I watched in fear and horror as their lives unraveled and the loneliness of their existences was exposed: They spoke their regrets about their lives, acknowledging paths they had not taken. Seeing this, I knew how precious life is; it is not a dress rehearsal, I realized, but the real thing. Two friends set out on spiritual searches that coincided with my own. Like me, they hoped for assurance that there is a God and a Heaven and, more important, that God is forgiving and merciful. But we never talked about that. I just watched them, and learned, and murmured, "Lord, I am not worthy, but only say the word and I shall be healed."

I was a city girl whose idea of the great outdoors was dining *al fresco*. A Midwestern outdoorsman with a deep need to see mountains and hike in the woods was hardly the man with whom I would have expected to fall in love. But I met Larry at a St. Patrick's Day dance party on Capitol Hill in 1984. He was a non-practicing Baptist from Kansas City, Missouri, recently back from service with the Peace Corps in Africa and now on his own spiritual quest. He was—and is—a kind, generous, sweet, self-giving man of high standards and solid ethics. We fell in love and within seven months were married in a civil ceremony. Four months later, on April 15, 1985, we married again, in the Catholic Church.

During our courtship, I had begun a tentative return to Catholicism. A sympathetic parish priest encouraged me to seek a Church annulment, which I eventually did. The annulment process demanded a profound self-examination, but not one in which I ever felt myself a victim. Rather, it helped me to heal emotionally and to gain deep understanding and respect for marriage as a sacrament. Overcome by God's mercy in giving me this opportunity to begin my life with Larry within the fold of the Church that I was growing to love, I prayed in gratitude for my marriage, and I prayed for children. Almost three years after our marriage, our first daughter was born. The miracle of her birth reminded me how much I had taken for granted in the past.

Over the years, our lives have changed greatly. Far from the unencumbered existence I once projected, our marriage has been blessed with two young daughters, and when Jennie, the elder, was three, my parents, no longer able to live alone, moved in with us. In those early years, I often went to Mass without Larry, but he joined us ever more frequently, and, to my great joy, he became a Catholic the same year Jennie received her First Holy Communion.

Today, my life is much simpler than it was when I was a feminist, and I am a great deal happier than I ever was before. I still have a satisfying career, but now I see that God's plan is for us to live in community. To follow the teaching of Jesus is to share our lives with others. When we live this way, we continually discover new levels of meaning.

As Mother Teresa told us, meaning is to be found in the simple acts of daily living, when we put God, rather than ourselves, at the center of our lives. Now when I face a decision, I pray, "Lord, please do with me as You will. Help me to understand—but help me to do Your will even if I don't understand. May Your Will Be Done." We now pray as a family, too. Often, we ask each other, "What do you think God is asking you to do in this situation?" Putting everything in God's hands, I trust that all will go according to His plan, that things will unfold as they should.

The saddest irony of my former life is that its pain and alienation were so unnecessary. My desolation was self-imposed. I wasted time and anguish trying to determine what I was about, instead of trying to discover what God wants of me. Before I could do that, I had to acknowledge that doing God's will is more important than pursuing my own will. The answer I sought to the meaning of life really is as simple as doing what I know is right and leaving the rest to God.

In these pages I have briefly sketched where I have been. My chief purpose in writing, however, is not to review my history but to pass along the simple, basic, indispensable lessons I was so slow to learn in living it. They contravene all the principles of feminism, but they are true, and they lead away from death to eternal life.

First, just as my old catechism formulated it, the purpose of life really is to know, love, and serve God in this world so that we may be happy with Him forever in Heaven. Second, to do so we must accept the goodness of His natural order in creation, which means that we are to accept our womanhood or manhood as His good gift. Third, each of us has a vocation in life, a special assignment to do some aspect of His work. Fourth, Christ gave us His Church to be the channel of His grace and to preserve the sacred deposit of revelation that is always threatened by the errors of the age. Finally, and first in importance, we must dare to reach out for God's forgiveness. He wants to forgive us; He came to bring salvation to sinners.

The mistake that led to my long exile was not believing in His mercy. As soon as I trusted in its reality and invited Him into my heart, my life changed for the better. His mercy proved so rich and tender as to be almost incomprehensible. Like the father in Jesus' parable of the prodigal son, God was only waiting for me to turn homeward, and while I was still a long way off, He came out and embraced me.

❧

Under her legal name, Constance Buck lives in the Washington, D.C., area with her husband and daughters, and works on Capitol Hill.

Finding God Again, Step by Step

Kathleen Howley

From a staunch atheist to a practicing Roman Catholic who is devoted to the traditional Latin Mass—there aren't many bridges longer than that. It's no wonder I raised a few eyebrows among my friends, when I began that journey in my mid-twenties.

"Are you still into the God thing?" a college friend asked a few years ago, when we met for coffee. She had been among the most incredulous when I started attending Mass.

Without pondering her question, I responded, "Before I came back to the Church, I felt empty, and I had no sense of where I was going. Now, I'm at peace. I don't fear death. My life has eternal meaning. Yes, I'm still into the God thing."

My friend is a lapsed Catholic, so I wasn't surprised by her reaction. She said, "Well, it's not for me. I couldn't handle the guilt."

Ironic, isn't it? The deepest meaning of the Mass is that Jesus suffered at Calvary to pay for our sins. We get off scot-free. He picked up the bill. When we do err, as we so often do, we can go to confession, receive absolution, and be given a clean slate. Somehow, that's misconstrued as a "guilt trip". Yet being a practicing Catholic means having the potential of living guilt-free—something that even the best psychologist in the world can't bestow. The sacraments of the Catholic Church give us the option of walking around unfettered by the chains of sin.

On the other hand, being an atheist or an agnostic doesn't relieve one of guilt, in my experience. The laws of God are written on the human heart whether we accept them or not. Rejecting God, as I did for many years, is simply slamming the door on freedom. It's a simple formula: rebel against God, feel guilt. Live as He wills, feel freedom. If you live as God wills and still feel guilty, that's a psychological problem, not a religious one.

But I didn't know any of that when I was in college. During my years as a lapsed Catholic, I never missed an opportunity to denigrate religion. If the subject came up at a party, I would maintain that Catholicism was the refuge of the neurotic and the robotic, the cumulative product of generations of people who suffered from overactive imaginations.

Strangely, the topic seemed to surface on a regular basis, apparently of its own accord—even at a Saturday night party at my non-Catholic college, the University of Massachusetts at Amherst. That's odd, because no one in my circle of friends expressed the slightest bit of interest in seeking God. We never used the phrase "lapsed Catholic", but I assume that it would have fit many of us. About half of the residents of Massachusetts are Roman Catholic, and the students in my dormitory seemed to be a fair cross-section of the state's population. Yet I didn't know anyone who went to Mass. No one.

"Religion is a crutch", I used to say, not knowing that I had my own deadly crutch. I didn't realize it at the time, but I was already suffering from the disease of alcoholism during my college years. Numbed by dependence on alcohol, I didn't feel a need for God. In fact, I didn't think I needed anyone or anything, as long as I could drink.

My friends and I attended keg parties any day of the week. We had the energy to pull "all-nighters" to catch up on our schoolwork on the eve of big exams. But we had neither the time nor the inclination to attend Mass on Sundays. That was for nerds.

When ridiculing religion, though, there's one thing that I never, ever discussed: the Catholic faith of my parents and grandparents. It was inexplicable. It was rock solid. I knew it was the foundation of their lives. I couldn't explain that phenomenon. Before my return to the Catholic Church, I simply dismissed it without taking an honest look at it. It worked for them. But it wasn't for me. I was too smart.

Or so I thought.

The night I was born, a snowstorm raged in Boston. As my parents prepared to leave for the hospital, they tiptoed around the apartment, "as quiet as mice", my mother recalls. My father's mother lived below, on the first floor, and they didn't want to alarm her. My father planned to call her from the hospital after I was born.

They made their way silently down the stairs, Dad carrying Mother's suitcase. When they reached the first-floor landing, though, my grandmother opened her door. "I'm praying the Rosary", she whispered. "Everything will be fine."

Her name was Nora, but everyone, including her grandchildren, called her "Mamie". She was a sweet and gentle soul. I always picture her with Rosary beads in her hands.

She was not well educated, but she knew the teachings of the Catholic Church. She could define transubstantiation. She knew what really happened at Mass. My generation of Catholics, despite our college degrees, couldn't do as well. Her faith was simple—she believed that her sanctification could be gained through attending Mass, praying the Rosary, taking care of her family, and washing her kitchen floor. She died when I was young, but not before she taught me to pray the Hail Mary. When I came back to the faith as an adult, her long-ago example gave me an abiding love for the Rosary.

Recently, my father found some letters she wrote to him when he was a seventeen-year-old seaman in the South Pacific during World War II. The Irish are not known for displaying emotion. "I will miss you terribly at Easter, especially during Mass," she wrote, expressing her love for her son in the best way she could.

As a lapsed Catholic, I wouldn't have understood. Why not, "especially during Easter dinner"? As a believer, though, I realized what she was trying to say, and her words made my eyes fill with tears. She had learned, through her faith, that there is a supernatural aspect to relationships that is far more important than what goes on in the tangible realm. Catholics call it the Communion of Saints—the spiritual union of the faithful on earth, in Purgatory, and in Heaven. So, even though her teenage son was thousands of miles away, in the midst of a terrible war, she could be close to him. And, as she wrote, that bond of love was especially strong during Mass.

It's a connection that exists to this day. I have no doubt that she continues to pray, in the next world, for her children and grandchildren who remain in the earthly phase of their eternal lives. The world of the 1990s may, in fact, turn out to contain more perils than the battlegrounds of World War II. The death of a body is no tragedy at all when compared to the loss of an immortal soul.

The fact is, the Holy Sacrifice of the Mass, and the graces that flow from it, gave my forebears the courage to do amazing things. Among the greatest achievements of my parents, grandparents, and great-grandparents was their perseverance in the faith; they lived their entire lives as loyal Catholics. At times, that was a monumental feat. My ancestors survived the great famine in Ireland without "taking the soup"—converting, just to get free food from the Protestant soup kitchens. Like many of the Irish then, they would rather have faced death than betray the true Church.

In September of 1914, my grandparents left their Galway farm in hope of finding a better life in America. Before stepping on board the SS *Laconia*, they must have attended the Holy Sacrifice of the Mass and prayed for God's protection. A few years ago, during a trip to Ireland, I visited the emigration museum in Cobh, County Cork. It is located on the wharf that was the departure point for most of the Irish who came to America, including my grandparents.

"Where is the closest Catholic church?" I asked an attendant. Then I followed in their long-ago footsteps, half a mile up a steep hill to St. Colman's Cathedral. Thankfully, it remains untouched by renovators. I knelt at the marble railing in front of a depiction of the Blessed Mother, to the left of the high altar. There, I prayed for God's protection for our family and for the repose of their souls.

Technically, I am a pre-Vatican II Catholic. Two weeks after I was born, Pope John XXIII called the Second Vatican Council. I have shadowy memories of kneeling at the altar rail as a child, of jam-packed pews, the smell of incense, and the red-tinged sunlight streaming through stained glass windows. That era, though, disappeared before I consciously knew it.

My earliest, clearest memory of Mass is traumatically different: a Sunday "folk" Mass in a glaringly bright school cafeteria next to the church. There were no kneelers; a folding table substituted for an altar; there was lots of guitar music and a friendly priest who began the Holy Sacrifice of the Mass with, "Good morning. How is everybody?"

The Mass seemed to me, then, like a meeting of the "Do-Gooders Club". The prayers evoked no sense of the sacred, and the ritual demanded no acknowledgment of the majesty of God or the existence of the supernatural. The point of it all seemed to be: "Try to be a good person." To me, it was the liturgical equivalent of "Have a nice day." Frankly, I wasn't interested. One Sunday morning, in my teens, I simply locked myself in my room and refused to go to Mass. My parents objected, but to no avail.

Later, we reached an agreement: I didn't have to go to Mass, but I did have to attend a religious education class at my parish, taught by my father, a long-time CCD instructor.

That year, he tried a new approach.: "Let's assume that you don't believe in God", he announced to his students. "I'm going to show you, over the next few months, how His existence can be proven, using the human intellect."

I doubt my poor father will have to suffer a moment of Purgatory, given the opportunities for sanctification he encountered in that class. I was the most vocal student, arguing against the existence of God. His own daughter led the charge against the faith.

I supported the Big Bang theory—maintaining that our world is a result of the collision of two universes. He used phrases like "uncaused cause", arguing that nothing comes from a vacuum. He asked me how these two theoretical universes were created. My reply was that science hadn't explained everything to us—yet. But, someday, it would.

Luckily for me, my father is an easy-going man, who never holds a grudge. Years later, after my conversion, I told him how worried I was about someone else who was away from the Faith.

"Well, I'll do what I did with you", he said.

"And what was that?" I asked, intrigued,

"I'll spend some time in front of the Blessed Sacrament", he said, with a bit of a smile.

I had a two-tiered conversion. First, I came to believe in God. Then, several years later, I returned to the Catholic Church. Finally, I found my spiritual home within the Church.

In my early twenties, I was still a devout atheist. God was for the weak. Not for me. But life has a way of teaching humility—even to atheists.

My first job, after graduating from college, was in Liberia, West Africa, where my position was part of a newspaper development project. I had a degree in journalism and a wide streak of idealism. So, in September 1982, I arrived in Africa, fully believing that human will, alone, could triumph over any worldly problem.

My job was to coordinate the establishment of a newspaper in Monrovia, the capital of Liberia. In my spare time, I taught writing seminars to anyone who was interested. At that point, my professional experience consisted of a part-time stint for a wire service and a full-time job as an editor for the daily newspaper at college. By Third World standards, though, I was a seasoned journalist.

I had always mixed liberal amounts of alcohol with writing. But, in Africa, my alcoholism took a more serious turn. I drank every single day. Usually, I would meet friends at a local bar at noontime for "sundowning drinks", because that, technically, was when the sun started to go down. Once we started, we kept going. As the months went by, I started drinking in the mornings, to relieve my hangovers.

After forgetting to take my tablets, I caught malaria. An Irish friend came to my aid with a bottle of Johnny Walker Red—widely perceived, among the expatriates in Liberia, to be an effective cure for anything that ailed us. Alcoholism and a few bouts of tropical illness were effective in opening a crack in my defenses. As I lay in my bed at night, shivering in the African heat, I grew less sure that atheism was a good idea.

Eventually I returned to America, and when I did, I joined a twelve-step group and stopped drinking. I began working for a newspaper, but I couldn't shake a persistent feeling of depression. A cousin suggested I try praying for a few minutes each morning.

"I don't believe in God", I reminded her.

She was not deterred. "It doesn't matter", she said. "Prayer works whether you believe in it or not." She seemed to have a happy, peaceful life. And she was an alcoholic who had managed to stop drinking. So, with more prodding, I tried it.

Every morning, I got on my knees and asked God for help. That wasn't too hard. Then, I spent a few moments trying to figure out, in prayer, how to have a relationship with God. It seemed a bit odd, speaking to Someone I felt sure didn't exist.

For a time, nothing happened. But after several weeks, I had a life-changing experience. I needn't have worried about getting in touch with God; as it turned out, once I made an effort to till the soil, and made myself open to Him, He got in touch with me.

I didn't see anything. I just felt the presence of God inside of me. To my empty and thirsting soul, it felt quite dramatic, but I didn't know what it was. When I described it to my cousin, she understood immediately.

"That's what God feels like," she said.

One second, you could not have convinced me that God existed; the next, you could not have convinced me that He did not. If no one else on earth believed in Him, I still couldn't have denied His reality. For a few moments I had experienced God's presence as plainly as I experience the presence of a friend.

Previously, I had thought that deeply spiritual people based their faith purely on intellect or, in some cases, mere habit. It had never occurred to me that God's love could actually be felt, or that I could have a personal relationship with Him. Today, when I encounter people who don't believe in God but who are open to being proven wrong, I suggest the "Sixty-Day Plan".

"Make yourself available to God for a few minutes each day. Try to pray. For those few moments, toss away your pride. Humbly ask that, if there is a God, He help you", I tell them. "Try it for thirty days; if that doesn't work, try it for another thirty days. God appreciates persistence." I've even offered a guarantee: "Empty lives are cheerfully refunded if you are not completely satisfied", I say.

No one has ever told me that they've tried such a prayer schedule and been left untouched. In fact, I've never encountered anyone who persevered in prayer without her life being changed by it.

Now that I knew God existed, I wasn't sure what to do next. I continued to pray. I read spiritual literature but—given my antipathy toward the Church—never anything Catholic. I bought New Age books, read a Protestant Bible, and took a copy of the Koran to work, for lunchtime browsing.

I asked God each morning for knowledge of His will and the ability to carry it out. I was doing the best I could, but I wasn't getting the full picture. I didn't go to Mass. Believing in God and searching for Him was the best I could do, at that point. My cousin urged me to go back to confession, but I resisted stubbornly. I didn't think I could ever say the words, "Bless me, Father, for I have sinned. It has been ten years since my last confession . . ."

She twisted my arm, and twisted, and twisted, until I finally did it. I made the long walk into the confessional with fear and trepidation. I was absolved of everything, and the priest made no demands on me to change my life. "God loves you", I remember him saying.

So I continued living in the same way, praying every day and basing my life on the principle that I should be "nice", whatever that meant to me. It was still a long time before I returned to confession or attended a Mass.

A few years later, a series of three events brought me back to the Church. First, I went to Ireland, to visit my family in Galway, where a cousin, Fr. Ray Kelly, confronted me, privately, about my loss of faith.

"When are you going to start going to Mass?" he asked, out of concern for my immortal soul. He was a young priest with a light-hearted personality, and I had never seen him look so serious.

I assured him that I did, indeed, believe in God. This was a vast improvement over the last time we had spoken about it, and I expected him to be happy. "I'm just not the religious type", I explained to him. "I'm spiritual, but not religious."

That line drove him as frantic as it now drives me when I hear people say it. Those who say it don't realize that it makes no sense. How can you love God but neglect His Mystical Body, the Catholic Church?

"This is the faith that your ancestors died for!" Fr. Kelly told me, getting uncharacteristically hot under the collar.

I replied: "Yes, I know, and that was good for them. But it's not for me."

Fr. Ray's distress was evident, and it made a deep impression on me. He surely didn't think he had won that argument, but, as it turns out, he had. Sadly, I never saw him again. A few years later, before I had a chance to return to Ireland, he was diagnosed with cancer and soon died.

My next push toward the Church came as I watched television one Sunday night. I was "channel surfing", and came across an elderly nun, conducting a Bible study. She reminded me of the nuns I had had in grade school, so I stayed, thinking the show might be good for a laugh.

She was talking about Hell.

If I were to ask a group of Catholics, "What should we do to bring lapsed Catholics back to the Church?" I'm sure many would say, "First of all, don't mention Hell, or any of that negative stuff. Just talk about love and goodness, sweetness and light."

But the television nun turned out to be Mother Angelica, foundress of EWTN, the national Catholic television network. And she didn't pull any punches. She wagged a finger at the screen. "It doesn't matter whether you believe in Hell or not. There IS a Hell, and you ARE going there, if you don't change the way you're living", she said.

It was a startling thought: that Hell exists, even though I didn't believe in it. It made me confront the dilemma that all dissenters face. If I'm correct, I come out ahead of the game because I got to live exactly as I wanted. If I'm wrong, I'm in deep trouble, and I will be, for all eternity.

A few days later, I was walking in downtown Boston and decided, on the spur of the moment, to pop into the Arch Street Chapel for confession. I got a priest who was more concerned with saving my immortal soul than with being nice. I didn't list my sins, because at the time I didn't believe in the concept of sin. But I told him everything else that was on my mind.

"Do you go to Mass on Sunday?" he asked, when I finished. I thought that perhaps he had missed the point.

"No, Father," I replied, "but I don't really think that's important."

"You have got to go to Mass on Sunday," he said, firmly but charitably. "First, because that is the starting point for your spiritual life, and, second, because it's a mortal sin to miss it."

I was polite, of course, but I was mad. As I left the confessional, I remember muttering something about "those Catholics and their stupid rules".

But, soon afterward, I did start going to Mass. Because that courageous priest dared to speak the truth to me, this sheep was able to hear the Shepherd's voice. He made me angry at first, but in the end, he saved my soul. I never had a chance to thank him. I hadn't even noticed his name on the placard outside the confessional.

For the next five years, I wandered from parish to parish. I was writing for a Boston daily newspaper and living in a carriage house on the ocean, but I used to tell my friends that I was "spiritually homeless". My soul craved a Mass that was unabashedly Catholic. I needed a reminder, during the Holy Sacrifice, of the majesty of God and of the supernatural aspect of the holy event that was occurring. Instead, I found Masses that were completely one-dimensional, with all the emphasis on the tangible. I knew a miracle was occurring, and bread and wine were being transformed into the Body and Blood of Christ. But, to my human eyes it looked more like we were sharing some sort of earthly meal.

I had a phrase that I used to repeat to myself while the priest spoke to the congregation across the "eucharistic table", as the altar was now called by many people. "I know it's really You, Jesus", I would say, over and over.

In fact, I didn't feel my homecoming to the Church at a profoundly moving level until the first time I watched the priest ascend to the high altar at a traditional Latin Mass. Like many other young people, I can truthfully say I never understood the new until I experienced the old. There could be no doubt that he was offering a Holy Sacrifice, not presiding at a communal supper. I felt a sense of sadness, as though the ritual spoke directly to my soul in a way I had never known before.

In 1988, while I was still fallen away, Pope John Paul II wrote an apostolic letter, *Ecclesia Dei*, directing that the traditional Latin Mass, as used in the Roman Missal of 1962, be made "widely and generously" available to "all those Catholic faithful who feel attached" to it. Some people are surprised that so many of those who have responded to this invitation are young. But I am not surprised. I know that many Catholics like the new form of the Mass and either have no wish to change or simply want to see it offered with greater reverence. Those who thrive on the modern form of the Mass are evident in the pews of local parishes. In many cases, however, those who do not so thrive aren't there to be counted. Several studies have shown that fewer than 25 percent of Catholics now attend Mass every Sunday. Many of the missing are young people who never had an opportunity to experience the rich liturgical tradition that is their patrimony.

As it turns out, I am one of those who seem to react viscerally to the traditional Latin Mass. When I see the priest offer the sacrifice in the same ritual that Catholics of the Middle Ages would have recognized, I am better able to dispose myself to receive the multitude of graces that are poured out at Mass. At this final step of my return to God, my heart lifts with joy.

ൠ

Kathleen Howley lives in Boston, where she reports for the *Boston Globe*, writes a featured column in *National Catholic Register*, and works on a first novel. Her articles appear in the *New York Times, Reader's Digest*, the *Boston Herald, Catholic World Report*, and many other publications.

Escaping the Pied Piper of Lies

Rosemary Hugo Fielding

In 1993, with *Veritatis Splendor*, Pope John Paul II reminded a jaded world of the imperative authority of truth. Reading what he wrote, I nodded in vigorous agreement. Only a few years earlier, while struggling to my feet from my latest emotional, intellectual, spiritual tumble, I had recognized the painful consequences of living as though truth were whatever I wanted it to be. I had seen at last that objective truth exists and that one must conform his desires to it or he will distort truth to fit his desires. I had done so all too often, following the Pied Piper of lies, with catastrophic consequences.

In many ways, my story exemplifies the history of my generation. I was caught up in the same adventures that seduced my peers and kept us wandering from idea to idea, experience to experience, spiritually homeless. I dived into middle-class American hedonism, surfaced in Eastern mysticism, raced back to Christianity, vacillated between Catholicism and Protestantism, drifted into modernist heresy, and then tied up at radical feminism, before falling into the abyss of deconstructionism, the most lethal of all assaults on my mental and spiritual well-being.

Before I discovered orthodoxy, the lies of the twentieth century nearly destroyed me. Providentially, just at the moment of despair, I encountered the orthodox claim that truth has

authority transcending any individual's opinion or desire—
one of the best-kept secrets in American Catholicism. Once
I accepted it, I returned to the faith.

How did all this happen to a good Catholic girl?

Growing Up Catholic in the Age of Aquarius

I was a late baby-boomer, the youngest of five children. My
parents, grandparents, aunts, and uncles were good, devout,
liberal, intellectual Irish Catholics. My father, a professor of
sociology at Duquesne University, taught his subject from a
Catholic perspective. My uncle, Fr. John Hugo, was a noted
retreat master and writer on the spiritual life. Priests often
visited our home.

During my childhood, my parents lived their faith: we
prayed, helped the poor, attended Mass, read Bible stories and
lives of the saints, and were taught right from wrong. My
grandparents prayed the Rosary nightly and spoke to us often
of God and His Providence. But my knowledge of doctrine
was slim. Except for two years in a parochial grammar school,
I attended public schools, where I learned more about the
ways of the world than catechism class could combat. With
Confirmation, at age eleven, my catechetical instruction
ended.

As I grew older, my happy, stable, Catholic family life was
gradually blighted by a combination of influences. First, my
parents adopted the gospel of permissiveness from the theo-
ries of popular pediatrician Dr. Benjamin Spock, with strong
support from my mother's relatives, who enthusiastically embraced all the liberal ideas flourishing in the culture and in
their political base, the Democratic party. Soon they were ad-
vocating dissent within the Church as well.

Another factor was my father's increasing isolation. Always
family-centered, he worked hard for us, at home as well as

outside, but his progressive hearing loss and growing dependence on alcohol removed him more and more from real involvement in our lives.

Finally, my older brothers introduced me to the ways of rebellion at an early age. From college, they brought student-radical notions home, where our permissive parents, quicker to adapt to their children's notions than to impose their own, allowed them ample latitude to preach and practice insurrection. As a result, I entered my teens surrounded by the slogans, language, ideas, regalia, and immoral attitudes of the radical left. Soon I espoused them, too. When my oldest brother dismissed the Mass as irrelevant and stopped going, so did I.

My trusting parents had no idea their sons were using and selling drugs while attending the very university where my father taught. When their arrest for drug possession made the evening news, our parents were devastated. The boys dropped out of college and plunged full-tilt into the counterculture. Unprepared and alarmed, my parents tried to institute a measure of damage control over me, but it was too late. I had already effectively abandoned the doctrine, and much of the morality, I had learned as a child.

For a long time, I saw my rejection of the Church as a normal youthful rebellion against authority. Now I know that apostasy and reckless self-indulgence are not inevitable in the young. But they become likely when adult society abandons its children to an autonomous search for sensation. The messages echoing through my culture said, "Seek experience. Seek pleasure. Find your own way. Make your own rules."

The First Lie: Moral Relativism

The first lie I learned from the spirit of the age was moral relativism. Ignorant of distinctions between legitimate and

illegitimate authority, I cultivated a reflexive disdain for authority of every kind and became a bourgeois American
hedonist.

The autumn after high school, I followed my brothers west
to live as a hippie on an old mining claim in the Cascade
Mountains near Medford, Oregon. Sharing the house were
my two brothers, a sister-in-law, a cousin, and my best girl
friend. Now and then I worked at a local agricultural plant,
but most of the time I read, gardened, and hiked in the mountains above beautiful, wild Applegate River. After nine
months, I was bored with the counterculture. Reflective and
much alone, I had come to crave some direction in my life
and to yearn for culture. I decided to go back to school.

I wanted to enroll in a progressive West Coast college, but
my parents gave me no choice: as a faculty member's daughter,
I had free tuition at Duquesne University. Later I thanked God
that I had been directed there, as I received a traditional liberal
arts education, if only sporadically Catholic. A major in English literature, I loved my studies. I cut out the marijuana and
hungered after the things of the mind. But old habits die hard;
outside classes, I continued to pursue worldly pleasure.

Then, in my junior year, the tragic death of someone near
me called hard reality to my attention, and I listened again for
the voice of my childhood God. The Holy Spirit seemed to
be calling me to a way of life more substantial than either the
mainstream culture or the counterculture I saw around me.
He nudged me gently during a lecture on Milton's *Paradise
Lost*, when a new film, *Jesus of Nazareth*, reminded me of my
childhood love for the Lord, and again when I read Dorothy
Day's autobiography, *The Long Loneliness*, and trembled to
think that God could call anyone, even me, from a life of self-
gratification to one of sacrifice. For the first time in years, I
attended Easter Vigil Mass with my mother.

But those tentative stirrings did not prevail. Philosophy class never hinted that perennial moral questions might have answers. I took no religion classes, so there was not even the possibility that I might learn any doctrine. So I came out of adolescence with my prejudices and assumptions intact: Democrats were good, Republicans bad; established institutions were hopelessly outdated; liberal solutions were the only kind worth considering; change was always better than the status quo, religion was for self-fulfillment, and feelings were the highest standard of judgment. Entirely ignorant of its substance, I scorned conservative thought. Despite the disastrous consequences I had seen in my own experience, I continued to live by impulse rather than by principle.

On graduation in 1978, I agreed to go to Afghanistan as a representative of a small clothing import company. Once enveloped in the blessed silence of that media-free country, and moved by the sight of Muslims praying in the streets, I formed a prime goal: to find out who God is.

The Second Lie: We Are Gods

Given my age and my long soak in the counterculture, it was probably predictable that I turned for an answer to Eastern religions, not to Christianity. I went to India, lived in an ashram for four weeks, and was "initiated" into *satmat* as a disciple of Darshan Sing, the sect's "living master" and a Sikh purported to be the apotheosis of the omnipotent God. Jesus Christ, I was taught, had once been a living master, too, but was no longer.

What I retained of Christian perception kept me from swallowing the part about this little man being God. But I was uninformed and open-minded, and so I accepted the false premise that all religions can be distilled into one universal spirituality. A Christian, for example, could follow Master

Darshan as his living master because such a master simply taught a "science of spirituality" common to all religions. Doctrine was unimportant; what counted was mystical experience, the only guarantee of *authentic* religion. So, once again, I was to seek experiences: this time, visions, sounds, out-of-body travel, or conversation with spirits.

Veiled under that spurious neutrality, however, was the central lie of Eastern mysticism, the claim that we are all gods. Along with other Western disciples, I swallowed it and so made myself the author of my own truth. Fortunately, the Holy Spirit saved me from complete idolatry. I could meditate two hours daily, eat a strictly vegetarian diet, and follow the other rigorous rules of asceticism. But I never could worship Master Darshan as I was directed to and as many disciples said they did. When I prayed, I still prayed to God the Father, the God of my childhood.

After a four-month junket, I returned to the United States still unsure what to do with my education. I landed a reporting job on a daily newspaper. Over the next two years, American life cooled my practice of Eastern spirituality, but that fact alarmed me, as I had really thought it could lead me to God.

"Why don't you make your uncle's retreat?" my parents proposed. "He teaches the kind of asceticism and simplicity of life you picked up in India." They were referring to Fr. John Hugo, and I bless them for their direction.

His week-long retreat was a seminal moment in my Christian life. It became, first, the means of a powerful conversion to Jesus Christ, and later, it lingered in my memory, calling me back time after time when I stumbled and strayed. At the time, however, I was planning to ignore the Christian influences. I expected the silence to serve as a way to revisit the ashram and revitalize my Eastern religion. Though Fr. Hugo had asked that the Bible be our only reading material during the retreat, my suitcase was full of books by Master Darshan and his peers.

Fr. Hugo's first conference waylaid my plans. On that hot Sunday evening in 1981, as he spoke to us of silence and of Christ, I had my first taste of the somber beauty of Christianity. Over the next seven days I fell in love with Jesus Christ. Though Fr. Hugo's family visits had been so rare that I hardly knew him, I came to love and revere him, too, as he preached the Gospel passionately. Fr. Hugo had been a powerful influence on Dorothy Day, founder of the Catholic Worker movement, and he figures prominently in her autobiography. He evangelized hundreds more through what Dorothy called "the famous retreat", which he called "Encounter with Silence".[1] Clearly, he was a man who would die for Christ.

During that April week, as the air conditioner hummed, I listened with a budding sense of destiny while he spoke of "two ways", God's way and mankind's way. These were roads through life, the very thing I had been trying to find as I stumbled about. I had thought of the world as divided between the permitted and the forbidden. But in God's plan, Father Hugo explained, the choice is more formidable; it is between Christian holiness and mere pagan goodness, which is necessary but not sufficient for eternal life. Natural good takes reason as its essential guide, and human happiness and rectitude are its worthy goals. These are not contrary to faith, he said, but more is asked of the Christian: God asks us to follow a supernatural path set high above the natural way. Faith becomes the guide, agape love and holiness the goals.

---

[1] *Weapons of the Spirit*, an anthology of excerpts from Fr. John Hugo's many books and articles, was published by Our Sunday Visitor in 1997.

Listening, I underwent a profound adjustment in perspective and hungered to hear more about this purpose of life. I shoved my suitcase full of books under the bed and consumed the Gospels, growing more and more excited. Here was the truth I had been seeking. "Why didn't I ever know you before, Jesus?" I asked.

That Wednesday afternoon, I knelt in silence before the Blessed Sacrament. My Catholic identity reawakened, I believed Jesus Christ was truly present there, Body, Blood, Soul, and Divinity. In a whisper, I said, "I believe you are God. I will follow you for the rest of my life. My life is yours." His Real Presence in the Blessed Sacrament was an embrace.

Fr. Hugo's retreat did not claim to teach any new doctrine or even new insights; it simply presented what he called "applied Christianity": Christianity lived to its deepest implications. Its most important element was "the folly of the Cross". To follow Christ, I learned, I must die to self and sacrifice my will to the will of God. A Christian's life is supernatural, he said, and should be quite different from the life of a merely "natural" man. It should bear fruit in action, in deep prayer, love for one's enemy, detachment from the world, and joy in all circumstances, even in poverty. With delight I learned that the goal of my life should be sainthood and my destination Heaven.

After the exaltation of that retreat week, however, when I tried to "die to self", I entered on a lifelong struggle against my old ways. When Fr. Hugo had revised his retreat after Vatican II, he had not addressed in detail the problems that were becoming manifest, and he still presumed his retreatants would be well-catechized Catholics. Sadly for me, this assumed a knowledge of fundamental doctrine that I simply did not have. Still, the retreat stayed with me like a glimpse of a lighted castle glimmering high on a distant mountain. It was where I wanted to be, I knew, though I didn't know how to get there. While the experience was not capable of keeping me on course, it remained a beacon in my memory, guiding me back again and again when I was swept into perilous and bewildering currents.

The retreat also left me with an ardent devotion to Jesus and to Scripture. It impressed on me the necessity of living as though the Beatitudes were to be followed and convinced me that "progressive" concerns like working for social justice, opposing war and violence, and voluntarily choosing simplicity of life are grounded in the Gospels and the teachings of the Church. But my immature faith could not overcome my deeply rooted moral relativism and rebellion, so I also continued to resist teachings of the Church that conflicted with my own personal opinions.

National Catholic Reporter became my chief source of religious instruction, by way of a gift subscription from my only brother still in the Church. What I read there was written by dissidents who indicated that modern Catholicism embraced all progressive causes, and so I became a "cafeteria Catholic" who was equivocal on chastity, autonomous when it came to doctrine, and confirmed in moral relativism. My understanding of the sacraments was so deficient that I was able to walk away from them only a few years after this conversion.

The Third Lie: It's All the Same

By then I had left journalism and earned a master's degree that certified me to teach. My first position, in 1983, was at Greater Works Academy, a nondenominational, charismatic, Christian school. Thus, like many of my Catholic peers, I met Protestantism through the charismatic movement.

Unlike most of the Catholics I knew, the Protestant friends I made there showed deep commitment to the Bible and to discipleship. Their ordinary conversation centered on Scripture and God. Ironically, under their influence I began to live my Catholic faith more conscientiously, trying to measure my actions by absolute standards and striving for purity of mind and heart. Early in the feminist era I had assimilated the standard progressive contempt for conservatives who opposed "women's liberation". When my new Protestant friends proved to be strong, compassionate, funny, and faithful, I revised my stereotypes, though I kept my liberal politics.

It was in this atmosphere that I accepted the third lie. Though my admirable Protestant friends disagreed, I privately concluded that denominations made little difference to one's faith. Their zeal convinced me that such distinctions were man-made, that their churches were as right as mine, as long as we all had a "personal relationship" with Jesus Christ.

They themselves maintained that Catholicism is a sect or cult. All the ex-Catholics I knew predicted that I would abandon the heretical Catholic Church as I became more knowledgeable in Scripture and "freer" in the Lord. But I didn't. Not then.

While at Greater Works, I held on to my Catholicism. But when I took my next job, teaching in Venezuela, I began to attend a Protestant church instead of the English-speaking Catholic church. I still thought of myself as a Catholic, and I fully intended to return to Catholic practice when I returned to the United States. It was Bible study that drew me to the Protestant church, and once there I stayed for the two years I lived in Venezuela. Scripture had become my source of strength, guiding me through painful decisions and tough times. In day-to-day American Catholicism, I had found little intimate knowledge of the Bible. Articulate, Bible-literate Protestantism moved in to fill this vacuum. And my knowledge of Catholic doctrine was so shaky that I didn't know I was forbidden to receive communion in a Protestant church.

However, some effects of Fr. Hugo's retreat were still clinging to life. I knew that Protestantism lacked something. Rarely did the message of the Cross carry with it a call for visible acts of sacrifice and mortification; constrained by *sola fide*, Protestants shunned those as works. I also missed the Eucharist, and when the longing grew too strong to ignore, I would attend a Spanish-language Mass at the parish church.

After two years I returned to the States. Still believing Protestant and Catholic services had different but equal value, I attended both. While taking more education classes and filling in as a substitute teacher, I prayed and read my Bible daily, attended some tepid retreats, and sought God's will in making practical decisions.

In that autumn, hoping to live my Christian life more radically, I accepted an invitation to move to inner-city Washington, D.C., and join a nondenominational "intentional community" called Sojourners. The group offered me a twelve-month internship program on formation in community life and an unpaid position as assistant to the publisher of *Sojourners* magazine.

I had first heard of Sojourners in their magazine, shortly after Fr Hugo's retreat, and I soon idealized this community bred from an unlikely blend of evangelical Protestantism with the antiwar and civil rights movements. In the early 1980s, the image presented by the magazine had been that of a theologically conservative but politically progressive fellowship. By 1989, the political focus of both magazine and community was on social justice. The members' decision to live, work, and raise families among the poor in the high-crime section of Columbia Heights told me that they took the gospel seriously.

Now I realize that Sojourners' form of government was Protestant to an extreme. Though founder Jim Wallis had more influence than anyone else, leadership by authority and hierarchy was fiercely rejected. Church and community issues were decided by consensus, and, as in many nondenominational Protestant churches, divisions often resulted.

Very soon I discovered that Sojourners was no longer theologically conservative. Process theology dominated scriptural exegesis in both study and worship. New scriptural interpretations and innovative doctrine and practice were welcomed, provided they fell within the realm of the religious left. The religious right, including orthodox Catholicism, was definitely unwelcome.

Living in this community, however, I found not only progressive politics and religion but also a warm social group of articulate, engaging, educated thirty-somethings. Their community life emphasized conflict resolution, consensus-making, honest sharing, and the kind of emotional support that comes from attentive nonjudgmental listening. In retrospect, I see that their ordinary interactions were similar to those of a support group or, at best, a loving family; they cared for each other admirably.

I had come to the community with a number of low-key emotional problems, some resulting simply from the extended adolescence that let me postpone maturity to some indefinite future, others springing from genuine anguish over my troubled family. In a sense, I was searching for a surrogate family to give me the attention, recognition, and guidance I longed for. The Sojourners community supplied exactly the kind of therapy I craved. They praised my humor, intelligence, integrity, and sincerity. They were interested in my views and sought my counsel. They affirmed me.

The friendships I formed, however, made me vulnerable to

the heterodoxy common among these post-Christians, ideas that eventually led me astray in my moral, intellectual, and religious life. From the very first "sharing of stories", I heard disturbing moral defenses of fornication and active homosexuality, along with accounts of "Creation Spirituality", "conversions" to gender feminism, and of a "third way" of life—between celibacy and matrimony—that some nuns and priests were exploring together.

During the year, my own attitudes swung from moderately conservative to radically progressive. Modernist exegesis, especially process theology, was presented, not as merely acceptable, but as the sole intelligent way to interpret Scripture. The supernatural element gradually vanished in the hands of process theologians. Condemnations of fornication, active homosexuality, and abortion were vague or absent. There was virtually no emphasis on sustained prayer, little formation in mortification or detachment, and no real expectation, as there is in evangelical Protestantism and orthodox Catholicism, that community members or interns would remain chaste or avoid inappropriate activities.

What I witnessed, I gradually came to accept. To some degree, that was because I yearned to be embraced by this warm communal family. Any misgivings I felt about doctrine and practice, I quickly suppressed. As happens in cults, love wanted to be blind. But the chief reasons were that I was a moral relativist, disdainful of authority, and I was attracted to these amiable dissenters. To put it in Protestant language, I backslid, to where I had been before my transitory conversion.

The Fourth Lie: The Second Lie in Modern Dress

The most vehement form of dissent at Sojourners was radical feminism, and it was fast dividing the community. Adherents charged that sexism infected even this stridently democratic church. Gender feminism, the ruling lie at Sojourners, is essentially the same lie found in Eastern mysticism and in moral relativism: that we are gods: *We* are in charge, and *we* will decide how things are to be done. Although it correctly observes that things are askew between the sexes, it dismisses the guidance of divine revelation on these matters.

Other feminists agreed that men and women are different, but, rather than accept any traditional definition, they insisted on defining such differences themselves. Searching for "divine authority" compatible with their tastes, they rejected Scripture and the Church and turned for instruction to such sources as New Age religions, secular feminism, goddess worship, modernist scriptural exegesis. and, most frequently, to what they called their "own inner authority".

Lacking a strong relationship with my father, and sometimes bruised in relationships with other men, I was a prime candidate for infection with the feminist world view. Feminism can be convincing to confused, wounded, or angry women. With my inbred liberal leanings, it easily convinced me. It promised compensation for my deprivations, excuses for my failures, and support as I turned myself into an aggressive, independent woman.

Setting out to change myself, I read avidly in feminist writing. One particular book, *Kiss Sleeping Beauty Goodbye*, by Sr. Madonna Kolbenschlag, O.H.M., transformed my perception of everything. Kolbenschlag identifies patriarchy as the original sin, the root of all injustice. That idea made me suddenly see every traditional distinction between men and women as another example of an unjust, man-made order that must be overturned. In religion, I focused especially on "inclusive" language and male priesthood. Scripture was an obstacle to changing both, so Scripture must be changed.

Both Scripture and the Church teach that God created men and women as equals, but with distinctive roles and vocations. Gender feminists claim that these differences did not originate as gifts from the Creator but as cruel cultural impositions. Thus they deny the authority of Scripture and the Church.

When I accepted the feminist lie, I didn't know all this. Without having read one word of Catholic doctrine on women, ordination, or hierarchy, I believed that the Church had discriminated against women down the centuries. I had little idea what the Church actually teaches and no concept whatever that her authority is supernatural.

Sojourners' feminists often experimented with prayer and ritual. The idea, they said, was to find "another way of doing" something that had once been grounded in doctrine and tradition. For example, reading a book that evoked strong feelings was simply "another way of doing" an examination of conscience. Lost in the exchange was repentance for and vigilance against one's actual sins.

In this subversive training ground, I began to divorce spirituality from sound doctrine. More and more, my attention centered on feelings. At the same time, ritual novelties conditioned me to the displacement of the sacred from the divine to the human. Scripture verses were used to give a Christian flavor to texts whose focus was not on God but on self, not on God's mercy but on one's empowerment. A neo-pagan religion was being fashioned out of familiar Christian terms with completely transposed meanings.

Meanwhile, I continued to attend both Catholic and Protestant worship services, taking from each whatever doctrine or practice suited me. The sacraments were just some among the many choices available and, to my distorted way of thinking, not even the most important. I took no special care to seek the Sacrament of Penance before receiving Holy Communion.

In my laxity, I fitted well with other Catholics I met at Sojourners, many of whom were consecrated religious. The neo-pagan prayers and rituals we used often were actually written by Catholic religious. This formalized detraction of Christianity reached a climax near the end of my stay, when some twenty-five of us acted out a feminist ritual designed by Sr. Madonna Kolbenschlag herself. We sat in a circle and read Scripture passages that distinguish between men and women. As each passage ended, participants chanted, "*This* is not the word of God! *This* is not the will of God!" Then, in a gesture of solidarity with Eve's disobedience, we each took a bite of an apple.

It was a thoroughly evil ritual. I knew better. A small voice within my heart warned me that once I blasphemed against the word of God, I would have nowhere left to stand. Deep inside, I knew I was trampling the Sacred Scriptures that had sustained and nurtured me. I knew I had profoundly offended God.

Yet I was able to muffle my conscience by recalling that many of the nuns and priests, lay Catholics and Protestants, whom I had met in D.C. blithely endorsed the repudiation of particular Scripture passages. A nun had written this very ritual, after all, and another nun had helped to facilitate it. My friends and I were not evil, I thought, we were ordinary: wives, mothers, professionals. And so we were. But we were overwhelmingly presumptuous, and our presumption impelled us to tell God how He was to speak, when we should have been hearing His word and keeping it.

Having seen the Sojourners community's quasi-monastic way of life decay into a perverse kind of spiritual therapy, I can understand how so many Catholic religious elsewhere were drawn into the same kind of decadence. In many Catholic communities today, women religious enjoy extraordinary personal freedom and situations of a kind that religious life used to guard against: special friendships, constant group interaction, and consensus decision making done with little reference to traditional rules or hierarchical authority. In creatures marred by original sin, the desire for acceptance can create powerful pressure to go along with the peer group in such situations, even a peer group that lives in a convent.

I am convinced that evil forces flowed into my life as we sat there cheering Satan's defiance toward God. The ritual critically wounded my faith and my prayer life. Within three months of it, I was in the steel grip of a severe emotional crisis, afraid for my life.

The Fifth Lie: From the Belly of the Beast

Directly after my Sojourners internship, in August 1989, I moved to the University of New Hampshire in Durham, planning to earn an advanced degree in English, with an eye to teaching again. Little did I know that I was going into the belly of the beast, the dark source of many of the currents of thought in which I had been dabbling.

During my absence from the field, English studies had been taken over by the philosophical system called deconstructionism. At first I was pleased; deconstructionism is the academic tool of radical feminists and marxists. *Hey*, I thought, *I recognize these comrades! These are the enemies of the white male imperialists!*

But on deeper investigation, I encountered raw nihilism. Words, I was told, refer to no reality—because there *is* no reality. There is no truth. There are no higher principles, eternal values, or universal mores. No God. Those ideas had all been "constructed" by elite groups ("interpretive communities") as means to gain and hold power by deluding the destitute masses. In order for the masses to take that power back, all absolutes must be demolished. Welcome to the People's Revolution.

Many people in academia seem able to stomach the idea that life is meaningless. But I couldn't. I was staring into the abyss of reason, and I was frightened. My warm, vague ambivalence evaporated before the ultimate question: What is the First Cause of reality? Is it the human will to power, as deconstructionists said, or God's sovereignty?

Deconstructionism is moral relativism taken to its logical end. Confronted with its stark clarity, I realized that I had been dabbling in evil, and I pulled back from study of this false literary criticism. But my faith had already been so weakened, and my thinking so infected by the feminist and process-theology variants of deconstructionism, that I had little resistance now to these black ideas. Anxious and depressed, I started attending daily Mass, hoping to find in the homilies some supernatural antidote to these lies, but all I heard were pep-talk platitudes.

With the feminist ritual at Sojourners, I believe I gave the devil an opening, and now his darkness descended on me with supernatural strength. I lost control of my emotional and moral life. I began and ended a most inappropriate affair, then suffered terrible remorse when the man threatened suicide. I grew so alarmed about family relationships that I feared to see my family at all. Oppressed with the required readings in deconstructionism, I struggled to pray, or read the Bible, or even to sit in peace, as I once had done. I was in a free fall, desperately lashing out for help.

It came from two sources. Fr. Hugo had died in 1985, but I began listening to tapes of his retreat conferences. And I called one of my charismatic Protestant friends. By speaking words of divinely revealed truth, both helped me to see where I had gone wrong. I repented of my sins.

But by then the crisis had built up a head of steam, and it was not easy to regain peace of mind. Pathological fear gripped me. I was afraid to teach, afraid to write, afraid to be alone, afraid I would end up homeless, deranged, or dead, afraid I'd commit suicide. Panic attacks struck daily: my heart pounded, my mouth went dry, my stomach knotted, my mind accelerated in a confused frenzy, latching on to a horrifying image I could not banish. As an ironic comment on my state, a friend who had never experienced a panic attack sent a copy of Edvard Munch's "The Scream". The picture hit so close to home it almost pushed me over the brink.

In this condition, after a single semester in New Hampshire, I returned to Pittsburgh to prepare for an assistantship at the University of Pittsburgh. On settling in Pittsburgh, I started Al Anon, a twelve-step program for families of alcoholics. It was a lifesaver, showing me how to understand and handle my emotions. I learned to think more clearly, to respond more serenely, to quell the panic attacks.

Still, I knew my anxiety was essentially a symptom of a spiritual crisis and a consequence of sin. I went to confession and began to attend Mass again. I thirsted for truth, immutable truth not indebted to "interpretive communities" or situation ethics, the divine Truth that is the Word of God. I also needed to hear about the enemies of truth, for I had been wounded because I failed to recognize them. But the Catholic teaching I heard, from the pulpit and in the confessional, did not deliver what I was seeking, that is, true, powerful, orthodox Catholicism. Instead I heard the watered-down variety of preaching so common in American Catholic churches today. It was lukewarm indeed.

Many priests seem unwilling to preach that there is only One who saves. They must not realize that there may be many in their congregation who are desperate to hear the truth and who will continue to suffer if they do not hear it from the one source they trust to preach it.

My Protestant friends seemed to understand more clearly that I had encountered lies and succumbed to evil. Once more they invited me to a nondenominational church, and it was from that Protestant pulpit that I at least heard acknowledgment of the great evil forces bearing down on truth today and was encouraged to fight against them.

Finally, I recognized the principle of contradiction. In the past I had held Protestantism and Catholicism to be equally valid, with the Catholic Church vaguely superior. Now I realized that Protestantism and Catholicism contradict each other and demand a choice. In the same way, I saw at last that radical feminism contradicts Christianity; one was true and one false. I chose Christianity. Unfortunately, in that desperate hour, I also concluded that the American Catholic Church had abandoned the truth and power of the Scriptures—as Protestant friends had so often told me. So I formally joined a Protestant church.

My new recognition of the need for philosophical consistency coincided with my entrance into the University of Pittsburgh, a virtual sanctuary for deconstructionists, feminists, atheists, and other anti-Christian radicals. My first semester began just as I was starting to climb out of my prison of fear.

The year that followed was hellish, not only for me, but also for most students. Deconstructionists had taken over the composition seminars. Only marxists and feminists seemed to enjoy the program. They preyed like sharks on timid, polite humanists, scouring our language of aestheticism and similar signs of elitism. Their job was to re-educate us.

A Dawning Hunger for Truth

But it was also a year of profound insight and change for me. I had already seen how my liberal prejudice against authority had shuttered my intelligence and led me to an inner hell. I was ready to listen to some new ideas.

Among the best I found were those of the late Richard M. Weaver, philosopher, rhetorician, and social critic. It seems miraculous that I came upon his books at the university, as he stands for all that deconstructionists hate. His *Ideas Have Consequences* clarified what my generation was never taught: that one must decide "whether there is a source of truth higher than and independent of man". If there is, one must live by this truth. "For four centuries every man has been not only his own priest but his own professor of ethics", and the consequence is anarchy, Weaver wrote. "A source of authority must be found."

Reading him, I understood for the first time the cultural waves I had been riding. I saw the foundational differences between liberal and conservative thought and recognized that I was deeply wrong in much of my critical reasoning. His ideas pinpointed the errors underlying radical feminism. Most important, he defined and exemplified right reasoning for me, leading me from the crazy rationalizations of post-modernism to the clarity of medieval scholasticism. To paraphrase William James, I realized that I had previously mistaken rearranging my prejudices for thinking.

In addition, Weaver's argument for the necessity of hierarchy and authority opened the door to my first real understanding of the Roman Catholic Church.

A Powerful Teacher of Truth

Providentially, it was at this time that an aunt gave me a copy of Scott Hahn's conversion tape. There, with great skill, this

Presbyterian minister, theologian, and convert to Catholicism proved *with* Scripture that the "twin pillars of the Protestant Reformation", *sola fide* and *sola scriptura*, are unscriptural. Once those collapsed, all the other Protestant arguments I had heard against the Church could not stand. With my new understanding, I could see that the claims of the Catholic Church were entirely sound.

The afternoon that I heard Dr. Hahn's tape, I practically danced around my living room. So many things made sense at last. Questions that had been open for years now closed, as I learned that one can make a firm and permanent choice if one uses reason along with faith.

In the spring of 1991, within days of hearing Dr. Hahn's tape, I returned with joy to the Church. Next I hungrily read other books that exposed feminism's false reasoning and specious anthropology[2] and followed up with works by other Catholic apologists,[3] exhilarated by their well-reasoned arguments.

Intellectually, I had moved to higher ground. Weaver had straightened me out on philosophical concepts; Catholic apologists and Church documents were straightening me out on Church doctrine. Now I had a compass and a guidebook for my continuing odyssey through the postmodern, post-Christian world.

Knowing the Church for who she really is, I experienced a second conversion. As I had once knelt and accepted Jesus Christ as my Lord, I now knelt and accepted the Roman

[2] Among the most important: *Of Men and Marriage*, by George Gilder; *Women and the Priesthood*, by Alice von Hildebrand and Peter Kreeft; *Ungodly Rage*, by Donna Steichen; *Mulieris Dignitatem*, by Pope John Paul II; *Inter Insigniores* (Declaration on the Question of the Admission of Women to the Ministerial Priesthood) from the Congregation for the Doctrine of the Faith.

[3] Among them, *Fundamentalism and Catholicism*, by Karl Keating, and *Where We Got the Bible*, by Henry Graham.

Catholic Church as the one true Church that Christ established.

Orthodoxy—The Straight and Narrow Way

When I first met David Fielding, my future husband, and told him about my tortuous spiritual journey, he asked, "How do I know this is your final change?"

"Because *I* know it is," I told him.

I can be confident because I now accept something that I had never understood before—that the truth has living authority that requires my obedience. Lacking that foundational mentality, one risks having his beliefs remolded by any number of forces. My mental habits, misshapen by moral relativism and a pride that scorned all authority, had reshaped every religious idea that had entered my mind—even the authority of Scripture. All the lies I lived by had one common characteristic. Some aspect of each asserted the absolute autonomy of the individual. In each, to varying degrees, man, the creature, attempted to usurp the authority of God, the Creator, by denying His right to tell man how to live.

Hedonism, Eastern mysticism, and radical feminism all maintain the complete autonomy of the individual. Protestantism, in accepting Scripture as its sole authority, rejects the authority of the Church's Sacred Tradition. Essentially, this means that each individual decides the meaning of Scripture for himself. Since the Reformation we have seen that such decisions grow increasingly subjective, resulting in thousands of different interpretations and at last in thousands of Protestant factions. Without the Church, one may lay claim to a higher authority than the self, and may even seem willing to submit to a true authority, yet in fact one remains the final authority.

Many Catholics today have never even heard the case for

orthodoxy. It contradicts the modernist mind. Having once been a thoroughly modern thinker myself, I know how foreign obedience is to our mentality. One or the other has to go. I will be grateful forever that when I finally understood this, I was given the grace to jettison modernism. As for my family of origin, my parents never left the Church, but only one of my siblings is still a practicing Catholic. God grant that all those still wandering may turn away from the Pied Piper of lies and come home to stay.

After a year of resisting what I was learning at Pitt, and hating the way I had to teach composition, I withdrew from the program. My life needed an altogether new direction, so I took a position teaching junior high English, religion, and Spanish at a Catholic school in Pittsburgh.

David and I married in 1995. He is a convert to Catholicism whose first ambition is to live a holy life. A writer and illustrator, he founded Brightstar Publishing, with which he hopes to achieve his second ambition: to teach sound doctrine to Catholic children. Under the Brightstar label, he has produced *The Light of the World* series, combining comic-strip illustrations with text firmly based in the catechism, to tell children the full life of Christ in a vivid form.

To our joy, a daughter, Helen Rose, was born to us on October 5, 1997. We are grateful each day that God has given us so great a blessing, so late in our lives. We both thank God for the Roman Catholic Church, and we hope to serve Him always, in our work and in our family life.

જ

Rosemary Hugo Fielding was born and raised in Pittsburgh and graduated from Duquesne University. During her years of searching, she sampled Eastern spirituality in an Indian ashram, taught in Protestant schools, and lived with a liberal, post-Christian, Sojourners community in Washington, D.C. For her conversion she credits her uncle Fr. John Hugo, Richard Weaver, and Scott Hahn. Afterward she taught in Catholic schools in Pittsburgh. Currently, she works with her husband, David Fielding, and they are rearing their daughter, Helen.

Led Homeward by God's Hand

Kathleen Brown Robbins

I am a cradle Catholic who left the Church twice before finally returning to stay. I pray that I will always remember the sins I am capable of committing, so that I will never repeat them. I wasted and threw away the faith that was my inheritance. Yet, like a true prodigal daughter, I was forgiven and welcomed when I came home.

I am the elder of two daughters in an Irish Catholic family. My parents were devout and faithful Catholics, who made sure we never missed Mass unless we were sick. Dad sang in the men's choir, held every office in the Knights of Columbus, and did a lot of volunteer work in the parish. Mother attended novenas regularly and was active in the parish women's club. We grew up knowing that our parish was important to our lives.

One of my earliest memories is discovering a book of Bible stories for children in the bookcase. Until I was able to read them myself, I spent hours looking at the pictures. Later, as an avid reader, I was a member of the Catholic Youth Book Club, which every month sent me a new Vision Book about yet another great saint. When I was about to enter the sixth grade, my sister and I were transferred to Catholic school. It was there we first learned about Family Rosaries, First Friday devotions, and other traditional Catholic practices. I attended Catholic high school and college, and as I was dutiful about practicing the externals of my faith, I considered myself to be devout.

During my college years, the Mass changed from Latin to English. I found the change tolerable, although the Mass in Latin had always seemed elevated above the ordinary. Now I became focused on the Eucharist, and I remember telling a Protestant boyfriend that I could never be anything but a Catholic.

Then, on retreat during my senior year, the priest to whom I confessed told me that I needn't go to confession in the future unless I "felt like it" or had something very serious to confess. His advice opened the door to greater spiritual pride, a vice to which I had always been prone. As a counter-influence, however, I met a most exceptional man at this time: Richard Cardinal Cushing, who was to become a friend and a measure of my spiritual condition, even after his death. He gave me an autographed picture, and I proudly hung it in my room. Wherever I moved, my Cardinal went with me. But during the years when I was away from the Church, I found that I could not look at his kind face with its piercing eyes. Depending on my state of grace at the moment, that portrait was either on my wall or in the back of the closet.

I went to graduate school at a secular university, still practicing the externals of my faith. Then I met my future husband. Steward is the son of a secular Jew and an inactive Methodist. A practicing Catholic was a new experience for him. As our relationship grew, he took it upon himself to investigate Canon Law regarding mixed marriages and learned that it was a canonical impediment that he had never been baptized. So off he went to the Episcopal chaplain, took instructions, and was baptized. Occasionally, after attending Mass at a local parish, I went to church with him. I was surprised to find that "their Mass" and "our Mass" were so much alike and that the priest and his young congregation were so enthusiastic about their faith.

I began to enjoy worshipping together so much that, shortly before our wedding, without any forethought, prayer, or discussion, I announced to Steward that I was going to become an Episcopalian too. It was something I *wanted*, after all, and I thought I was such a good person that God would understand. Besides, the original split from the Catholic Church had been political, not theological. At least that is what these good Episcopalians believed. They thought they were Catholics.

Still, because the wedding was already planned, this "good" Catholic girl was married in the Catholic Church, where, because she was expected to, she received Communion. It was sacrilege, pure and simple. But I had what I wanted. Had I lost my faith? No, I don't think I ever really did. But at that time it was only skin deep. My parents had given me their faith, and I had assented to it; but it hadn't yet become fully mine. When what I wanted conflicted with my faith, my desires took precedence. That was the first time that Cardinal Cushing's picture went into the closet.

After graduation, we joined a friendly Episcopal parish. But I can honestly say that it seemed superficial to me compared to the Catholic Church; I never had the feeling that I was in God's presence when I entered the church. Eventually I went to talk to the pastor, who agreed with me that I was not at home in the Episcopal church. With the help of a friend, I gradually worked up the courage to go to confession and return to the Catholic Church. Steward was very supportive. After all, he had never asked me to leave the Church in the first place. Soon I was once again practicing all the externals of my faith, but on a little deeper level this time around. I still didn't go to confession very often, but once in a while I would remember something from the past and confess; progress, at least.

Suddenly, out of the blue, Steward woke me up one night with an ashen face and told me he had just had a very vivid and frightening dream. It made him KNOW that Satan really exists, and that he felt he had no alternative but to become a Catholic. He has never told me the details of his dream, and I don't think I need to know. It was enough for me that he took instructions and converted.

It was a joyous day, and afterward our lives became a little less chaotic—for a time.

Then, in August of 1971, we moved to a small town in southwest Washington. There was only one Catholic Church there. The Mass was sloppy and the servers were inattentive. The sermons were boring. The church building was ugly. It took all of our immature faith to keep going there week after week. Steward lasted less than a year before he stopped attending Mass. With my background, I was more determined: I lasted one year longer. Then Archbishop Hunthausen decreed that priests were forbidden to say Mass in Latin anywhere in the Seattle Archdiocese.

Up to that time, the parish had made the Latin Mass available once a month, and this had kept alive my love for the Mass. Those Latin Masses were the only ones not "directed" by a teenage girl with a guitar. Once they were gone, there was no way to escape her performance. She would stand in the sanctuary, apparently chewing gum, and say things like, "Okay, now we're all gonna sing 'Kumbaya'." Meanwhile, no one in the sanctuary acted as though anything sacred was happening. Horrified and distracted, I usually left Mass angry.

Twice I spoke to the pastor about it. He was a man in his eighties who should have been retired, but there was no one to take his place. The first time we spoke, he admitted that he didn't know why the archbishop had ruled the way he had. The second time I asked him if there was any hope for a change, he said that people like me were "holding the Church back" and that I had better get with the program. Looking back, I suspect the poor man had heard the same speech from some diocesan bureaucrat, if not from the archbishop himself. But at the time, this conversation left me feeling as distraught as an abandoned child.

As the weeks progressed, I grew angrier. Steward observed that anger was not the desired effect of going to Mass. He wondered why I continued to attend when it had clearly become an occasion of sin for me.

At about this time, I read Raymond Moody's *Life after Life*. The similarity in the stories struck me. All the people reported that they had felt total love and compassion after their "death" experiences and had only been asked what they had learned. This gave me some kind of strange confidence and led me to my next mistake, which was to seek religious experience, mere *feeling*, instead of seeking Christ first.

The following Sunday I attended the Episcopal church again. This time my first impression was better. The acting rector was an Anglo-Catholic who had once considered entering the Catholic Church but found he could not overcome his objections to papal authority. He believed and taught everything I had always believed, so it was easy for me to rationalize again that the original division of the churches had been merely political and that apostolic succession still existed within the Episcopal church. It looked to me as though Rome must have gone crazy now, anyway, throwing out so much at once, while offering nothing beautiful to replace it. Again, Steward followed me, and we began to attend the Episcopal church together.

There was a stronger sense of community in this church than in the previous one, but, as we got to know people, I became aware that each one believed his own little "package" of doctrines. No two people had the same faith, though they belonged to the same church. While this was a foreign experience to me, in all fairness I would have to say that I, too, with my traditional Catholic beliefs, was accepted there with open arms by everyone, whether they agreed with me or not. Even after a new rector was hired who wasn't from an Anglo-Catholic background, things remained stable for a time.

Then our lives changed. Steward's mother, Lolly, who had chronic emphysema, entered the terminal phase of her illness and was no longer able to live by herself. We moved her into our home. She needed someone with her twenty-four hours a day, so we hired a nurse's aide to stay with her while we worked and took care of her ourselves on evenings and weekends. For two years we dropped all social activities. At first, Steward would stay home on Sunday while I went to church. But the time came when he was no longer able to cope with her alone, and then I had to stay at home on Sundays as well.

This was when I first questioned my membership in the Episcopal church. At no time during that last year did the rector or anyone else offer to bring me communion, although they knew that I was a regular communicant and that I could no longer get to church. Of course, I should have asked, but it was striking that no one thought communion could be of help to me, could be a source of grace and strength during a difficult time. Lolly herself was a "non-practicing Methodist" and had declined our offer to find a Methodist minister to visit her. So at the end, she was visited by an Episcopal priest who was visibly uncomfortable in the presence of a dying woman. Steward and I both questioned the depth of the Episcopal faith at that point. When she died, we had a memorial service for her in the Episcopal church, but, after that, I didn't go to church regularly any more.

A few months after Lolly's death, we took a trip to Japan, where we visited a few Buddhist monasteries. On our return, Steward told me that he had felt peace at those Zen monasteries and was going to find a Buddhist group to join. He found a Sangha in Portland and began studying Zen and meditating. Soon I noticed that he was beginning to change, developing patience and understanding even beyond what he had learned while caring for his mother. I was impressed. I was no longer active in the Episcopal church, and I didn't even consider going back to the same Catholic Church where I had felt rejected.

The Zen priest was quite willing to teach a Christian how to meditate. I took to it easily; after all, I had previous experience meditating during many visits to the Blessed Sacrament.

Over time, I found that I was learning more about myself from my Buddhist practice. It even brought me to the point where I was able to let go of my anger toward the Catholic Church and to appreciate the things I had learned there. As Buddhists, we were all encouraged to keep visible in our homes a symbol of the faith in which we grew up: a crucifix, or a Star of David, for example. Most Zen Buddhists don't believe in a Supreme Being. During meditation, one is supposed to empty one's mind of all conscious thought, but my meditations always focused on my Creator. I did not call Him by a name, but I was aware of His presence. I did not attempt to learn Buddhist "theology"; I simply meditated. During this time, I continued to "make progress as a person" and "gain confidence as a woman". I came to the conclusion that I could never be a Catholic again.

One reason for this conclusion was the Church's refusal to ordain women, of course. One of the three Buddhist priests I studied with was female, and I found her to be as compassionate as any male Catholic priest; in some ways more so. Then I attended a memorial service at an Episcopal Church for a group of people who had died in a tragic mountain-climbing accident. Several clergymen spoke, but the only one who said anything helpful or hopeful was the priestess. I took this as proof that women should be priests. With our nurturing natures, we were naturals, I thought.

The other problem I had with the Catholic Church concerned authority. I had come to believe that only the uneducated need someone to tell them what is right. *I* was well educated, of course, and had made *so* much progress as a person that I was entirely capable of making my own spiritual decisions. I didn't recognize my old problem with pride.

After I had turned my back completely on the Catholic Church, we moved to a city that did not have an active Zen group of our sect. (Buddhists are every bit as sectarian as Protestants.) We spent eighteen months there, gradually falling away from our Buddhist spiritual practices. Then we moved to our present location, which also lacked a Zen group. Soon we became accustomed to a completely secular life, though I never completely gave up my Christian beliefs. Occasionally, we experienced moments of remorse over our lack of a spiritual life. Once we visited an Episcopal church, but the experience left us cold. We both felt it wasn't worth waking up early on Sundays for that. I never considered that any of the other Protestant churches had anything to offer: no Eucharist; no sacramental life after Baptism. I would say things like "It's too bad there aren't any *good* churches around here." In retrospect I can see that my pride was experiencing a growth spurt during this time.

Eventually I began to feel a serious lack in my life, though I wouldn't admit what it was. Up to this time, my so-called spiritual life had been completely self-centered and willful. My mind and heart were closed to the Holy Spirit. But there were a few things beginning to nag at me enough to make me doubt my path.

When Pope John Paul II visited the United States, I recognized him as a very holy man who radiated love, and I loved him in return. If it could be said that I prayed during this time, my prayers were back-handed, along the lines of, "I wish I could believe in what John Paul II represents." Little did I consider that God listens to all prayers, even poorly phrased ones.

After we bought a new television set that allowed channel blocking, Steward became a true channel surfer, looking to see which ones to block. "There's a Catholic channel on here", he said. "Do you want me to block it out?"

A voice that sounded like mine but surely couldn't have been, answered, "No, leave it on."

And so Steward started watching Mother Angelica. One day he told me, "There's this neat old nun on this Catholic channel, and she is a riot! You should listen to her."

So I listened and put her into the same mental category where I kept Pope John Paul II: I loved them both, but I could not believe wholeheartedly in what they represented.

Then I was diagnosed with ovarian cancer. Only a small number of women survive it, and I am one of the lucky ones because I was diagnosed early. Why God was sparing me, when so many other women had died of this disease was a question I puzzled over during the time I spent in the hospital. There must be some purpose for the rest of my life, I realized, but I did not know what it could be.

KATHLEEN BROWN ROBBINS 157

My cancer was treated at a Catholic hospital, with a Catholic chaplain or chaplain's assistant on every floor. Most of them were retired nursing nuns from the order that owned the hospital. I had declared myself a Buddhist on the admission form. Still, after my surgery, the Sister on my floor visited me and said that if I wanted her to pray with me or for me, I only had to say the word.

Open to prayers from every corner at that point, I said, "Yes, please come and pray with me." She came every day and held me in her arms as she prayed. Although I don't know her name—after the morphine wore off, I couldn't remember—I will never forget her kindness. She was blessed with an ability to pray extemporaneously and simply say the right thing. This was the first time in many years that my heart opened completely to anyone from the Catholic Church. Still, I reminded myself, papal authority and the refusal to ordain women would keep me away.

Over the following six months, I put no effort into finding a church. My chemotherapy was debilitating, causing short-term memory loss and an inability to concentrate. Each session required a two-day stay in the hospital. During the weeks when I had no treatment, I worked ten hours a week and slept most of the rest of the time, unable to read or do anything creative. Even after my treatments were finished, I suffered from lingering post-chemo fatigue.

Though I did not take any big steps toward God during this difficult period, I did learn something. Often, while lying helpless in my bed, I was awed with gratitude that Steward could tend me so lovingly at a time when I was completely incapable of returning his love. I felt unworthy. I wondered whether I would ever be capable of returning his care to the same degree. Looking back, I realize that the Holy Spirit never misses an opportunity to make progress with a sinner; I was being prepared to accept God's forgiveness for my sins, no matter how unworthy I might feel.

Several months passed, and we began to think again about going to "a church" regularly. Steward had been doing a lot of reading. He told me that the Catholic Church was the only one that could possibly be right and then asked me which Catholic church we should visit on Sunday.

Suddenly I remembered something one of my college roommates had said when I told her I was no longer a Catholic: "You would never have left the Church if you'd had a Jesuit to talk to." So I suggested we attend Mass at the Jesuit parish and we did. Reverence was something I was looking for after my last experience in a Catholic Church, and the tall, thin priest who said Mass was very devout. Another priest gave the homily, and it was of better quality than most of the sermons I remembered from times past. After Mass, I asked Steward where he wanted to go the next week, when it would be his turn to choose.

"I don't see any reason to look any farther", he said.

I was surprised but filled with joy at his words. I still had to overcome my problems with papal authority and the male priesthood. I prayed that God would give me the humility I needed to understand these things. Papal authority was easy; I had not questioned it when I was a Catholic, and I had great love and respect for Pope John Paul II. If I admired the Pope for his holiness, and seemed to agree with him about most things, I told myself, then surely he was closer to God than I was. If I didn't agree with the Pope about something, who was more likely to be right: this holy man, whom I believed to be so close to God, or I? So what was my problem, anyway, other than pride?

Once I had stumbled through that question, it was a short step to the realization that I would have to surrender my attachment to the idea of women priests. It was the same question after all, wasn't it? As I turned my resistance over to the Lord, I felt a greater sense of spiritual freedom than I had ever felt in my life. That was the first time I experienced the power of the words "Thy will, not mine, be done."

So I made a call to the church offices. "My husband and I have been away from the church for over twenty years", I said. "We would like to talk to a priest about returning."

The voice at the other end of the line told me that a Fr. Tom Williams was standing right next to her. In one of many circumstances that fitted smoothly together, Fr. Williams seemed to have been appointed by the Holy Spirit to the task of restoring us to the Church. He agreed to see us right away, and when we met him he proved to be the kind and devout celebrant of our first Sunday Mass at the Jesuit parish. Later we learned that he was rarely in the parish offices. Because of his duties as superior of a community of retired priests, he said Mass in the parish only once every three or four weeks. Yet there he was, waiting by the phone when I called.

We couldn't have hoped for a more understanding priest to welcome us back. I asked him to hear my confession right away, so that I would not have to attend Mass on Sunday without the privilege of receiving the Body and Blood of Christ. Fr. Tom referred Steward to his own confessor, a kind and wise priest who became our mutual friend.

I went home and rehung Cardinal Cushing's picture in the bedroom, finally happy to look at it again, and conscious that I had felt guilty deep inside through all those twenty years that I had been away from the Church!

When I called my parents to tell them that we had returned to the Church, Mother said, in her matter-of-fact way, that it must have been Daddy who did it. All through those years, he had been making regular retreats and novenas, praying for his daughters. Between Daddy's prayers, Mother Angelica's witness, and the inspiration of the Pope, the Holy Spirit guided me back home and taught me what a powerful weapon for good we have in prayer.

The biggest change I noticed from the Catholic Church of the past was that everyone we met said "Welcome home!" when we were introduced. People were reaching out to each other on a daily basis, it seemed. Perhaps the pendulum had swung back toward the center after Vatican II, after all.

The first time I received Holy Communion, I had to struggle very hard to keep from sobbing. I could not get enough of my Blessed Lord, and attended Mass as often as I could. I had so much lost time to make up for!

Daily, hourly, constantly, I thank the Lord for His great love for me, for not giving up on me, for continuing to call me, first by softly nagging and, when that didn't work, by sending me a message I could not ignore—until at last I noticed Him!

Kathleen Brown Robbins works as a reference librarian and designs jewelry. Born and raised in New Britain, Connecticut, she holds a B.A. from Emmanuel College, Boston, and an M.A. from the University of Denver. Married for more than thirty years, she lives with her husband in Spokane, Washington, serves as a eucharistic minister to the homebound in her parish, and volunteers on a cancer hot-line. An enthusiastic dog trainer, Kathleen makes regular pet therapy visits to nursing homes with her amiable Bouvier.

Back to the Beginning

Marcella Trujillo Melendez

My problems with God began on August 17, 1949, on the night my childhood ended.

The first seven years of my life had been the stuff wholesome movies used to be made of. I lived with my mother, Isabelita, whom we called Mommy, and my five brothers and sisters—Bernie, Junie, Godey, and the two baby boys—in Bosque, New Mexico, a small farming village in the middle of nowhere. My father worked in the city and would visit us on weekends. Although we were more impoverished than church mice, there was nothing we wanted for. I say "we" because it would be many years before I would begin to see myself as a separate individual. In my world and in my culture, mothers and their babies were a unit, inseparable.

I was born at home in the spring of 1942. Doña Rumalda Moya, the village midwife who delivered generations of children, helped bring me into the world. And what a beautiful world it was.

Our home was a tiny three-room adobe hut with a dirt floor and a flat roof made of sticks and mud. For furniture we had only the bare necessities: a free-standing kitchen cupboard painted cobalt blue, a wood-burning stove, a wood bin, a bin that held food stuff, a homemade table, and two benches. The other two rooms each had a double bed. One had a crib and a free-standing closet, and the other had a couple of straight-backed wooden chairs with rush seats. The room with the baby crib was my parents'. As soon as a new baby arrived, the previous occupant of the crib would be moved into the double bed in the other room, where all of us children slept together.

I earned the nickname "brinca-charcos" (one who jumps puddles) because of my boundless energy. I was always the first child out of bed in the morning, but Mommy would already be at the stove making tortillas by the time I got up. The kitchen had two windows. One was a narrow, horizontal window that faced north. During the winter my mother would use that window to make jello and to keep foods cold. The other window was vertical, low to the floor, and faced east. Adobe walls, being as thick as they are, made this window sill a perfect window bench for me.

Having no electricity to bring us entertainment, we children had to entertain ourselves. My little window bench doubled well as my stage. From there I would regale my older sister Bernie and brother Junie with my antics and storytelling. I was very silly, and they were a very appreciative audience.

By the age of three I would accompany Junie, who was a year older, into the fields to collect armloads of quelites and verdolagas, very delicious and nutritious weeds we called food. Mommy would cook them and serve them with beans, chile, and tortillas. We were all chubby, healthy, happy children.

Our Catholic Faith

I did not realize it at the time, but our lives were permeated with Catholicism. To be Indian (American) and Spanish (European), that is, Hispanic, was to be Catholic. I took it for granted that the whole world was Catholic. Because we were Catholic, we observed wonderful traditions. First came Lent, with its special foods that were kept exclusive to the season. Even as children we would hear about some village men, known as *penitentes*, who would go secretly to *Moradas*, where they would flog themselves as penance for their sins. This practice, which came to America with our Spanish ancestors, was forbidden by the Catholic Church but continued in secret.

Everything about *Cuaresma* (Lent) was considered to be very special, particularly *Semana Santa* (Holy Week). Until our village church was built in 1929, Masses were celebrated at my great-grandmother's house on the few occasions when a priest visited. During the rest of the year she would lead community prayers in her home.

Perhaps that is the reason why, after her mother's death, Grandma continued the Lenten traditions in her home. Grandma Ramona, otherwise known as "Mamagrande", would create an altar in the living room by draping lace curtains from the *vigas* (ceiling beams) to form a canopy. The curtains would hang down the back of the altar. Fresh flowers, wildflowers, paper flowers, crochet doilies, candles, and statues of saints would fill the altar, with the crucifix in the center.

Entertainment was not allowed any time during Lent, but especially during Holy Week, which was devoted to concentrated prayer. Everything intensified during the three days of the Triduum: *Jueves Santo*, *Viernes Santo*, and *Sábado Santo*. The feeding of farm animals was about the only work permitted. The work of cooking and cleaning had been done beforehand in preparation.

On Holy Thursday family members and other villagers would arrive early, dressed in their Sunday best. Children played quietly, without much running or laughing. The men talked softly, with no heated discussions. The women silently served up the food in the kitchen, without the usual ruckus of joking, banter, and gossip.

Ramona would lead prayers in which the Last Supper and the Agony in the Garden would be recalled. Haunting, droning hymns were sung, verbally depicting the sufferings of Christ. Tears streamed down many a face, even those of the most macho men, as Mamagrande led the Sorrowful Mysteries. Breaks from praying would be taken throughout the day and evening while the delicacies of meatless *Cuaresma* cuisine were served. This went on all day and into the night.

Holy Friday began like the day before, only more so. The fervor built up into a crescendo, which peaked at 3:00 P.M., when the Crucifixion was recalled in vivid detail. Tears flowed again as the high-pitched sound of the women's lamentations joined the men's deep, sorrowful rumble in Spanish hymns that described Jesus' suffering and death.

On Holy Saturday people stayed home and cleaned all day, observing it as a meditative day of mourning. They swept their yards up to the corrals where the animals were kept. In the afternoon everyone took baths and got ready for the *Sábado El De Gloria* dance. As soon as nighttime arrived, joy and excitement burst forth. It was like a new beginning. After forty days of sacrifice, with no music or entertainment, followed by three days of intense prayer, everyone agreed that this was the best dance of the year.

On Easter Sunday we attended Mass, and then the entire extended family would go on a picnic. That's the way it was done if you were a direct descendant of Ramona, who, following in her mother's footsteps, held the position of matriarch in our village. I have always assumed that other families in our village celebrated Easter Sunday the same way we did.

The month of May was also known as the month of Mary. Mamagrande would walk two miles of dirt road to the church, where she would lead the villagers in the daily Rosary. On the last day of May, fields were scavenged in search of wild roses and asparagus ferns, which were arranged in Mason jars so that we little village girls would have something lovely to present to Mary. Dressed in white First Communion dresses, we marched up in turn and carefully put down our jars, surrounding the statue of Mary with flowers. An older village girl would have the honor of ending the procession, carrying a tiny, exquisite crown of flowers, which she placed on Mary's head. All the while, the village women and men sang beautiful songs in honor of our Mother Mary.

The village fiesta, La Fiesta del Bosque, was celebrated on the Feast of Christ the King. Mass would be said that day. The statue of Cristo Rey would be taken in procession around the church, as everyone, including those from neighboring villages, sang the inspiring hymn "Yo soy soldado de Cristo Rey, en esta lucha contra el pecado, en primer fila siempre estaré" (I am a soldier of Christ the King, in this battle against sin, I will always be on the front lines). There would be plenty of food and bottled sodas in all colors: green, red, purple, and orange, which were kept cold in tin tubs filled with chunks of ice.

Then came the Advent season and Christmas. Las Posadas, the reenactment of Mary and Joseph's search for a room to stay in, the nine-day Novena and the Rosary at midnight on Christmas Eve were all part and parcel of Christmas.

There could be no extraction of our culture and traditions from Catholicism. They were all one and the same.

Our Mother, Our Everything

Mommy was an uncomplaining person with lots of joy. She

must have worried about many things, but you never would have known it. She sang and hummed a lot. She told us stories and fables and never showed weariness with us children. I felt loved and treasured, as I'm sure all the others did, as well.

Several fields separated our home from our nearest neighbors. Junie and I spent many hours playing there, discovering the outdoors. Bernie, being our mother's little helper, never left Mommy's side, and the babies were always with them. But whenever we went to visit a neighbor and were otherwise out of our immediate surroundings, even Junie and I clung to Mommy. She walked with everyone attached to her. Up until the fateful Wednesday night when Mommy died, we children had known nothing but love. Suddenly she was gone. We were devastated.

To this day, no one seems to know the cause of my mother's death. Some think she must have had a heart attack; others, a stroke. We only know that she was seven months pregnant with a little girl, who also died and was placed at her feet and buried with her in the same casket.

As I grew older, I came to suspect that there may have been foul play involved in my mother's death. I learned that my father had been cheating on her at the time she died, that she had gone to her parents for support in leaving him but had been turned down. She already had six children and another on the way; my grandparents themselves were too poor to support us financially, and besides, the Church did not permit divorce. My grandmother died regretting this decision.

On the evening of Mommy's death, we all had dinner together, and after dinner her parents came for a visit. They would later describe her behavior as happy—as was her nature. After they left, we children were put to bed. A couple of hours later she was dead. My father was the only one with her when she died. There were no doctors in our village. No autopsy was done.

The World against Us

Tremendous, indescribable suffering followed. My father took us from our village, the only place we'd ever known, to Albuquerque, a strange place they called the city. His plans to dispose of his children by putting us all in orphanages soon unraveled. He finally offered the two babies to our maternal grandparents.

The rest of us lived in a garage for a time. I was eight when I fell sick with rheumatic fever, which caused damage to my heart, and Chorea, or St. Vitus' Dance, which affected my nervous system. Unable to get out of bed, much less attend school, I stayed alone; Bernie would lock me in as she, Junie, and Godey left for school. I would be alone all day, in that cold place, with no food until ten-year-old Bernie would return to heat up a can of beans for dinner.

After a time, my father found a convalescent home for me. He told me that because I was so sick he was taking me for a ride. We drove through the city and across a river. I had no idea where I was, but I was happy to be with him, until I realized that he had taken me to the home of strangers and was leaving me there. I was without any of my family, all alone with people with whom I could not communicate. I spoke only a little English that I had learned in my two and a half years of school, and I believed these people could not speak Spanish. I had felt abandoned by my mother when she died and now I felt abandoned by my father. I went into a deep depression, lasting week after week. For a couple of months I was kept in a darkened room. This did not help my mental state.

The lady in charge operated her house as a convalescent home for children with heart problems in need of bed rest. She was a widow known to me only as Mrs. Tapia, who lived on Tapia Road. Her niece, Loretta, a teenager whom she had raised as her own daughter, also lived there, along with up to three other children at a time. I can remember at least seven other children living there during the two years and more that I was there.

I will never forget the day I came out of my depression. It was spring. I was moved into a different room, and through the open window of the bedroom I could see the Chinese elms lining Tapia Road. They were starting to sprout leaves that made the trees look lime green. Even today when I see that color I remember the day when I felt life begin to return to me.

I remained bedridden for about two years with severe heart damage. The doctors' predictions for my future were dismal. I was told that I would never be able to participate in any physical activity and that I was not to marry because my heart could not take the stress of childbirth. They told me I would not live past the age of thirty.

The Sacraments

I had been baptized as an infant and confirmed as a toddler. The bishop would visit our village every five years, and all the unconfirmed would be confirmed at once. While we lived in the garage, Bernie had taught me from the Baltimore Catechism. One day, while I was living in the convalescent home, a priest came to visit and gave me my First Communion. He never visited me again, and I learned no more about God or the Church.

Anger, Rage, and Rebellion

By the time I returned to my family and to school, my father had married an unpleasant woman who did not welcome us children. Miserable, I began to spend every hour of daylight away from the house. I made friends with two sisters whose parents both left home for work by five in the morning. During the summer, when I was not in school, I would be at their home as soon as their parents left and would usually remain until dark. Being without supervision, we spent our time "hanging-out". These girls starting smoking by the age of twelve, and they cursed and walked with a swagger. I thought they were cool. I did not start smoking until I was sixteen, and I never did curse, but I managed to develop a giant chip on my shoulder, along with a nasty attitude.

Life with my stepmother finally became so intolerable that Bernie arranged for the four of us, brother and sisters, to join our two little brothers on our grandparents' farm. Of everyone involved, I believe I had the hardest time adjusting to our new living arrangements. After having lived virtually on my own, doing my own thing, it was not easy for me to have to do exactly what I was told if I wanted to keep the privilege of a roof over my head. My poor grandmother found it very difficult to have a sulking pre-teen with bad street habits living in her home.

Fortunately, Mamagrande was a woman with a deep faith and a strong prayer life. She spent many hours praying for me, because it was easy to see that my life was headed for disaster. We were all required to pray the Rosary on our knees every evening, and we were not permitted ever to miss Mass on Sunday. Though Mamagrande always prayed, she never tried to explain why. Considering my attitude at the time, it was probably best she didn't.

A New Start in California

On the day following high school graduation, my two sisters, my best friend, and I all boarded the Santa Fe train and headed for Los Angeles to start anew. We quickly found jobs, an apartment, and friends.

This period of time can best be described as happy and carefree. For once, we had all the food we wanted to eat, and we had enough income to buy new clothes. No one made much money, but whatever we made multiplied by four was more than we could have imagined having. We did a lot of dancing, spent a lot of time at the beach, and we did plenty of dating. What saved us from ruination was that we were judgmental. Years before we had judged ourselves to be "good girls". While at school we often heard of "bad girls", and we knew we were not like them. This "good girl" concept kept us accountable to each other. Not wanting to "let the others down" was one powerful control. Another was the fact that when we did date, we insisted on double dating. Many times we simply went places together as a group without anyone pairing off. We enjoyed what every young person should have: the opportunity to experience a season of fun and laughter.

At the age of twenty-three I got married, and my husband, Eddie, insisted I stay home to be a wife and mother. This was during the sixties, when women were in revolt. The feminists managed to get on all the television talk shows, where they spouted their ideas. They preached empowerment, equality, and freedom for women. They encouraged women to leave their homes and go to work. Not having gotten over my own sense of being a victim, I found myself receptive to their talk. My husband, however, would not hear of me going to work and leaving our babies.

Religion was the least of my concerns at this time in my life. I simply did not bother with it. I was convinced that God did not exist, or that, if He did, He was a cruel God.

Searching for God

Although Eddie and I were not attending Sunday Mass, we somehow managed to have our children baptized. It was probably the cultural thing to do. We didn't question it, we just did it.

Eventually, though, I found myself searching for truth. I began to read and study transcendental meditation and Hinduism, and I even attended the Church of Scientology a few times with a friend who had joined it. They expected me to pay for expensive programming sessions they called "clearing". I was very troubled with things I saw there. One was what appeared to be a private military force: men from the "Sea Org" walking around dressed in navy-style uniforms and watching everyone. At that time the founder of Scientology, L. Ron Hubbard, was still alive and living in a large ship in international waters. My understanding was that these men from the "Sea Org" would carry out any orders given by Hubbard.

Another disturbing thing was the behavior of Hubbard's followers toward the pictures of their leader that hung on all the walls. The way they acted at the mere mention of the name "Ron Hubbard" bothered me; the person saying the name would almost swoon. It was eerie and made me very uncomfortable. When I decided I had had enough, I discovered it was not simple to walk away. A young man was assigned to come to my house to convince me to go back. For members of the Scientology group, failure to complete an assignment is not acceptable. They believe in "human potential", which means that man can accomplish anything he sets out to do. When I refused to go back, the young man was worried for himself. He could not return without having accomplished the mission he had been assigned. I don't know what became of him.

My friend was not as lucky as I. She remained under the groups' influence for more than ten years, during which she almost worked herself and her two small daughters to death. She was assigned an impossible task of running a school and making it profitable. She ended up in the hospital in total exhaustion. When she got out of the hospital, she was at last somehow able to disconnect from the group.

Around this time my children began asking questions about God for which I had no answers. I signed them up for CCD (Confraternity of Christian Doctrine) classes on Saturday mornings and soon found myself being asked to volunteer. Although I knew practically nothing about my own Church's teachings, I was swiftly moved from being a teacher's helper to actually teaching my own class. I followed the lesson plans, which taught that God's love is "like a warm puppy". We sang a lot of tunes by ex-priest Carey Landry, who was described on the cover of his *Hi God* record album as part of an "Ecumenical Program based on the Human Growth and Development of Children". I even found myself foolishly telling my grandmother that her God was dead and that the new God was the God of love.

I'm afraid the class was a waste of time for my poor students, who could not possibly have learned anything of value from me. It was a case of the blind leading the blind. In a futile attempt to be a few steps ahead of the pupils, I attended several Los Angeles Archdiocesan Religious Education Congresses, which made me even more confused about Church teachings. Many New Age ideas were being introduced there, but I was too naïve at the time to recognize that.

Then, around 1974, I heard that a philosophy professor from Loyola University in Westchester, a woman named Dr. Ronda Chervin, was holding teaching sessions for housewives. Because I realized that I needed help, I began to attend.

We would all gather around a long table in a small room adjacent to the church on campus, and Ronda would sit at the head. She would read from the Bible, teach, and pray. That was the first time I truly became aware of the Holy Spirit and His gifts, and that's where I heard God described as a loving Father. My own experience with God, who had taken my mother and caused all the suffering that followed, was certainly not one of a loving father and my biological father was the opposite of loving, protective, and caring.

At one point Ronda invited us to ask for a spiritual gift. I asked for the gift of love, because I thought I had little to give, yet, at the same time, I could see my children's eyes asking for it. Although I kept them clean and fed, I felt that I could not give them what I myself did not possess. So I prayed: "God, if you are truly a loving father, I need you; but if you are not, forget it, I don't need any more pain." Shortly after I prayed my prayer asking God to come into my life, I began to sense a slow and gradual change taking place.

There was no dramatic awakening, nothing I can actually put my finger on, but somehow an awareness of God and His goodness as revealed in Holy Scripture began to take shape in me. Finally I came to understand that the Catholic Church is the one true Church established by Christ Himself, that Christ will not abandon His Church, that my role is "to know Him, to love Him and to serve Him", and that His will for all of us is sanctification. We are to be set apart for a sacred purpose.

Since then I have regularly attended prayer meetings and continued to study the Bible. Now I know that the Holy Eucharist is not merely a "symbol" of Christ's body and blood but the actual Body and Blood of our Lord and Savior, Jesus Christ, who died that we might have life everlasting. It was then that I accepted all the doctrinal teachings of our Holy Mother Church, of the Holy Father and the Magisterium.

Called to Battle

My husband and I had purchased a home in a nice neighbor-hood with a reputation for good schools. While my children attended school, I was working, naïvely thinking everything was okay. In 1986 the business where I had worked for six years began going through financial troubles, and I was laid off. I got on my knees to offer my new-found time, my energy, and my financial resources to God, asking that He do with me as He willed. Little did I know this would result in the roller-coaster ride of my life.

Almost immediately after that prayer, a priest from another parish came to St. Augustine's Church in Culver City to inform us that our local public high and middle schools were getting a school-based clinic on the joint campus, for the purpose of dispensing contraceptives and arranging for abortions. I was shocked. How could that be? I had one son in college, my daughter was in high school, and my youngest son was in middle school. Two of my children would be affected by this clinic, but I had received no information from the school. I began to attend school board meetings and to ask questions.

Shortly afterward, because of my involvement in opposing the school-based clinic, I came to the attention of Monsignor Charles Fortier, who at the time was the director of the Archdiocesan Family Life Office. A young Spanish-speaking woman he knew about had experienced a brutal abortion and wanted someone to talk to. He called and asked me if I would go to visit her. She lived in a city with a reputation for gang violence, where I had never been. Since I had made myself available to God, I felt I could not say No. It took two free-ways to get me there, and I prayed all the way. I had no idea how one would approach a total stranger and say, "Tell me about your abortion." Amazingly, the young woman, whose name was Raquel, was very willing to tell all.

Raquel claimed that, although nearly seven months pregnant, she had been unaware of her pregnancy. She said she had done a home test, and the results had been negative. She had not gained much weight and did not look pregnant. One day she passed out at the local market, and a woman handed her a card with the address of a "health clinic". She went there. A doctor touched her abdomen but did not examine her. The receptionist told her that she would need an operation, and that she had to come back on a certain day with a certain amount of money.

When Raquel returned, she found out she was getting an abortion. The abortionist proceeded to pull on the baby for hours, but for all his effort only managed to take one arm, one leg, and the intestines. When it was obvious that he was not going to be able to remove the rest of the baby, he had the receptionist take Raquel to the local county hospital where the rest of the baby's body was removed. The police were called in to do a report, and the coroner's office took the body.

I knew she was telling the truth, but it was hard to believe the horror of it all. Somehow, along the line, I had never been informed about the evils of abortion. I knew that Catholics did not approve of abortion, but I had no concrete idea of what abortion really meant. This young woman's story left me aghast. I suggested that I try to get an appointment with the District Attorney's office so that she could tell him her story. Raquel agreed to let me take her to downtown Los Angeles on the day of the appointment. After repeating her story, the District Attorney's only comment was, "I hear these stories every day. It's legal." I was stunned!

I went to my pastor and told him, "They're killing babies. Someone's got to do something about it." In response, he made me the Respect Life chairman of our parish. I tried holding educational events and many other activities without much success, and without much cooperation from my pastor. In February 1989, I discovered that Operation Rescue, a direct action organization, was going to be in town and was looking for participants. I decided that I needed to join. I talked to my family and warned them it could mean my being arrested and put in jail. They all gave me the "go-ahead". Next I talked to my pastor and told him that I had decided to make this sacrifice as "an atonement for the inaction of our parish". He was very upset and told me that as my pastor he forbade me to break the laws that make abortion legal. Pointing skyward, I responded, "I love you and I respect you, but I must obey Him."

At the first Rescue we blockaded two abortion clinics located on Pico Boulevard in Los Angeles, a block away from each other. As we sat all day on the sidewalk in front of the abortion clinic doors, we sang and prayed. I was not surprised to see women wearing Planned Parenthood T-shirts parading in front of us as they screamed and chanted "pro-choice" slogans, but I was very surprised to see the lesbians and gays who joined in with Planned Parenthood. I failed to see why lesbians and gays needed to worry about abortion. However, I immediately identified with the anger they displayed, and I realized that it was only by the grace of God I was not marching with them. I knew I was on the right side, and I thanked God that my grandmother's prayers had saved me from making the mistake of fighting for the right to kill unborn babies.

I chose to focus on the feet of the opposition as they walked back and forth in front of us all day. I realized that they had come from God as beautiful newborn babies and something awful must have happened to them in the meantime. I spent most of the day praying for the healing and restoration of those poor lost souls filled with rage, and I thanked God that my own anger was gone.

All around me I could hear the prayers of the many humble young men who sat with me on the sidewalk that day. They prayed for men, that they would respect and protect women, not use them for their own pleasure. They prayed for women; they prayed for children; and they prayed for themselves, that God would forgive them for not having humbled themselves before. They sat there in repentance, risking pain, humiliation, financial ruin, ridicule, and rejection by their friends, co-workers, and even family members for the sake of "the least" among us. That day, when I saw humility in action, I joyfully realized that there are still "real men" left in our society.

After participating in several Rescues, I eventually ended up getting arrested. The judge sentenced me to one month at Sybil Brand women's jail in East Los Angeles. I served twelve days. I was locked up with 180 women who were in for prostitution and drug related crimes. They were pretty tough women, but when they found out what I was in for they treated me with respect. Those twelve days were very intense. I saw things, heard things and experienced things I never would have even dreamed of. It was as if all the sufferings of my entire life had prepared me for this moment. If I had still had any doubts of God's existence, these twelve days removed all doubt. God's presence was very powerful. I felt as if I had a shield of protection all around me. I would go to bed in peace, would get a good night's sleep, and wake up filled with joy. I did not get homesick, as I felt completely at home. The only thing that was difficult to witness was the concentrated lesbian recruitment and activity that went on constantly and successfully, as young women were held captive and intimidated by their recruiters until, in the interest of survival, they eventually made the transition to identifying with their captors.

It was after this experience that various small groups and scattered individuals spontaneously came together and eventually formed the organization known today as Hispanics for Life and Human Rights, of which I am a founding member. The main purpose of HFL is to educate the Hispanic community about life issues, according to the teachings of the Catholic Church: that life begins at conception, that each life is sacred and must be protected until natural death. By doing presentations in churches, in public schools, and wherever we are invited, we expose the reality of abortion and those who promote and profit from it.

Looking back, I cannot blame the Church for my rejection of God. It was not her fault that my mother died or that we children suffered the way we did. However, I do see pastoral problems in the Church today that I believe contribute to the tragic loss of so many other Hispanics whose heritage, like mine, was inseparable from the Catholic faith.

One reason so many Hispanics are joining Protestant churches, I believe, is that they are looking for direction and often not finding it in Catholic parishes. I think many priests do not adequately use the pulpit to give solid teaching and moral direction. Sermons rarely talk about the difference between good and evil. It seems almost as though there is more interest in not offending anyone than in saving souls.

A strong attraction in many Protestant churches is the sermon that teaches clearly and specifically what is pleasing and what is displeasing to God: abortion is wrong; the practice of homosexuality is wrong. Most do not preach that contraception is wrong, but, the fact is, we Catholics rarely hear that in sermons either.

Even worse, I have been offended several times in the last few years by well-meaning but terribly misguided people in the Church who told me that European Catholicism stole the culture and traditions of the American Indians. In order to compensate them for this perceived loss, Hispanics in some places are being reintroduced to old forms of pagan worship. I do not condemn my Indian ancestors for worshipping nature when they had not heard the truth revealed by Jesus. But we have heard and embraced the truth. Why would we want to give up the light of truth and deliberately return to darkness?

As our liturgy tends to de-emphasize the Holy Eucharist and discard the traditional practices that dramatized the distinctiveness of Catholicism, it shouldn't surprise us if Hispanics go to where they are being offered Bible-based teaching.

Maturity of Faith

As for me, instead of blaming God for the suffering in my life, I now thank Him. I used to think I was abandoned, but now I know that God never abandoned me. He sent people into my life to teach me. It was Ronda Chervin who taught me much of what I know about my faith. It was Raquel who taught me what abortion really is. I have come to believe that I was re-awakened to the faith largely because my mother and grandmother prayed for me while they were on earth and continue to pray for me in Heaven.

So far, I have lived twenty-six more years than doctors had predicted I would. I had three, big, healthy children without any complications. When I reached the age of thirty and was still alive, I decided I was not going to restrict my activities any longer, so I began to ride a bicycle and live a fully active life. I have four wonderful, baptized grandchildren who live nearby, and now I can keep up with them. A few years ago I asked my doctor to do an ultrasound of my heart, to see what kind of damage I still had. To my grateful surprise, we found that my heart had healed itself. Who says miracles don't happen?

So I continue to pray that our Church and her teachings will someday be as important to my husband, children, and grandchildren as they are to me.

With so much to be thankful for, I now share the joy that was so evident in my mother. The words of the old Quaker hymn resound in my head:

> Through all the tumult and the strife,
> I hear that music ringing;
> It sounds and echoes in my soul;
> How can I keep from singing?

The End. And this is only the beginning!

ë.

Marcella Trujillo Melendez lives in Culver City, California. In the late 1980s, on learning that a school-based contraceptive clinic would be established in her children's' school, she ran for a seat on the public school board and lost. That experience helped to propel her into a long career in the pro-life movement. She was a founding member of Hispanics for Life and still serves on its board of directors. Appointed by Cardinal Roger Mahony, she has served on the Los Angeles Archdiocesan Commission on Catholic Life Issues since its foundation. For six years, she directed La Cuna Pregnancy Services in Wilmington, California. She was co-producer of *Dura Realidad*, a Spanish-language video version of Greg

Cunningham's *Hard Truth*. Marcella also served a term as president of the northwestern district of the Archdiocesan Council of Catholic Women.

Hunting the Hound of Heaven

Deborah Beauman Harvey

Conversion is a complex and personal journey. Reflecting on my return to the Catholic Church, I catch glimpses of the mystery of God's work. For so very long, I searched for truth without knowing where to find it.

I was born on the East Coast and raised as a Catholic. In my family, Catholicism was more a culture than the spiritual center of our lives. We received the sacraments and went to Mass regularly, but our faith was not personal. We did not pray together or read Scripture together as a family, and if my parents did so privately, we children did not know about it. Our faith was not integrated as a vital component of our daily lives. When my family went through the various challenges that may confront any family, we were not taught to turn to the Lord.

My parents depended on the parish religious education program to teach us the faith. On Wednesdays, Catholic students wore pink bus buttons that allowed us to leave our public school early to attend catechism classes. We were eager to get out of school, but I remember thinking that the instruction itself seemed disconnected from the rest of life. Despite this lack of integration, however, I loved Jesus at an early age and thought of Him often.

While I was in high school, my father had a change of conviction. Disillusioned by the turmoil of change in the

Church, he decided that Catholicism was unbiblical and some of its doctrines erroneous. He read books referring to the Pope as the Antichrist. With that, he set out on a quest for a "better" church, bringing his children with him. Every Sunday we would visit a different church: Baptist, Episcopal, Methodist, et cetera. After months of searching, he decided that the Lutheran church was the one he wanted to join. The first time we went there, the pastor began a prayer with the words, "In the name of the Father, Son and Holy Spirit". Automatically I began to make the Sign of the Cross. My father grabbed my hand and whispered that they did not do that here. He was plainly relieved that he had managed to prevent an "embarrassing mistake".

"Church shopping" was an unsettling experience for me. I learned that there were many other churches besides our Catholic Church. What was my father seeking that I could not see? Why was the Lutheran church chosen, I wondered? Was everything we had learned at our old Church wrong?

The impression I retained was that *church* had little to do with following Jesus. I still believed in God, and in Christ, but religion had come to seem contradictory and superfluous.

When my college years began, I set aside church and other religious activities and focused on education and friends. It was not long, however, before I sensed an internal void and longed for a spiritual dimension to my life. Pondering the reality of God and what He meant for my life, I asked myself the same questions many other college students raise: *What is the purpose of life? What am I doing here?* Life seemed so finite and futile: people go to school, graduate, find a job, get married, have children, get old, and die. What was there to keep us from despair?

In my elective comparative religion class, I was attracted to Eastern philosophies and religious thought. These ideas appeared very different from those of Western culture and seemed more freeing and integrated to me. Hatha Yoga and meditation classes were available on campus, and I joined them as a natural extension of what I was learning in class about Eastern religions. A guru in white Indian-style robes directed the yoga class, which was filled with people who, like me, were yearning for inner fulfillment.[1] Along with stretching and physical postures, he taught us meditative techniques, including mantras, breathing, and mental imagery. Purification of the body was emphasized as important for achieving holiness of mind and spirit. We were given instructions on vegetarian diet, cleansing, and fasting. I enjoyed the ostensibly rejuvenating effects of those practices and of this new way of thinking.

The guru discussed religion and introduced us to the various Hindu gods. I wondered how Jesus Christ would fit into this Eastern system of thought.

"All paths lead to the same goal", the guru explained. Jesus was just one of many paths that took us to the same transcendent place. Buddhism, Hinduism, Primitivism were all equal. Without feeling a need to choose between the various world religions, I integrated samplings from each one and dedicated myself to this path toward nirvana.

After college graduation, while many of my peers settled into adult responsibilities, I decided to travel across the country. I wanted time and freedom to concentrate on seeking answers to my ultimate questions. I was in pursuit of meaning and

---

[1] Let me declare at this point my conviction that there needs to be a much more active Catholic presence on American college campuses. Young people are yearning for truth. Many of them are away from home for the first time and vulnerable to deception. Yet often there is no one to invite them to examine Catholicism, in which Christ's truth is encountered in its fullness.

truth, and anything that could distract me from that purpose seemed trivial.

During these travels, I became increasingly troubled with spiritual questions. I mused about the guru's explanation that all paths lead to the same goal. *What exactly was the goal? Was it really just a state of "nothingness and peace"? Is purity of mind and spirit actually possible? How does God fit in? Is the suffering we encounter in life just a distraction that needs to be transcended, or does it have deeper purpose? Are all religions truly equal, or is one more right than the others? May some actually be wrong?* Lacking answers, I felt agitated and very lost.

Wrestling with those questions, I sought out and joined a community in Northern California that was an extension of the group with which I had been associated at college. Somehow I thought I could find answers there. We were united by our mental and spiritual goals, which were rooted in Eastern philosophies and practices.

At first I enjoyed the atmosphere and the alternative lifestyle, but after a time I developed suspicions about the situation. The people who had been there longest did not seem happy. Neither did they seem unhappy. They went through the motions of their daily work, but they were so detached as to seem almost void of themselves. If this was "purification and enlightenment", I did not want it. Feeling frightened and trapped, I became increasingly concerned for my soul, and I knew I had to get out. One day I packed and left and never looked back.

I moved to Southern California, where I had family living, began working as a teacher, and pursued a higher academic degree. My life settled into an ordinary routine, yet my internal confusion continued. Troubled that the true meaning and purpose of life still eluded me, I decided to explore some

churches near where I was living. It was a profoundly important move. Looking back, I know that it was the Holy Spirit
who prodded me to make it. At the time, however, it seemed
like a desperate move by a desperate person.

Like my father before me, I visited a different Protestant
church each Sunday. It took courage and resolution to do
this, for the diversity of worship services available was nearly
endless. One Sunday evening I went to a service at the Church
of the Nazarene. As the pastor preached from Ephesians, his
words brought relief to my weary soul.

I went back to hear more. The Eastern notions I had been
pursuing were gradually challenged and put in perspective by
the word of God. Light began to shine where there had been
darkness. It is hard to describe the liberation I experienced. I
encountered Jesus, and it was like meeting a long-forgotten
friend. He was not merely a philosophy or an optional path;
He was God made man, who is alive and still with us. He was
the Source of light: the Way and the Truth and the Life. This
discovery was phenomenal in its effects. He touched my mind,
my heart, and my soul.

As time went by, I learned to rest in Christ and settled into
a deepening relationship with Him. I attended Bible studies,
where I read and memorized Scripture. Kind and loving believers welcomed me into their fellowship, and I enjoyed becoming involved in various church activities. This was a
nurturing and healing time.

In light of my own previous experiences, my heart was
burdened for others who did not yet know the living Lord. I
grieved so much for those who were trapped in false religions
that much of my prayer life focused on the unsaved. Increasingly drawn toward missionary work, I set a course toward
bringing God's word to the unevangelized peoples of the
world.

There are still many regions of the world where Christianity is marginal or absent. Though Catholicism is widespread, it is believed by many Protestants to be a distortion of truth. It is commonly assumed among them that the Catholic Church somehow went astray and became filled with error and "traditions of men". They see Catholicism as, at best, a ritualistic, watered-down Christianity, and at worst, as an apostasy rife with falsity and evil intentions. They hold the Reformation to have been a great move by the Holy Spirit to bring pure, true faith back to Christianity. Therefore, the many nations that are predominantly Catholic are lumped with the other "unreached" as needing to be evangelized.

Many Protestant denominations are doing missionary work throughout the world, especially in Third World regions. Sadly, some of these denominations are in competition with each other for converts. I wondered whether that could hinder our Christian witness and create confusion among potential converts. Couldn't we just be generic "Christians", rather than Baptist, or Methodist, or Pentecostal?

While I pursued studies in the missionary field, I was also taking classes to become a member of the Church of the Nazarene. In the class, we discussed the history of the denomination and its creed. One night we were given a map tracing the history of Christian churches. In a branching pattern, it showed where the different denominations had first arisen. I was astonished at the number of sects and their connections with each other. I had already known there were a variety of churches, but why were there *so many*? How did they differ from one another? Was it simply style of worship, or were there doctrinal differences as well? I remembered Jesus' words urging us to unity.[2] Could all these churches claim

---

[2] Jn 17:20–23.

to be following Christ? If so, what kept them from merging together? If there were doctrinal differences, was it possible that some churches were wrong and, unintentionally, misleading their members? Was there one church that best understood, interpreted, and applied God's word?

As I read on about these various denominations, I saw that there were indeed doctrinal differences. One matter of particular concern was the understanding of salvation. There were differing opinions as to who is considered "saved" and who "unsaved". Each faction cited Bible passages to support its point of view. While some denominations believed that Baptism had a role in salvation, others did not. It was generally believed, in evangelical and fundamentalist churches, that to be saved a person must say the "sinner's prayer" and ask Jesus into his heart. Some believed that it was possible to lose one's salvation, while others claimed, "Once saved, always saved." Calvin taught that God predestined each person to either Heaven or Hell, regardless of his personal merits. If one is predestined for Heaven, his salvation is assured. If someone "saved" should turn from Christ, it meant that he probably was not saved to begin with.

I would have expected God to make all this a little clearer. After all, salvation is the crucial objective of our faith. If Christian churches are all following the Bible, why is there such disagreement? Other doctrines were in dispute as well, along with styles of worship and moral precepts such as the possibility of divorce. If I was to be a missionary, I must know which creed was true so that I could share it with others.

To understand some of these issues better, I began to study post-Reformation church history. It was interesting, and unsettling, to look in depth at the different Reformation leaders. Although Luther, Calvin, Zwingli, and the rest all protested against the Catholic Church to varying degrees, they also disputed doctrine among themselves. There was much controversy among them, and sometimes they denounced each other as heretics.

Once the original split from the Catholic Church had taken place, a precedent had been set for continual splintering off by those of different persuasions/opinions. There was, I learned, no uniform body of Protestant doctrine and practice that all agreed on. Although the Bible was acclaimed as the only authority for all our lives, opinions varied widely as to what the Bible actually said. Each Reformer, assuming that he himself grasped its true meaning, appealed to the Bible to prove his splinter group correct in its beliefs. Each had his own particular set of Scripture verses that he and his followers emphasized to that purpose, while other passages were ignored or glossed over. Those favored items of belief were then assembled into particular creeds, forming sectarian filters through which the rest of Scripture was interpreted and applied.

In more recent times, I observed, there had been a movement away from denominationalism. In an effort to practice the "pure" faith of the early Church, people had begun to found "nondenominational" churches. Unencumbered by divisive creeds and human traditions, they professed to look to the Bible alone for truth and to follow the prompting of the Holy Spirit. These congregations came to be guided by individual pastors, each with his own subjective system of belief. The flock had simply traded one system of belief and interpretation for another.

The well-intended expression "just following the Bible" began to sound hollow to me. The Bible is God's word and His priceless gift to us, but its meaning is not always self-evident. Whose interpretation was to be relied upon? Was there no final authority to rule on important theological issues? Were other documents available that offered further insight into the beliefs and practices of the early Church? Was this disunity and individualism truly the work of the Holy Spirit? Could Christ have left us orphans, to flounder this way?

During this time, I met a man who was studying for the Catholic priesthood. *What a waste,* I thought; *another young man throwing his life away to serve misinformed Catholics.* My initial intention was to evangelize him and lead him to Christ. Although I myself was wrestling with problems in Protestantism, I assumed that Catholicism must present even more problems. Hoping he would see the errancy of his beliefs, I shared Scripture with him at every possible occasion. Well-versed in Scripture and a model Christian himself, he would listen patiently as I challenged his beliefs, and then he would explain the Catholic position. When I admitted my concern about the lack of unity among Protestant denominations, he smiled sympathetically. He encouraged me to read Church history and to include pre-Reformation history in my reading. He also suggested books by Catholic authors for me to read, in order to comprehend better what the Catholic Church really believes and teaches.

Proceeding cautiously at first, I acted on his advice. It did not take me long to discover that I had stumbled onto something big. Contrary to the Protestant perception that Catholicism is unbiblical, I found that Catholic theologians referred to Scripture continually. The Bible was held to be God's word, and it had been highly regarded by the Catholic Church over the centuries. In fact, these writers said, it was the Catholic Church, guided by the Holy Spirit, that compiled, guarded, and carefully transmitted the Scriptures down the centuries. *How can this be?* I exclaimed. *The Bible is our book—a Protestant book!*

Soon I discovered that while Protestants look to the Bible alone for their theology, the Catholic Church approaches Scripture within the context of Christian tradition. The early Church existed and flourished before the New Testament was ever written. The oral teachings of Christ and His Apostles were carefully preserved and passed down, along with Scripture.[3] Tradition did not contradict Scripture but rather supported it and made it clearer. It was carefully transmitted through the centuries by a succession of bishops who can be traced all the way back to the Apostles. While the Church Fathers appealed to biblical authority, they did not base their theological case on the Bible alone but also looked to the Church's tradition to discover the intent of Christ and His Apostles. Tradition is not a collection of man-made extras but an essential part of the *full* deposit of faith.

In the writings of the Church Fathers, I discovered that the earliest Christian interpretation of Scripture was Catholic. In fact, all the doctrine and practice of the early Church sounded much more Catholic than Protestant. The early Church believed in salvation by faith and good works done through grace, in free will (including the freedom to reject God's grace), in the Real Presence of Christ in the Eucharist, in confession, in the bishop of Rome as the head of the Church, and in intercessory prayer by the Blessed Virgin Mary and the saints.

Certain beliefs that Christians now take for granted were not defined immediately. For example, the doctrines of the Trinity and of the divinity of Christ, although rooted in Scripture, are not specifically articulated there. It was Church councils, responding to the heresies of their day, that defined and defended those dogmas.

[3] 2 Thess 2:15; 2 Tim 2:2.

Many present-day Protestants, even some Protestant theologians, believe that the Catholic Church withheld the Bible from the people up to the sixteenth century and that it was only with the Reformation that the Bible was finally made available to lay people, freeing them to really know Christ. A close look at Church history reveals this as a sad example of revisionist and prejudicial history.

Before and during the Middle Ages, most people were illiterate and had to depend on the well-educated clergy to read them the Gospel and the Old Testament stories. The Church carefully copied the Scriptures by hand, guarded them, and passed them down. It was not until the invention of the printing press that books began to become available to the common people.

After the Reformation, when Bibles and theology tracts were distributed, the Church did object, but this was not because she wanted to keep the Bible from the people. It was because poor and inaccurate translations of the Bible were being distributed along with heretical tracts. She was protecting her sheep.

Catholic authors, I found, had a much different view of the Reformation than did Protestant authors. The Catholics held that the Reformation was not strictly a spiritual enlightenment, as so many present-day Protestants assume, but a complex series of events initiated by spiritual concern. The Roman Catholic Church of the sixteenth century was in need of renewal. However, Luther and the other Reformers chose an unbiblical approach to dealing with the problems they saw in the Church. Instead of following the way of prayer, patience, and humility, they followed the path of pride, dissent, and rebellion. The rise of nationalism, fueled by political and economic causes, gave the Reformation momentum. Protestantism was often spread among the common people by fear and coercion rather than by spiritual conversion.

I read and read, prayed and prayed, and talked to pastors and priests. Many of my misconceptions and prejudices about the Catholic Church were dispersed, and I began to see her depth, beauty, and truth. The Catholic faith filled in gaps and made me aware of other deficiencies in Protestant theology that I had not even noticed until I saw the contrast.

The Catholic understanding of salvation was particularly refreshing to me. Contrary to Calvin, it balances free will and God's grace, acknowledging that God continually gives us opportunities to turn and embrace Him yet also leaves us free to say No to Him. We have the freedom and responsibility to cooperate with the Holy Spirit. Contrary to Luther's belief, Christ does not merely cover over our sins with His blood; we are actually transformed and enabled to grow in virtue and grace with His divine help. We are not only saved but also urged toward a deepening transformation in His love and grace. We are "saved and being saved". This Catholic understanding of salvation and sanctification was the most reasonable, balanced, and mature I had ever heard. It was faithful to *all* the passages of Scripture.

I welcomed other discoveries about the Church as well. Christ left us a visible Church with tangible ways to guide her sheep. She is universal in that she reaches across centuries and cultures with a profound sense of rootedness. She is unified in doctrine, which is clearly defined and expressed. Her theology of suffering offers resolution and consolation. Her liturgical year recognizes the ebb and flow of our growth and meets our spiritual, psychological, and social needs. Her deposit of sacred art and music lifts our hearts and minds. The Church is the Mystical Body of Christ, and her development demonstrates the working of the Holy Spirit through time.[4]

What a surprise! The Catholic "cult" was after all the truest of all Christian Churches. I am not sure at what point I knew this, but discovering it was another profound favor granted by the Holy Spirit.

One Sunday, my Catholic seminarian friend asked whether he could attend my church service because he was doing a paper on Protestant liturgies. It happened to be the one Sunday a month when we had a communion service. As the crackers and grape juice were passed around, my friend did not accept them but respectfully passed them along. When I asked him later why he had not taken part in this memorial feast, he told me he was unable to share this communion because that action would profess a union of faith that is not yet a reality.

The sacraments are channels of God's grace, he explained. They exemplify the incarnational way in which God deals with us. He does not share His life with us only in invisible, spiritual ways but also through material means. He changes ordinary bread and wine into His real Body and Blood to nourish us.[5] The greatest gift of Himself that He offers us is the Holy Eucharist, my friend said. In a flash, I saw the hollowness of matzo crackers and grape juice. I hungered for Christ and the Real Food that He offers.

This brought me to a painful crossroad. Part of me did not want the Catholic Church to be the answer. I was happy at the Church of the Nazarene. It was small, familiar, safe, and comfortable. I had grown as a Christian there, and I was

---

[4] Some of the books I recommend are: John Laux, *Church History* (TAN Books, 1989); Alan Schreck, *Catholic and Christian* (Servant Publications, 1984); and Hilaire Belloc, *How the Reformation Happened* (Peter Smith, 1979).

[5] Mk 14:22–24; Jn 6:51–58.

warmly grateful for all the good things I had experienced. The pastor was wonderful, and I had grown to love the people of this community, where I felt like an integral part of an extended family. I did not want to be uprooted, but the deeper issues gnawed at me. I had to follow Jesus all the way, whatever the cost.

My mind and heart knew that I had found the fullness of truth and of the Christian faith in the Catholic Church. The Church I had believed to be unbiblical was truly the Church of the Bible, Christ's Church. I surrendered myself to God's will and stepped toward the Catholic Church. I entered a convert class and so at last came home.

The divisions in the Body of Christ are still painful to me. They separate families, friends, and nations and are a stumbling block to non-Christians. I keep my Protestant friends close to my heart, and pray that we will someday know the joy of full communion in Him.

Since reentering the Church, I have married and established a family of my own. I am thankful for all the tangible expressions of God's presence the Church offers us. It is a joy to see my children receive the sacraments and grow in faith, developing a relationship of trust and certitude with Christ and His Church.

God has been generous and patient with me. He planted in my heart an early longing for truth. Although I had been raised a Catholic, I had not recognized the rich spiritual heritage that was mine. For a long time I seemed to be a spiritual wanderer, yet His Providence led me safely through many obstacles to the point where I could see the truth clearly. I am deeply grateful to my parents for the seeds of my Catholic faith, which were planted by the sacraments so many years ago. The graces I received then surely sustained me until I finally found the crucified and risen Lord, who had been waiting for me in His Church all along, and I came all the way back to Christ's open arms.

Every conversion is a mystery. Though we may seem to be pursuing God, it is always He who is pursuing us. My hope is that this testimony will be a blessing to others who seek the fullness He offers. Most of all, I desire to give thanks and praise to God for His gracious mercy and His faithfulness.

Deborah Beauman Harvey was born and raised in New York State and now lives in Ventura, California, with her husband, Andrew, and their four children. A B.S. graduate of Rutgers University, she also holds an M.S. degree and a teaching credential from California Lutheran University. A former public high school teacher and counselor, she is now educating her own children at home.

Giving Jesus a Fair Chance

Zoe Romanowsky

If you've read *Anne of Green Gables* or seen the television series based on that book, you've glimpsed the charm and beauty of my childhood world. The Atlantic Ocean's gray-blue waters could be seen from my living room, and acres of fields, woods, swamps, and brooks were my playgrounds. Unlike the book's protagonist, orphaned Anne Shirley, I was the first of nine children born to a Canadian mother of Celtic ancestry and an American father of French, Latvian, and Russian background.

Born in Halifax, Nova Scotia, I spent my early years in New England. When I was seven, we moved to our summer property on Nova Scotia's north shore. My parents thought a simple rural life would provide a wholesome environment in which to raise a large family.

Across the road from our old farmhouse was a one-room schoolhouse, which my father converted into his medical office. It allowed us to see him far more often than we would have in another setting. He always looked ten years younger than his real age, so it wasn't easy for him to win the immediate confidence of the locals, but soon his practice boomed, and his patients came to love him. Intelligent and jovial, he always had interesting hobbies going, from raising goats and turkeys to practicing acupuncture.

Mother's background is Irish on her dad's side, Scottish on

her mum's. She was brought up a Catholic and did what most good Catholic girls expected to do if they didn't enter the convent: marry a Catholic "good provider" and raise a big family. My mum was exceptionally bright, academically keen, and had more radical bones in her body than conventional ones. She acquired a kind of notoriety in our county over various moral and social issues.

I was baptized a Catholic on New Year's Eve, 1967, and went on to receive all my sacraments, but my catechetical instruction seems not to have made a deep impression on me. In the early years I memorized the Apostles' Creed, the Our Father, and the Guardian Angel prayer, I remember, and learned about why God made me, and about sin and virtue, but the picture captions in my Baltimore Catechism sometimes puzzled me. Under a picture of a family it said, "This is good." Under the picture of a priest it said, "This is better." No one ever explained why. At my First Communion, I recall being so anxious about holding my hands without interlocking fingers that I almost forgot my disappointment with my veil, which was less regal than I had hoped.

Because I attended public schools, I received some religious instruction through our parish, where the classes I took were dull and insubstantial. As the bishop placed his hand on my head during Confirmation, I had an idea something special was happening, but I didn't know exactly what that was. It wasn't fashionable at the time to take a saint's name, but I had a little book of saints that I loved to read. I knew about the Rosary but didn't pray it.

At home, we were taught to be kind, loving, and true to our principles. But for all that my parents did provide, I received little formation in the Catholic faith. As I look back, my mother had very little time to do much more than feed, clothe, and diaper her children and tuck them into bed. Her faith was lived but not discussed. We did celebrate the season of Advent with a wreath and calendar, and we knew Christmas was about Baby Jesus. But Easter was largely about the Easter bunny and egg decorating.

Bedtime prayers and grace before holiday meals were the norms in my family, but as I grew older, I experienced God more powerfully in nature and in the love of family and friends than in our parish church. The Creator, whose power and presence I sensed, seemed too mysterious and grand to have much to do with a boring old Mass on Sundays. God seemed to me more like a clockmaker who makes a clock, winds it up, and lets it run on its own. Maybe once in a while, if the clock breaks down, he might come around and fix it and then disappear again. My security was my family—particularly my mother—and my safe, tranquil environment. Jesus Christ was someone I heard about now and then, but He didn't have much relevance to my life.

My siblings and a few neighbors were my playmates, and our imaginative games kept us too busy to care that our television, when we eventually got a set, provided only one channel. The stillness of the country encouraged wonder and reflection; I actually scheduled "thinking time" into my daily life. Lying in a field under the clouds or in my bed at night, I considered the mysteries of existence. *What's life about? Where does the wind go? Why do people and creatures have to suffer? Why do I never quite feel "at home"?* As I grew, the answers in my childhood catechism seemed naïve and simplistic and soon faded into the recesses of my memory.

The nearest Catholic church was thirty kilometers away. When I was twelve, my parents separated, and, as Mum couldn't drive, Mass attendance became less frequent. With expert planning, along with some help from the few Catholics in our community, my mother got us to Mass most

Sundays, and to classes for sacramental preparation. When I turned sixteen, we bought a former undercover car from the Royal Canadian Mounted Police (the Mounties), and I drove us to Mass when the weather was fair.

I loved the conversations I had with my mother about life and other interesting matters, from poverty to abortion. During my early teens, Mum stopped practicing the Catholic faith, but still she had laid the foundation for what God would eventually do in my life, because her entire life was a testimony to sacrificial love. By word and example, she taught the importance of honesty, integrity, and charity. Since she was right about most things, however, I gradually adopted her distaste for the Church.

Eager to be on my own, I left for university at seventeen. The school I attended was owned by the Sisters of Charity, and my dormitory housed a chapel where Mass was offered every Sunday. Since it was so convenient, I felt at first that I should go. *After all,* I thought, *I'm a Catholic.* But one autumn day, I found myself listening skeptically to the words of the Mass. *I really don't believe a word of this,* I said to myself. *I don't believe in Jesus Christ. If I keep coming I'll be a hypocrite.* And with that, I cut my ties to Catholicism.

Soon I discovered that St. Augustine wasn't all wrong: my heart was restless. Life itself was one big question, but I wasn't interested in Christian answers. Christianity couldn't be the truth; it just didn't go deep enough, and the Catholic Church seemed nothing more than a rule-making, guilt-inducing institution. I wasn't even much interested in rational answers to my questions. For a while, I preferred searching to finding. New Age thought and Eastern philosophies seemed to satisfy my need for mystery, asked nothing of me, and kept me entertained and "connected" to the spiritual world. I even read

Shirley MacLaine's books and liked them. Atlantis, aliens, astral projection—why not? At the time, they seemed as plausible as belief in an obscure Jewish carpenter who died on a cross to save the world.

Although my undergraduate program consisted mainly of communications courses, I preferred discussing philosophy and theology. But I was too busy with my daily affairs to think through my spiritual quest. My life, like that of most modern young adults, was devoted to looking for love in some of the wrong places and trying to juggle diverse demands. Pursuing my cherished dream of being a performer and winning an Oscar some day, I became an actress in university stage productions—mostly in musical theater—and did some modeling on the side. After graduation, I dived into professional theater. Directors, fellow actors, friends, and family all heartily encouraged my plan to go on to theater school.

Just before I graduated and started my theater career, however, my interior life started to change. During my university days, I had become close friends with Patrick, a man I first met during rehearsals for a production of *A Chorus Line*, when I was a freshman and he was a senior. After he graduated, we stayed in touch. Whenever we were together, we seemed to skip over trivial topics like the weather and head straight into such contentious matters as God, religion, angels, art, philosophy, and sexuality. Patrick was a practicing Catholic with lots of zeal and a heart to evangelize. Often, he invited me to retreats, talks, and Sunday Mass, and whenever he saw an opening in the conversation, he would try to bring up Jesus. I say "try" because that's when the conversation would stop for me.

"Our friendship would go much better if you'd stop talking about Jesus", I'd groan.

One day, he threw down a gauntlet. "You're not really

interested in finding the truth", he challenged. "If you were, you'd give Jesus a fair chance."

If we hadn't been such close friends I might have found a way to avoid him, but I thought about it and realized he was right. I *did* prefer to ignore Christ, and I *was* hostile toward the Church. No one I knew ever talked about Jesus, but I had heard lots about the Church, and not in admiring terms.

The Chinese say even the longest journey begins with a single step. To "give Jesus a fair chance", I took a baby step; I agreed to go on a young adult retreat known as an Antioch Weekend, which is modeled on the Cursillo retreat. Ironically enough, it was held at the convent where my late great-aunt had lived as a nun all her adult life. The convent Motherhouse, set on a hill overlooking the Bedford Basin in Halifax, is still quite beautiful.

Sleeping bag in tow, I rode to the retreat with my atheist roommate, who couldn't understand why I was doing this and almost convinced me to turn back. My earnest search for religious truth had begun to drive a wedge in our friendship, and I was at a loss to remedy that. But I knew that Patrick, who was my retreat sponsor, was waiting for me at the Motherhouse, and I believed it would be rude not to show up. *It's only one weekend,* I thought. *When I get through this, I can say I gave it a fair chance and move on.*

On my arrival, Patrick told me that there would be confession on Saturday evening, the last night of the retreat. I frowned.

"Look pal," I said, "you got me here, but I won't be going to confession. I don't believe in confession!"

He smiled, gave me a hug, and said good-bye.

I had sincerely asked my Creator to show me what He (She? They? It?) wanted me to see and know. I tried to be open and prayed for wisdom. And I found I admired the honesty and openness of my peers at the retreat. The talks were inspiring; the discussions were interesting; I enjoyed the creative projects we did. The *palanca*—personal letters to each retreatant from people who were praying for us that weekend—moved me. Then Saturday night came in the upper room of the Motherhouse. Quite against my own feelings, but in answer to a strange call, I found myself standing in the line-up for confession. I didn't know what I was going to say. I hadn't been to confession for years. There I was treading down the hall to a waiting priest. I could hardly believe it. I needed help!

Help came quickly. Father was kind. He explained what the sacrament was all about. When he said the words of absolution, something unexpected happened. Suddenly, I felt the presence of God in a way I'd never known, powerful yet gentle. My head and eyes, as well as the whole room, seemed to be bathed in light. *Surely the priest can see it too*, I thought.

When I returned to the larger gathering, another *palanca* was delivered to me, a letter from my friend Patrick, written as though he had anticipated exactly what had happened to me in confession. His words spoke to my heart all that I needed to hear at that moment. To this day he remains an irreplaceable brother in Christ.

It is difficult to articulate what happened to me during that retreat. I experienced the love and power of the Holy Spirit. I never expected it, and I didn't understand it, but I left the weekend a changed woman and one committed to going back to Mass.

As I began to frequent the sacraments, I still had questions and no lack of emotional baggage concerning the Church. The Lord had to work gradually with me. Determined not to have the wool pulled over my eyes, I wanted the truth, not a crutch. So it took a lot to convince me.

I started reading the Bible and got my hands on some good Catholic books. Although I'd always been pro-life, I had a problem with almost every other Catholic moral teaching. *Premarital sex always wrong? Contraception always evil? Homosexuality always disordered? Come on.* I had other questions too: why intelligent, articulate, compassionate "Jane Smith" couldn't be ordained to the priesthood but gruff, aloof, lackluster "John Smith" could. That didn't seem right. One thing was clear, however. I couldn't pick and choose what suited me. If I were to embrace the Catholic faith, I would have to assent to its doctrines. Issue by issue, obstacle by obstacle, I read, discussed, and prayed my way to understanding and accepting the teachings of the Catholic Church. I discovered that the Church wasn't in the business of rule-making to oppress us, but of providing us with a road map to true freedom, peace, and joy.

Around the time that the Catholic faith began making more sense, something serious was troubling me. I still had doubts that Jesus Christ was God. For all the books I had read, and all the convincing arguments I'd heard, I couldn't seem to really believe, deep down, in Jesus. Could anyone prove that He was God? Sure, the Bible told me so, but how could I know that the Bible was true—that it had any authority? I could see that Scripture was reliable only if the Church had authority to deem it so, since the Church wrote it and put it together in the first place. And the Church had authority only if Jesus Christ was the Son of God. I fretted myself into a distressing quandary and spent many an hour in tears.

I was teetering at the top of a precipice. Part of me wanted to forget it all and head back to adventures in the Andes with Shirley. I kept on going to Mass, and often I would sit in church at odd hours feeling isolated and alone, begging for God's help. I couldn't share my struggles with my family or friends; I thought they'd never understand.

One day over the phone I admitted my doubts to Patrick. He suggested the agnostic prayer, which goes something like: "Lord Jesus, if you are who they say you are, reveal yourself to me in a way that I can know it's you." Worrying I'd never escape the funk I was in, I prayed this every day. I knew that I needed the gift of faith—and that I couldn't conjure it up myself. What would I do if God didn't come through?

A few months later, one ordinary evening, I was in my bedroom folding laundry and listening to music when suddenly Jesus walked into my room. I didn't see Him, I didn't hear Him, but in a split second my spirit knew Him, and I instantly burst into tears. It was over in a matter of seconds, but from that moment on I was able to believe that Jesus Christ was indeed God. This grace of faith was pure gift. I had sought the Lord with all my heart, and He had let me find Him (Jer 29:13).

Since then I have learned that God does not generally give extraordinary mystical experiences. Spiritual "highs" have actually been rather sparse in my journey of faith; that has been frustrating at times, but it has taught me to see Jesus in the ordinary, and not to confuse emotional highs or ecstatic experiences with true, abiding faith.

During the time I was investigating the Church I was a full-time actress, and I expected that I would be one for the rest of my days. For all its dark spots, I loved the theater world. Among my warmest memories are the magic times I experienced onstage with fellow actors, some of whom I grew to admire and love. Still, after my conversion, I began to wonder whether or not the theater was where I belonged. My approach to life had shifted; my own will no longer held the trump card. Did God have a plan for my life? A path for me that would give Him more glory?

Providence has a way of throwing me into situations before I think I'm ready for them. In a perfect introduction to a theater career, I was offered a coveted part in a big musical production, *Man of La Mancha*, with some of the top actors in Canada. I had planned to work for six months in Kenya, with Canada Crossroads International, an overseas volunteer program, but I decided to take the theater job, believing the experience would help me to know for sure whether this was the life for me.

As the youngest cast member, I felt intimidated every day of rehearsals by the enormous talent around me. I learned a lot from my dressing-room companions: one was an experienced opera singer; the other an actress who went on to play Fantine in the Toronto and Los Angeles productions of *Les Misérables*. Listening to their histories, hearing about their heartaches and sacrifices, brought me face-to-face with the reality of life as a professional actress. For all the delight I had in doing it, by the end of that show I wasn't so sure I should throw all my eggs into the theater basket. I took another role in a cabaret show and spent more time thinking about my options.

Inspired by the work of Crossroads, I grew more interested in serving people directly, in a way that could bring them to God and let them know His love. That desire moved me to pursue a degree in psychology with a view to further education in counseling. I ended up at Franciscan University in Steubenville, Ohio. It was there that I began to understand St. Paul's exhortation to "renew your mind in Christ" (Rom 12:2).

My first few months in Steubenville brought dramatic change and an experience of culture shock. I'd been living in downtown Toronto, Canada, in an artsy, liberal environment

with unconventional people, where I was accustomed to
being the only Christian everywhere I went. Now I was in
a small, conventional midwestern American town, on a
vibrantly Catholic campus where Christ was at the center of
classes and student life. At first it was overwhelming and,
frankly, almost annoying. Did everything have to be so
spiritual?

But I came to see that I needed a new world view. My
heart belonged to Christ before I got to Franciscan University, but my mind still belonged to the world. Not only had I
not received a solid liberal arts education during six years of
undergraduate studies, but my professors had been atheist,
agnostic, marxist, feminist, in fact, almost everything but
Christian. Approaching life from a Christian mindset was foreign to me.

While in the counseling program, I enrolled in a few
theology courses and found them enlightening and tremendously stimulating. Dr. Scott Hahn, a well-known convert
who is a theology professor at the university, made Scripture
come alive for me. I began to see the many levels of meaning
in Scripture and how the Word of God could be God's own
advice, consolation, and direction *to me.*

There were times when my ideas of God were challenged
by what I was hearing in class or in conversations or reading
in theological texts and the Bible. For example, I was shocked
to discover the God of the Old Testament: the Yahweh who
ordered Abraham to sacrifice his son, slew Israel's enemies,
and allowed Job to be put through the wringer didn't seem to
be a God I should trust. Sometimes my roommate would
come home to find me in tears over something I had learned
in class that day. The complementarity of men and women—
especially as regards the role of women in the Church—was
an issue that could raise my hackles. The opinions of some of

my fellow students came across as sexist or rigid. Yet when I read the actual Church teachings and discussed them with wiser and more learned people, I was surprised and delighted at the depth and beauty of the Catholic view. As Archbishop Fulton Sheen once observed, there are millions who hate what they think the Catholic Church is, but not a handful who hate the real thing.

During dark days when I wondered if I could continue on the "Catholic" journey, I would cling to the Lord and place myself in His hands. He is real, I knew, and I knew that He is the center and source of all, so I trusted Him and kept walking. Those struggles brought me to my knees and challenged me to go deeper in my faith. I would take my questions and concerns to prayer and lay them at the foot of the tabernacle, where I believed His grace would penetrate my confusion and frustration.

My temptation was to get off the narrow road and take an easier path, or to go sit in the shade forever. But I always came back to Jesus and the fact that He established a Church to continue His mission and to teach with authority. When the going got tough, I clung to Him and learned to live with unresolved tension while I continued praying, learning, reflecting, walking, and crying out to God. I came to accept that not everything had to be figured out all at once.

It took time before my daily life and attitudes reflected my beliefs. For example, I already believed that sex outside of marriage was wrong, but I didn't understand that the virtue of chastity was more about a disposition than about behavioral dos and don'ts. I knew Jesus was working in my life, but I didn't know the importance of daily prayer.

I learned there was more to prayer than reciting an Our Father and asking for the things I wanted. Prayer can be praise, worship, intercession, meditation, contemplation, and adoration. I could pray with Scripture, read spiritual works, spend time before Jesus in the Eucharist, pray with friends, offer a novena, celebrate feast days in my own home, go on a Rosary walk. I loved the childlike enthusiasm of the charismatic expression of faith as well as the reverence of more traditional celebrations and rituals.

Since my faith journey felt more roller-coaster than hayride, I needed different forms of prayer at different times. The Psalms helped me to express my feelings to God, rote prayers were there when I had no words, Scripture passages gave me guidance when there was none, and eucharistic adoration let me sit before the Son and be immersed in His presence.

For the first five years of my Christian life, I had few sisters and brothers in Christ. I wasn't a "joiner", identified with any particular group; my acquaintances were an eclectic bunch. I had a few close friends, and otherwise I enjoyed being alone. Often I seemed to have more in common with non-Christians I met and befriended than with church-going Christians.

One of my greatest joys, however, was finally meeting likeminded women from different parts of world who shared my faith. Our love for Christ and the Catholic Church bonded us together in a way I had not experienced in other friendships. Even today, these spiritual sisters are my supports, sounding boards, and sources of encouragement. Their faithfulness, courage, and love are visible signs of God's nurturing care for me.

After an eye-opening season working at the United Nations in New York in preparation for the Beijing Conference on Women in 1995, I attended a pro-life conference in Washington jointly sponsored by the Respect Life office of the National Conference of Catholic Bishops and Women Affirming Life, a Boston group. Those experiences moved me to start Women toward the Third Millennium, with

Katrina Zeno, another Steubenville alumna. Our vision for this apostolate is to implement the Holy Father's call for Christian women to join together in considering our role in building a culture of life in a civilization of love. WTTM is a project under development; we are still small and poor. Currently, I am a contributing editor of *Envoy Magazine*, and my full-time job is as producer and hostess of *Envoy*'s new Catholic radio magazine.

My own Christian journey has not been entirely a holiday picnic. But I remain a Catholic because I know the love of Jesus Christ through the Church He died to found. I could never live a set of doctrines, or teachings, or commandments, without His love at the center of my commitment. I could not stay in the Church, filled as she is with faulty human beings, if I didn't believe in her divine origin and in the constant, guiding presence of the Holy Spirit. Although I have found my spiritual home in the Catholic Church, my heart remains, in a sense, still restless. I desire more of God, and I long to be counted among His saints, to be welcomed at last into the place He has prepared for me.

இ

A Canadian native with honors degrees in public relations and psychology, Zoe Romanowsky was an actress in legitimate theater when she came to believe in Christ and returned to the embrace of His Church. Subsequently, she earned a master's degree in counseling at Franciscan University of Steubenville, where she also studied in the graduate theology program. Her articles have appeared in *New Covenant, Lay Witness, Credo, Our Sunday Visitor*, and *Pittsburgh Catholic*. Currently she is a contributing editor of *Envoy Magazine* and the producer-hostess of *Envoy*'s new Catholic radio magazine.

A Little Child Shall Lead Them

Julie Baker Maguire

God was an important presence in my childhood. I can't say when I became conscious of Him; it seems that an awareness was always there. At about seven I became aware of it in a distinct way. For some time I had been terrified that our house might burn down in the night, and I prayed fervently that God would prevent it. One night, during my prayers, Mother let me light a votive candle just below my crucifix, promising to blow it out after I went to sleep. Distracted with a new baby, she forgot to come back. The next morning I awoke to a blackened wall above my head. After brisk cleaning, the only permanent damage was to the crucifix. The feet on the corpus were melted and misshapen, and the end of the wooden cross was charred. Afterward, I no longer worried about the house burning. I had been given an obvious sign of grace, a pledge that Jesus would protect me.

His signs have not always been so conspicuous, but in my soul I know from Whom they come. I don't always understand their meaning, but I know I am to take notice of them, and I sense the wonder of His watchful care.

My parents had entered the Catholic Church when I was six, and we were all baptized together: my mother and father, my younger sister, and I. Nearly everyone we knew in Phoenix then was Catholic, and I couldn't imagine why anyone would not want to be Catholic. Our godparents' daughter was my best friend. I still remember the awe I felt those first few times I went to Mass. For me, there was no other Church.

By today's standards, my parents were very young when I was born. Perhaps because of their youth, my sister and I endured a great deal of verbal abuse while we were growing up, and so I did not feel that I was a bright or capable little girl. But when I began attending St. Jerome Catholic school, just inside the city limits of Phoenix, Mother Aidan instilled in me a conviction that God really loved me, no matter what I couldn't do. It became a foundation that saved me at many low points in my life.

I spent ten years in Catholic schools, and during that time staff transitions seemed to mirror those of the entire American church. The Second Vatican Council was under way in 1965, when I entered second grade, and St. Jerome's school was brand new. Originally, it was staffed by Sisters of Loretto, most of them Irish, who marched us to Mass on Monday, Wednesday, and Friday. But the following year, the "spirit of Vatican II" began blowing through our school, and we went to Mass only a few times each month. Though we children didn't pay much attention to administrative matters, we knew there was controversy between the Sisters and our pastor. When I was in fifth grade, these Sisters were replaced by Dominicans, whose somewhat abbreviated white habits were in sharp contrast to the black habits of our lost Lorettos. There were more lay teachers, too. By 1970, when I was in seventh grade, our principal was a married woman with six children, and all the nuns were gone.

Religious education became experiential and experimental. In a special room filled with bright pillows, we lounged while one of the parish priests showed us multi-projector slide shows to the music from *Jesus Christ Superstar*. We thought this was cool. Soon we were "celebrating" Mass by standing around the altar during the Consecration. No one talked seriously about the sacredness of this principal part of the Mass anymore; we were one happy family, sharing a meal with Christ. Sometime during this period I made the last confession I would make for more than twenty years.

Many parents pulled their children out of St. Jerome's and drove them longer distances to schools still graced, they thought, by nuns. I wanted to graduate with my friends, so my parents let me and my sisters stay. After graduation, I moved on to an all-girl high school, while my sisters transferred to the Cathedral school where our beloved Loretto sisters had gone.

Unhappily, this pattern of hectic transitions was also reflected in my growing confusion about Church teaching. I encountered no sense of Catholic tradition, or even of continuity. Everything about the Church, it seemed, must continually be reinvented. As a family of converts, with little knowledge to fall back on, we had no idea that the changes flooding the Church did not always issue from the Magisterium. My neophyte parents established a pattern of Sunday Mass attendance in our early years, adopted some Catholic traditions in our home, and relied on the Catholic schools to teach us the faith. Beyond that, they depended on the example of their peers, a dubious source in those tumultuous times. Because of those circumstances, they had difficulty maintaining their original excitement about the faith, and our practices at home were observed inconsistently.

While I was in high school, I became confused about the morality of abortion. During free periods, I'd often visit Jane, a family friend who lived just steps from school. She was in her twenties, married, and expecting her first child. I was charmed by her conversation, and by her pregnancy, about which she kept me fully informed. Jane was involved in a charismatic group, and she became so evasive when I asked whether it was a Catholic group that the truth was obvious. Stimulating as it was, our friendship did nothing good for my religious formation; on the contrary, it played a part in launching me on years of perplexity.

The Phoenix city council was considering whether to permit an abortion clinic to be built a few blocks from our Catholic girls' high school. Some students planned to attend the council meeting in our conspicuous plaid uniform skirts. When I told Jane about it, she asked what I would do if I were I impregnated by rape, or if my life depended on ending a pregnancy. She manipulated my emotions with the specter of women dying from illegal abortions. Until then I had never been challenged on the issue, but afterward I was uncertain about the propriety of opposing abortion.

During my senior year in high school, we moved to a small town in northern Arizona, where Mass at the tiny country parish was nothing like the rowdy guitar Masses we had grown accustomed to in Phoenix. We slipped easily into a habit of infrequent Sunday Mass attendance, and at last, like the seed that fell on rocky soil, my family's connection to the Catholic Church effectively died out.

After high school, I attended a state college, where I went to Mass sporadically at the campus Newman Center. My relationship with God was much like that with my earthly parents: I would call on them from time to time to ask for something I needed or even just to check in. If anyone asked, I said I was Catholic, in the same way that I said I was a biology major; in neither case did I adequately understand what the term meant.

After graduation I moved to Denver, where a former roommate was in graduate school. My life was without direction; I had no plans for the future, beyond supporting myself. Now and then I would mutter a prayer for safe travel or for some family member. But I had stopped going to Mass, not because I ceased to believe or objected to the Church, but simply because I did not feel required to do so. There seemed no pressing need to recognize God's presence in my life; my working definition of Catholicism involved no element of obligation on my part. If I thought about God at all, I confidently presumed that He would continue to look out for me, as He had always done.

So I went heedlessly on, enjoying life, meeting my basic needs on my own initiative. For the first time, more than one young man was showing interest in me, and, as the eldest of five children, I found this a heady degree of appreciation. The life I was leading seemed good enough for me. I never wondered whether it was good enough for God.

Then God interrupted my frivolity with a momentous change. A young man I had met briefly in Arizona called and invited me to dinner. He had just finished a summer job in Phoenix and had moved back to Colorado to start working for the Forest Service. My feelings about his invitation were mixed. I was in no mood for adventure, having just endured a trip to Arizona made harrowing by mechanical troubles with my car. Besides, I suspected that my old college friend had given him my telephone number in hope of diverting my attention from her Protestant brother. The onset of a dismal cold gave me sufficient excuse to put him on hold.

Not until three weeks after his first call did I go out for an evening with Bob Maguire. As we drove home, each of ten traffic lights turned red at our approach. Braking for one of them, Bob leaned over in his micro-sized car and gave me a very light, casual peck, one that barely fell into the category of kiss, yet somehow completely changed the way I viewed him. It was nothing like the "falling in love" I had experienced in the past, but more like a window opening. I knew this was something important. Now I know it was grace. As it happened, Bob too had been raised as a Catholic, and he didn't go to Mass anymore either. We seemed to make the perfect couple.

Our relationship progressed, and we had grown very close by the time Bob was forced to consider a new career. His prospects for a permanent job with the Forest Service were threatened by funding cutbacks, so he took a temporary post as a deputy sheriff, complete with health insurance and a retirement plan. It seemed an excellent opportunity, despite the perils, stresses, and odd working hours it entailed. But visiting him soon wore down my patience, as it required a four-hour drive over two mountain passes. At last I issued an ultimatum: we would either live together or dissolve our relationship.

[Years later, when I read Scott Hahn's description of marriage as a covenant with God as the third partner, that truth put the nature of marriage into proper perspective at last, and I felt a keen sense of loss over my past behavior.]

Bob was fairly shocked at my announcement, but soon he conceded the practical advantages of such a plan. Since many of our friends were choosing the same sort of life-style, it would be socially acceptable. Neither of us had any moral concerns, never having been presented with Catholic teaching on sexual behavior—and frankly preferring ignorance to an investigation of such teaching. We embraced the popular logic that marriage is just a technicality involving a piece of paper; as long as we were committed to each other, marriage could come later.

Without much struggle, Bob agreed to my proposal, on condition that we not tell his parents, especially his traditionally Catholic mother. The ruse was easily effected, as they lived in Massachusetts, and Bob was expected to keep in touch with them, so they never called him.

After a year and a half of "trial marriage", we decided it was time for us to get really married. We even met with a priest and filled out a required questionnaire, thinking we might get married in the Catholic Church. Now I realize that the priest exuded disapproval; I am certain he was not deceived about our living arrangements. In any case, circumstances related to Bob's employment forced us to abandon our plan to be married in Colorado.

When he took a seasonal job with the National Park Service in Arizona, we learned that the Catholic diocese there would require us to wait a year before marrying. Abandoning all idea of a Church wedding, we arranged to exchange our nuptial vows on a paddlewheel boat on Lake Powell, with the captain, a mail-order minister, officiating. All four of our parents came, which meant that Bob's parents learned the truth about our premarital living arrangements. His father said he had known it all along, but it was plainly a shock to his mother.

The next morning, Bob and I went to Mass with his parents, and we received Holy Communion with no sense of the sin we were committing by doing so. We assumed that it was our right to participate; we regarded being Catholic as holding permanent membership in a sort of club, where we could drop by whenever we liked, use the facilities, and participate in daily events. We didn't even think it necessary to get involved with the other members, as long as we donated a little something when convenient. If we had sat in the confessional through Mass, we couldn't have been more in the dark. And once the festivities were over and the relatives gone, we reverted to inactive status in the Church.

Our next move took us to Massachusetts, where Bob hoped

to obtain a permanent job with the Park Service. Undeserving as we were, God was good to us, and this career goal became a reality. During our time in the East, I came to know Bob's family. I grew close to his sister, but my relationship with his mother was strained, with good reason. She knew her catechism thoroughly, having been well taught by nuns back in the 1930s. Now she was in pain to see that Bob and I were not living by that faith. But we were still in abject ignorance. One new friend advised me to go ahead and receive Holy Communion as long as I felt in my heart that it was the right thing to do. That was what her professor had taught her at Catholic Boston College, she assured me, so I gratefully took her advice.

Fourteen months after coming to New England, Bob was transferred to Corpus Christi, Texas. As the name of the city would suggest, there were plenty of Catholic churches there, but I didn't enter one for at least a year. After six months of job hunting, I was hired as a biology teacher at a Catholic high school, of all places.

During my interview I was asked, as a condition of employment, what I thought about abortion. "Well, I'm Catholic and—", I began.

"That's good enough", the Sister interrupted. So she didn't ever hear me say that I really was uncertain about abortion. I knew that I would never have one myself, but I wasn't sure what this had to do with anyone else's choice.

(I didn't learn the answer until 1996, when I read a short statement by Mother Teresa about "the culture of death." She pointed out that its origin can be traced to the legalization of abortion, because when a society permits the killing of the unborn baby, the most defenseless human life, the end result will be disrespect for all human lives. In other words, legal abortion is the root of this evil culture. Suddenly, I under-

stood that my refusal to judge gave tacit approval to the practice of abortion.)

School at Incarnate Word Academy had already been in
session for two weeks when the original teacher was called
away by a family emergency. So I began my first teaching
engagement in less than ideal circumstances. It was sink-or-
swim time for me, and a time of reacquaintance with the
customs of the Catholic Church. Once a month I attended
Mass with the whole school, where I continued to receive
Holy Communion in a state of sin and ignorance. Outside of
school, my religious life was entirely up to me, because Bob
worked weekends. Once I tried going to Mass, but I felt isolated and out of place.

Soon a transforming event came into our lives: I gave birth
to our first child. Simply by being present and being herself,
this little daughter was to change the way I looked at everything and to move me constantly closer to God.

As an infant, she was often inconsolable. Many nights I sat
rocking my tiny, wailing daughter, with no one to talk to but
God. Mostly, I begged Him for the patience to endure her
screaming without leaping out a window, with her or without her. Between the demands of part-time teaching and trying to be a perfect mother, I was nearly frantic.

Then the wife of a colleague of Bob's, in a well-meant
blunder, called one day to tell me how poorly I was succeeding. Baby Jill was not being properly nourished, she said. It
was obvious, because she was distraught and insecure, rather
than contented, and not gaining weight as she should. These
comments left me devastated. Despite the knowledge that Jill
had received glowing health reports at her checkups, I was
beside myself with anxiety, fearful that I was a negligent
mother.

Bob was a two-day journey away on a special assignment.

When he got home the following week, he found me an emotional wreck. Nothing he said could soothe my distress, so at last he stopped trying. I had never been in such despair. I felt as though someone had dumped me into a trash barrel, and in trying to dig myself out, I had clawed through the bottom instead, into an even deeper pit. My husband's consoling words seemed empty to me. It was then that I knew God was my only source of comfort, and I placed myself in His hands. That was a moment filled with grace, when healing began in many of my wounds, some of them very old and deeply buried, but made manifest again in this crisis.

Some months later, when my emotional condition was much restored, another teacher made an interesting prediction about my future. First she asked whether we went to Church.

I began to answer with the usual, "Well, we're Catholic . . .", but it didn't work this time.

"No", she interrupted, "I mean, do you attend Mass, as in actually belong to a parish?"

Of course, I made excuses: Bob always worked on Sundays, or he was on call, and living as we did some thirty miles from the city, it was next to impossible for us to get to Mass.

"I used to feel pretty much the same way," she said. "But as my children grew older, I got concerned with their spiritual welfare. I predict that the same thing will happen to you. Just wait and see."

Her comments stirred me to thought. Not long afterward, I packed up my baby and took her to Mass. Since Bob couldn't come, it seemed like an ordeal, and I felt so alone when I got there that I didn't try it again. But occasionally I would bring Jill along to a school Mass, where the students all loved to see her, and I loved to show her off.

We moved again, to Missouri, and then on to North

Dakota, making a feeble gesture each time toward becoming practicing Catholics, but never following through. In Missouri, part of the problem was living forty miles from the church, part was that Bob's work schedule still conflicted with Mass times, and part was laxity. Jill was only weeks away from turning five, and our second daughter was nine months old before we arranged for them to be baptized. Our reasons for proceeding were benign but spiritually shallow. "Well, this is something we're supposed to have done, isn't it?" we said to each other. "And wouldn't it make a nice memory to have them baptized in this historic mission church?"

Shortly after the baptism, we moved back to northern Arizona, near Lake Powell, where we had been married. Jill was entering kindergarten, and, as Divine Providence would have it, a catechism class for kindergartners was held during the 9 A.M. Sunday Mass. This moved us easily into regular attendance. So it was a little child who led us back, through our sense of obligation to her.

As Bob was now free most Sundays, we suddenly felt like a "normal" family. We still had not been married in the Church, but we did not let this prevent us from receiving Holy Communion. There were times when I thought maybe I should not go to Communion, and then I would stay behind in my pew. But the next Sunday I would be back in line again. Was I thinking that not receiving Jesus on one Sunday meant I had done my penance and was eligible to receive Him again? No, I was not thinking at all; I was simply making up my own rules on the basis of how I felt at any given moment. We were "cafeteria Catholics" who picked and chose what we cared to believe.

It was questions from Jill that finally moved us to have our marriage blessed. After several classes, we thought we were ready. But we felt no urgency about it; the birth of our third daughter delayed us for another year. Then, shortly before we were to receive the sacrament, Father Walter informed us that we needed to go to confession. With great trepidation and shame, we did so. My childhood memories were of stern priests who gave stiff penances. I couldn't guess how many hours I would need to work off my present long list of sins. At the least I feared a scolding, but it wasn't as bad as I had imagined.

I didn't realize it immediately, but that first confession only uncovered the tip of an iceberg. As I came to recognize my spiritual condition, it is true that I suffered spiritual anguish, but then I discovered the joy of conquering my iceberg, bit by bit, through the great Sacrament of Penance. Sometimes only small bits broke off, but at other times huge blocks came down, and I experienced a great sense of accomplishment. To actually look at my faults and be truly contrite about them, to admit them as something to be forgiven, was a new experience, and I found that I needed the guidance of the Holy Spirit and the help of a detailed examination of conscience booklet. Though I have made progress, there have been occasional regressions, too. Certainly I still have much to learn.

God gives us only what we can handle, and apparently what we accomplished during those first years in Arizona was all that we could handle at the time. Our faith had been reawakened, we had become conscientious about Sunday Mass attendance, we made sure that Jill attended catechism classes and received her First Communion. We even began to involve ourselves in the parish community.

One group that played a part early in my renewal of faith was not a Catholic one. It was "Mothers of Preschoolers", or MOPS, a branch of a national Christian organization, sponsored by a local Protestant church. Here I met women who were intensely serious about their faith.

I was embarrassed and a little sad for a young mother from my parish when I heard her tell the MOPS group, "Oh, you know us Catholics. We aren't too serious about our faith." Yet I had to admit to myself that she was exactly right about many of us, including me. By that time I was trying to be more serious about my faith, at least by doing what I thought I was required to do. More than that I did not have the motivation to do.

Unexpectedly, I was urged to become coordinator of the MOPS steering committee. The request was apparently made in desperation, as the woman who thrust the guidebooks and box of records into my arms had the look of someone fleeing a crime scene. My first committee task was to fill out forms, on which the major question seemed to be, "Have you been saved?" Then I was asked to explain the experience by writing something called my "testimony". The only episode I could think of that might fit was receiving the Sacrament of Confirmation, so I wrote all I could recall about becoming "a soldier of Christ". This must have been acceptable, because they didn't reject me.

From time to time the other women asked me questions about the Catholic Church, and for the most part I was able to answer them. Sometimes a question was simply puzzling, such as, "Catholics hate Jews, don't they?" This I flatly denied, of course, for no one had ever taught me anything of the sort. And I wondered where such ideas came from.

Many of the young MOPS mothers wanted to homeschool their children when they were old enough. I found this a strange notion, and tried to discourage it by defending the local schools. I was pleased with the education Jill was receiving, and I saw no need for anything different. Even though one of my friends was homeschooling her children, I never considered it as something I might do. It seemed logical in her case, because she lived fifty miles from town and the nearest school; I agreed that it would be madness to expect little children to ride a bus a hundred miles each day, though it was routine practice in that school district.

In any case, homeschooling seemed to me to be a Protestant thing, not something Catholics did. At least, I knew of no Catholics who were doing it.

My peers at MOPS sparked my interest in Bible reading. Their devotion to Jesus and their commitment to evangelization were inspiring to me. But, much as they would have loved to convert me, I never entertained a notion of leaving the Catholic Church, even if I didn't understand much about it.

I wanted to learn how to evangelize, too, especially how to develop the courage to open my mouth and actually speak about Jesus. So I watched their methods with warm interest and tried to analyze them. But I didn't find the courage to go any farther.

In retrospect, I see my time in Arizona as a season of spiritual repair and nurturance, sent to prepare me for what lay ahead. After four years in that pleasant climate, we moved to Jackson Hole, Wyoming, where winter lasts eight months. Each Sunday we attended Mass, as we had in Arizona, but we found it slow going to enter into the life of a new parish during the busy summer tourist season.

Then, in September, God's Providence began to initiate changes. First there was a sign-up sheet for Eucharistic Adoration on Thursdays, and I pledged to fill one slot, wondering silently how this was likely to work with a two-year-old in tow.

Shortly after that, I received a call from the parish religious education director, who hoped I would have room for her three home-schooled daughters in the Girl Scout troop I was forming. I was surprised to learn that there were Catholic homeschoolers, but her call meant more than that. It roused in me that old awareness of a nudge from God, as if to tell me the reason for my being in Wyoming.

A nomadic life like ours can sap one's sense of purpose. For several years I had comforted myself with a poem by Elizabeth Searle Lamb, "You Are Needed". It spoke of being required where you are, filling a spot where God needs you. When I felt displaced and in need of acceptance, I would murmur its reassuring last line: "Walk serene in grace; you are in your needed place." It had become my axiom as a park ranger's wife. Just so, the telephone call that day was solid assurance that I was in my needed place. But more was to come.

That first year in Wyoming, our daughter Jill became a source of concern. The previous year, because of her difficulties in third grade, we had arranged to switch her to a different classroom in midyear. Now she was starting over in new surroundings for a third time. Disappointed because we had had high hopes for the tiny three-room school, we watched and shared her misery as she suffered another unhappy year. Something went wrong almost every day.

One April afternoon, Jill burst through the door in tears, declaring that she was quitting school and would never go back. She felt she didn't fit in. Despite the determination in her eyes and voice, we persuaded her to return the next day, and hoped we would hear no more of such protests.

Her spiritual life was being shaken up as well. At catechism class, her general feeling of inadequacy was magnified by her growing friendship with Sarah, a daughter of the parish DRE who had telephoned me about Girl Scouts. Homeschooled Sarah was only a third-grader, but according to our Jill she knew far more about the faith than our daughter did. One day, overwhelmed by the discovery that she knew little about her faith, Jill could not make her feet take her into the confessional. As she came sobbing back to our car, saying she couldn't do it, Sarah and her mother drove up. Sarah talked to her and that helped calm her down. But I knew we had to take some action, though I was uncertain what it should be.

At my next Adoration hour, I prayed earnestly for direction, offering myself and my time for whatever God might need of me. So it should not have surprised me as it did when, that night as I tucked Jill into bed, she asked from a misery in the depths of her soul, "Mom, can't you please just homeschool me?"

"If you can convince your dad, I'll do it", I replied.

Soon I learned that a homeschooling conference was scheduled for the July fourth weekend, in Denver, and Bob agreed to attend it with me. While waiting for the day, I checked out Mary Kay Clark's book *Catholic Home Schooling* from our parish library. It took only a few pages to show me the flaws in my thinking about our children's education. Despite my two college degrees, one of them in education, I was brought to my knees by what I read. Swamped with guilt, I rushed to confession, where the kindly priest kept assuring me that I was a wonderful mother, and had nothing to worry about. Hadn't I made a conscientious effort to see that my children attended CCD classes? Weren't they well fed and well cared for? Yes, yes, and yes.

But when I read the words of Pope John Paul II, declaring that we are all called to be saints—*saints!*—and that our most important duty as parents is to be the primary educators of our children, I knew that I had failed miserably. In my devastation I recalled the time when Jill was an infant, and I was admonished for not feeding her properly. This time, the nourishment in question was spiritual, but I had no doubts about my negligence. True, we made sure our daughters were at Mass every Sunday and had even increased the occasions for confession. But I had been relying on the parish staff to educate them in their faith, while I stayed uninvolved. Did we recognize it as our primary duty to prepare our children for sainthood? I saw their chances of becoming saints as falling in the "slim to none" category. The gravity of my failure left me trembling.

Reflecting on the situation, I saw that we had not done what we should have because we had never been taught to do so. We had simply followed the pattern our culture set for us. Then my anger began to mount. I had been cheated by religious education so focused on saccharine, categorical, merely human affirmation that it left me as ignorant and presumptuous as a monkey. I had never acquired any sense that there are obligations I must meet, for which I will be held personally accountable by Jesus Himself.

The priest who blessed our marriage had spoken to us solemnly about the need to put God first in our lives, but the concept so puzzled me that I had prayed for enlightenment. That was why this new knowledge affected me as deeply as it did. Now I saw vividly *how* I should have been putting God first.

I finished Mrs. Clark's book and went on to read *Rome Sweet Home*, by Scott and Kimberly Hahn. Scarcely able to turn its pages fast enough, I took their book with me wherever I went. Light poured into my mind about the Church, the Scriptures, and related matters. Amazed, I realized I had spent ten years in Catholic schools without ever learning any of these truths about my faith. I felt as though I had accidentally bumped a lever on a shelf that opened behind it a secret door to the universe.

The Denver homeschooling conference arrived and gave me a clearer idea of what Catholic homeschooling was about and how it could be done. More important, it showed me the Catholic Church I had been reading about. There were families present with twelve or more children. At Mass, it was a pleasure for me to join in singing the Kyrie and the Agnus Dei, for I had loved Latin in high school. I learned a strange word that I did not recall ever having heard before: Magisterium. *Magister* means "teacher" in Latin, I knew, but it took some inquiry to find out that the word referred to the Church's teaching authority.

The Holy Spirit had surely taken a hand in our arrangements to stay with old friends in Denver, for in the end it was neither the excellent workshops nor the inspiring homily by then-Bishop Chaput that made up Bob's mind, but the conviction of our hosts that we could do nothing better for our children than to homeschool them. By the time July ended, Bob gave our home schooling plans his blessing.

My new role as my children's personal tutor has demanded a good deal of adjustment all around, but the fruits of our efforts are inestimable for all of us. As I work with our girls each day, I too gain increasing knowledge of the teachings, traditions, and history of our Church. My life as a Catholic has been like the children's game of Chutes and Ladders. My path took me up some ladders and down some chutes, and now I'm on a ladder again, climbing up after the riches that make up this glorious Church.

Looking back, I lament the ignorance that for so many years kept me from seeing and delighting in her splendor, from marveling at the wonder of God's love, and from understanding what He requires of me. It grieves me now to recognize the sins I committed. I wish I could undo them. Yet I have seen by God's astonishing mercy that He loves me still. He has brought me to "my needed place" and poured out on me, undeserving though I am, the treasures of the faith.

≈

Julie Baker Maguire was born in Phoenix, Arizona. A graduate of Northern Arizona University in Flagstaff, she also holds a degree in education from Dickinson State University in North Dakota. Today she lives in beautiful Jackson Hole, Wyoming, with her husband, a park ranger, and their three homeschooled daughters.

Finding the Face of Christ Again

Allyson Smith

My Protestant father agreed to let my Catholic mother raise their children as Catholics, so in July 1960, two months after my birth, I was baptized at Holy Trinity parish in San Diego. My godmother was my maternal grandmother, Nanna, who held me over the baptismal font as the priest poured the water and recited the prayers that filled my soul with sanctifying grace and welcomed me into the Catholic Church.

My mother took seriously her obligation to pass the faith on to her children. One of my earliest memories is of her kneeling on the floor by my bed, murmuring my favorite prayer, the Salve Regina: "Hail Holy Queen, mother of mercy, our life, our sweetness and our hope".

Nanna, who lived with us then, taught the faith by example. Every morning and every night, she would kneel and pray before the crucifix that hung above her bed. If her door was open, I would often join her. So, living in the domestic church, I first learned about Jesus and the Catholic faith.

That domestic church soon grew crowded with two little brothers, separated by a little sister, Alyssa, who has Down's Syndrome. To ease the stress, my parents looked for a class for pre-kindergarten students. They found one near home, so, before I turned four, I entered a preschool class at a school staffed by Sisters of the Society of the Sacred Heart, an order of internationally respected educators. The school's demanding curriculum included French, social studies, math, science, and Catholic doctrine, as well as the arts. I especially loved reading and writing. By second grade I discovered the library and spent hours there poring over lives of favorite saints like Maria Goretti.

Discipline, courtesy, and obedience were integral to a Sacred Heart education. Conduct was publicly graded every Friday at "Primes", a dreaded weekly assembly of students and religious. Mother Superior sat at the head of the class and pronounced each student's name and conduct grade. The student then walked up to receive her rating card from Mother, made a polite curtsy, and returned to her seat. This was easy enough to do when the rating was "Très bien" or "Bien" but utterly mortifying when the rating was "Bad". The prospect of public humiliation during Primes was normally terrifying enough to guarantee good behavior.

In second grade, I made my First Confession and First Holy Communion. I still remember the solemnity of the Mass and my awe as I knelt at the Communion rail and tasted the Body of Christ for the first time. The same "sense of the sacred" pervaded many occasions during my years at the convent. Devotions were always conducted with reverence, in beautiful surroundings. The nuns fulfilled well their mission of imparting a perception of transcendence and of rich Catholic traditions.

My years at Sacred Heart coincided with the Second Vatican Council, but as it took time for conciliar change to filter down through the Order, I caught the tail end of traditional Catholic culture. By the time I was transferred to public school in 1969, the formal black habits were gone. But, young as I was, the treasure I'd found in the Catholic faith was planted deep in my heart. Later, it was obscured for years by the muck of sin, but it never quite died. I always knew the Catholic Church was the true face of Christ in the world, even when I betrayed Him with my own behavior.

The year 1969 also marked the end of my parents' troubled marriage. Dad was a successful surgeon, able to provide us with anything money could buy, but he was emotionally unavailable for Mom and four small children. As a result of his remoteness, alcohol abuse, and episodes of infidelity, he and my mother separated when I was in fourth grade and divorced when I was in fifth. Divorce was still uncommon, and I remember the acute embarrassment of being the only child in my class whose parents had "untied the knot". Even after the divorce agreement was signed, their bitter quarreling continued for ten years, until I had graduated from high school and my father had remarried.

My leaving the Church was not the result of a deliberate decision; an accumulation of personal and cultural factors propelled me away. The divorce was the primary one. At first Mother took us to Mass each week, trying to keep the faith even through the divorce proceedings. But as her situation grew more difficult, and we acclimated more to the secular world, she gradually stopped trying. My original training in Church teachings, learned in the ordered beauty of Sacred Heart School, fell away like a dream in this new environment. There was not much order of any kind in my life now, and my conscience grew numb. Soon we children began objecting to Mass, and at last we stopped going completely, except for Christmas or Easter. Thus, at an age when most Catholics were making their Confirmation, I no longer practiced the faith.

At my father's urging, Mother went to Texas for nine months during my freshman year of high school, to take a refresher course in nursing. Dad had told her they might have a chance to reconcile if she started working again. While she was away, I lived with my father and two brothers. Alyssa had been living in an institutional setting for nearly four years, and as the only female in the household, I was suddenly charged with household responsibilities about which I knew next to nothing, in addition to attending school. During this time, my father drank heavily, and he was not a happy drinker. Many nights he would arrive home late, in a rage about my mother over imaginary wrongs. Even on school nights, he would wake us at 3 or 4 A.M. by knocking on our bedroom doors, to herd my brothers and me out to sit in the kitchen and listen while he pounded the counter and yelled in fury about Mom. Often I feared for my physical safety during these episodes, and I longed for the day I could leave.

Eventually, my mother's refresher course ended. She returned from Dallas, got a job as an operating room nurse at a local hospital, and rented a small apartment. Within a week of my sixteenth birthday, I got my driver's license, left my father's house, and went to live with her. This further enraged my father. Now, instead of getting my brothers out of bed when he was drinking, he started coming to our apartment in the middle of the night to pound on the door and yell at Mom and at me. Years later, Mom admitted that during those episodes, she was afraid for our lives.

The California life-style itself was a contributing factor in my drift to disaster. I easily assimilated the "sex and drugs and rock-and-roll" mentality common to many of my peers. Living with so much emotional tumult, I escalated my drug use, trying to blot out the pain of my parents' divorce through artificial highs. With few qualms, I discarded my virginity and sought a substitute for my father's love in a series of uncommitted romantic relationships. At that time, between the arrival of the Pill and the arrival of AIDS, many of my high school friends considered "having sex" the normal thing to do. By the time we graduated, few of us were virgins. Several had had abortions and referred to them almost as badges of honor.

Through those troubled years, one bright spot in my life was Mr. Murphy, the music teacher at Granite Hills High School and choir director at nearby St. Kieran's parish. I took piano lessons from him, sang in his high school choir, and joined the campus community service club he headed. Ray Murphy was a Harvard graduate and a solid Catholic family man, who showed me the face of Christ in those dark years. He and his wife, Patty, had four children near my age. Aware of my family turmoil and sensing that I was heading down the wrong road, he often invited me along on his family's outings. He also urged me to come to Mass at St. Kieran's. "I met Patty through Church", he said. "The Catholic Church is a good place to meet good people."

Recognizing his kindness, I listened politely while he talked, but I never took him up on the invitation to attend Mass. It was not until many years later that I realized that he was as wise as he was kind, while I was stubbornly unwise.

In the middle of my senior year, I got involved in my first serious sexual relationship, with a man a few years older than I. Long-haired Bryce was a non-conformist who liked Harley-Davidson motorcycles, disliked full-time jobs, and lived for the moment; I thought him the most exciting man imaginable. But I knew what my mother would think about him if she met him, so I made sure she didn't.

One morning the smell of breakfast made me bolt to the bathroom with sudden queasiness. That day I bought an in-home pregnancy test, and it told me what I already suspected: I was pregnant.

But I was determined not to have this baby, not with this man who could not provide even for himself, let alone for me and a child.

When I told Bryce of my condition the next day, he said, "Well, what do you want to do?" It sounded like a multiple choice question, but we both knew it wasn't, so the discussion was brief. Abortion seemed the perfect solution to the whole sordid mess, and I was not going to change my mind. At Planned Parenthood, I scheduled an appointment for the first available abortion date, which wasn't until August 11, some three weeks later.

The intervening days were excruciating, as my body changed and I considered my choice. Though I wasn't ready to commit my life to Bryce, I did love our baby. Yet I knew exactly what I was going to do to him: I was going to kill him. More than killing, I dreaded the shame I would suffer if I disappointed my family with an out-of-wedlock pregnancy. I did not see that my motive was cowardly "convenience", nor did I see that I was trying to conceal one sin by committing another far worse. I have never considered myself a "victim" of abortion, either then or now. Even at the age of eighteen, I knew I was premeditating a crime of the worst kind: the murder of my own helpless child.

The day of the abortion arrived at last. I proceeded with the loathsome deed. My memory has blocked out most of the details of the experience, but I will never forget the aftermath. Too late, I comprehended the terrible cost of evading embarrassment. For a year afterward, the sound of a crying infant would send me into uncontrollable spasms of tears. Not a day has gone by since when I have not thought of my abortion with pain, guilt, grief, and sorrow. Nor will I cease to think about it to the end of my life, though I have long since confessed my sin and been absolved.

Afterward, Bryce and I tried to go on together. Eventually, some two years after the abortion, he even proposed marriage, and I accepted. But three weeks before it was to take place, I called off the wedding, and we separated permanently.

Afterward, I resigned from my job and returned to college. Then, during my junior year at San Diego State University, I met Stan, and fell ardently in love with him. But Stan was unalterably in love with another woman. After a tempestuous nine-month affair, he ended our relationship to marry her. As I struggled with loss and rejection, my grades took a precipitous plunge that cost me several career opportunities. A mood of depression lingered in my spirit for nearly a year.

Having lost my chance for a more prestigious job, I settled, on graduation, for a post that eventually took me to the San Francisco Bay area. There I met Ron, a handsome coworker whose sense of humor invariably made me laugh. He paid marked attention to me and seemed to find me attractive. Before long I fell in love with him, but our relationship never seemed to progress beyond mere friendship. Frustrating months later, I began to guess what the problem was and finally confronted him with the question. Yes, Ron admitted, he was homosexual.

Once again, I was devastated. This time it took me even longer to recover, because I was overwhelmed with self-doubt. I was twenty-four. In the years when most other young women were finding husbands and marrying, I had experienced, in close succession, three devastating failures in serious relationships. The first cost the life of my baby and the life of grace in my immortal soul; the second wounded my confidence and stunted my career; the third left me in doubt that I was either lovable or capable of sound judgment. My depression was intensified by the awareness that my friends seemed to have no trouble finding the happiness that eluded me.

Seeing nothing ahead but a lifetime of loneliness, I lost weight and entertained thoughts of suicide.

Why does this happen to me? What does everyone else have that I don't have? Unreasonably, I blamed God, *Why are You so cruel to me? Why do You let others find happiness but snatch it away from me?* I felt as though He had abandoned me, that He was deaf to my desperation.

But He was listening.

In 1988, when I was offered an open-ended contract as a consultant in Honolulu, I didn't think twice before accepting. My mother and my darling Nanna, now seventy-four years old, helped me pack my belongings for storage, and they watched with tears as my plane took off across the Pacific Ocean. As I waved good-bye to them, I did not imagine that I might never see Nanna alive again.

In the fragrant beauty of my new environment, my heart began to heal. I felt happier and started to regain the weight I had lost. Occasionally, at the invitation of my client, Sulea, I even attended Sunday worship services. But those evangelical services, in an auditorium-like setting with a preacher dressed in street clothes, didn't feel right to me.

It was late September when I arrived in Hawaii. Uncertain how long I would be there, I decided not to go home for the holidays but to stay in Honolulu to experience a Hawaiian Christmas. Once more kind Sulea invited me to attend evangelical services with her on Christmas Day, but I politely declined. Instead, for first time in many years, I located a nearby Catholic Church and went alone to Midnight Mass.

My decision to attend was not the result of a recognizable flash of inspiration, but I believe the Holy Spirit planted the idea in my mind. During that Mass, a tiny light started to flicker again in my soul where darkness had ruled for so long.

The priest in his vestments, the incense, the moment of Consecration: suddenly all of it felt right. Though there were few
other Caucasian faces in the congregation, I knew I belonged
there. Surprised, I thought, "I've really missed this!" I was
further surprised to find myself returning to Mass at that
church the Sunday after Christmas, and the Sunday after that.
And the Sunday after that.

I wasn't fully back in the Church yet, but the spark of faith
rekindled in me that Christmas night marked an important
turn off the road to destruction that I'd been traveling. God
had seen this prodigal daughter while she was yet far off.

A month later, I called my mother one Friday afternoon, and
the moment she answered the phone, I knew by her voice
that something was dreadfully wrong.

"Nanna died today", she said. Death had come during the
afternoon, with a cardiac arrest, while Nanna was at home
alone.

I flew from Honolulu to San Diego the next morning, and
stayed with my mother as she arranged for Nanna's body to
be flown to Pennsylvania for burial. On Sunday, when we
knelt at Mass together at Holy Trinity Church, where Nanna
had held me when I was baptized nearly thirty years earlier,
both Mom and I wept in grief, but we were also comforted.
Because Nanna was a faithful Catholic, I felt assured that she
was with Jesus. Aware that she had always prayed for me, I
also hoped she knew, now, that I was edging my way back
into the Church.

The next day, we flew to Pennsylvania, on the same plane
with Nanna's body. The weather in the East was brutally cold,
in contrast to the Hawaiian warmth I had left only days previously. The atmosphere could not have been more funereal.
While staying at my uncle's house, waiting for the funeral, I

picked up a book of Catholic prayers and flipped it open. The first thing my eye fell on was the Salve Regina, my favorite childhood prayer.

"Hail Holy Queen, Mother of Mercy, our life, our sweetness, and our hope . . ." As I read it, I could hear in my memory my mother's voice, as I had heard it when I was a tiny girl.

At that moment, the little flicker of light brightened in my soul. It was like a gift from Nanna, that reminder of those days of lost security. I knew with certainty that the Catholic faith my mother had tried to teach me, despite the worst of circumstances, was real and alive. In the midst of sorrow, there was a promise of eternal life for Nanna and strong hope even for me.

We buried Nanna in a pink dress, with a Rosary in her hands. When I touched her hands and kissed her lips, her body was icy cold, but the expression on her face was peaceful, and I too felt a new sense of peace.

A new job opportunity took me to Chicago the following summer. The transition was not easy that first year, as I sought to learn my way around, adjust to the unfamiliar climate, find a parish, and make new friends. Soon after I arrived, I met Maureen Malone, an Irish Catholic high school teacher who haled from Detroit, and she quickly became my best friend. It was she who introduced me to my new parish, in Napierville, Illinois.

The moment I saw SS. Peter and Paul Church, I knew it was the place for me. I loved the beauty of its Gothic architecture, its stained glass windows and carved wooden reredos, the gold tabernacle in the marble sanctuary, the kneelers and Communion rail as well as the choir that performed at the 9:30 Mass every Sunday. I was conscious that some things had

changed in the decades I had been away. But the parishioners
were friendly and welcoming, and the general atmosphere was
far more relaxed than the strictly disciplined Catholicism I
recalled from Sacred Heart Convent School. I was also drawn
to one of the associate pastors there, Fr. Doug Hauber.

Fr. Doug gave new meaning to my definition of a priest.
Thirty years old and only recently ordained, he was handsome, engaging, and a wonderful homilist. Before meeting
him, I had always pictured priests as stern and elderly, the way
they had seemed when I was a child. Not only was Fr. Doug
near my own age, he was always smiling and vivacious. The
"joy of the Lord" was written all over his face, and on many
occasions over the next several years, I was to find in it the
face of Jesus Christ.

As months passed, the fact that I had never confessed my
abortion weighed ever more heavily on my mind. I knew that
if I was serious about practicing my Catholic faith again, I
would have to go to confession. I had not been to confession
for twenty years. After fretting about it for weeks, I finally
gathered up the courage to go one Saturday. First I called the
parish office and learned that Fr. Doug would be hearing confessions that afternoon.

Sweating profusely, I stood in his line, and, when my turn
came, I opened the confessional door with trembling hands.
What I saw next surprised me; there was an inviting chair
beyond the screen. "Wow, is this ever different from the last
time", I thought, as I sat down awkwardly.

Fr. Doug turned to face me as I settled into the chair. I told
him he had to help me, as I had not been to confession in so
very long. Everything came pouring out: my affairs, my abortion, and more. Father treated me gently, yet he probed my
conscience thoroughly. When I was finished, he took my
hands and asked if I needed post-abortion counseling. As he

pronounced the words of absolution, my Heavenly Father welcomed His prodigal daughter all the way home at last.

I walked out of the confessional feeling lighter than air. All the pain of those years of sin was lifted from me, and my heart was filled with the joy of Resurrection. From that day on, instead of dreading the Sacrament of Penance, as I had when I was a child, I have loved it, because now I understand its healing power.

Over the next few years in Chicago, God blessed my life in many wonderful ways. I began working toward my master's degree, bought a small townhouse, and made friends my own age through a Catholic singles group. Meeting friends through the Church was a new experience. Often we would attend Mass together at different churches around the diocese and afterward gather for brunch. Sometimes we helped out at a local food pantry. Those were happy times for me. As I enjoyed wholesome fun with people who shared my religious convictions, I realized that Ray Murphy, my old music teacher, had been right when he told me that the Church was a good place to meet good people. I was sorry it had taken me so long to see it.

By mid-1993, I had been going to Mass regularly for almost five years, and living in Chicago for four. The greatest fruit of my return to the Church was the interior peace of knowing that God loves me. It was really His love that I had sought so fruitlessly from my father and so destructively from other men for many years. I felt God's love in the blessings of my new friendships and in the fullness and contentment of my life. It was the secure center around which everything else now revolved: my Sunday Mass attendance, my work, my academic studies, the company I kept, and my general outlook. For about a year, I had a chaste dating relationship with one man, and after it ended, I didn't try to date anymore. Gradually, the urgent longing to be married faded, and I was content.

I was unaware that a great battle was raging all around me. But that was soon to change.

That July, for the first time in my life, I was laid off from my job. As I looked for new work over the next six weeks, I had a lot of free time but no money. Looking for inexpensive ways to fill my days, I discovered that the parish had Mass at 5:30 every afternoon. I had never gone to daily Mass before, but soon I realized that I loved it even more than Sunday Mass.

When Mass was over, I would check the book rack at the back of the church for reading material others had left. One day, I found six issues of *The Wanderer* newspaper. I had never seen it before, so I took them home and started reading. Within several hours I had devoured all six issues. As soon as I could afford to do so, I took out a subscription of my own.

Also in the book rack were copies of *HLI Reports*, a newsletter published by Human Life International. I was fascinated by what I read in them about the slippery slope of contraception and "the culture of death". I had never understood before the connections between contraception, fornication, marital infidelity, divorce, and abortion. But after reading a few issues, I recognized the good sense in their commentary. My own life provided all the evidence needed to show where contraception and illicit sexual behavior could lead.

God used those weeks of unemployment to instruct me in the basic teachings of the Catholic faith. Stirred by my new understanding of Church doctrine, and shocked by what I was learning about attacks on the Catholic Church in America, I began to see more clearly what had gone on in the years following the Second Vatican Council. The beautiful

Catholicism I had known as a little girl had been watered down in many places to fit contemporary tastes.

Thus in a period of personal and financial hardship, the Lord blessed me with more light than I could ever have expected. As I studied Church teachings, and as I contemplated the crucifix, I gained new insight into the infinite depth of God's love. I began to see that His laws and doctrines express His great love for us, His desire for our highest good. I was overwhelmed to realize that He loved me so much that He sent His Son to die on a cross for me. My love for him grew deeper, and I began to long for ways to show Him my love and gratitude in return.

The quiet little flame that had been burning in my heart those past few years blazed up like lightning as I finally understood the tragic condition of our world. Through His Church, the Son of God offers us the salvation He purchased at such terrible cost, yet the world rejects Him, defames His Church, and persecutes His defenders. Suddenly I recognized the great spiritual conflict St. Paul speaks of in Ephesians 6:12: "We are not contending against flesh and blood, but against the principalities, against the powers, against the world rulers of this present darkness, against the spiritual hosts of wickedness in the heavenly places."

It was a transforming experience, the kind you can never forget or turn back from. The five years since I began that spiritual journey into deepened conversion have brought a series of adventures, amazing coincidences, and answered prayers. The Holy Spirit, who had already changed me from a nonpracticing Catholic to a practicing one, began to change me from a relaxed, Sunday-only Catholic to a fully committed soldier on active duty in the Church Militant.

Conscious that God's army travels on its knees, rather than its stomach, I first added a daily Rosary to daily Mass and started making frequent Holy Hours before the Blessed Sacrament, asking to know God's will. Then, fired by a sense of sacred responsibility, I moved into an entirely new level of activism. I attended lectures and took courses in the faith, wrote letters and did telephone surveys in defense of the right to life, prayed and witnessed in front of abortion clinics, sponsored a little girl in a Chilean mission, visited convents, seminaries, and shrines, and considered whether God might want me to enter the religious life.

First, I remembered that I had never received the Sacrament of Confirmation. This put me in an unsuitable position; as a would-be defender of the faith, I would always need to stay as close as possible to the Holy Spirit. So the following fall, I enrolled in the RCIA program at SS. Peter and Paul's and tardily began the process that would make me an adult Catholic. I expected to enjoy the weekly class sessions. Certainly I did not expect to challenge publicly statements made by the Sister who led the group. But almost all the others in the class were converts from other faith traditions who did not know enough of the Catholic faith to question anything she taught. So when Sister said that Scripture does not make clear the existence of Hell and asserted, repeatedly, that traditional Catholics were "unenlightened" and "spiritually immature", I felt reluctantly obliged to challenge her, even if it made me look like the class black sheep.

A richer, more powerful preparation for this great Sacrament was the pilgrimage I made with my mother to the Holy Land in February. During Mass at the Shepherd's Cave in Bethlehem, I recognized a description of my own life when I read from Isaiah 9:2–4: "The people who walked in darkness have seen a great light; those who dwelt in a land of deep darkness, on them has light shined." Walking in the footsteps of Jesus for those fourteen days made the Lenten Scripture readings truly come alive for me when I came back home, just a few weeks before Easter.

My Confirmation, during the 1995 Easter Vigil, was a day of exaltation. There, in my beautiful parish church, in the presence of my mother and close friends, as well as all the priests, nuns, and parishioners who had helped me along so generously in my faith journey, I received the Holy Spirit from my pastor, Fr. James Burnett, and, at nearly thirty-five, became at last a full member of the Catholic Church.

In succeeding months, the thought of returning to San Diego was often on my mind and in my prayers. When I was laid off my job a second time the following winter, I decided this was the right occasion to go. I said reluctant good-byes to the close friends and parish family I had come to love, listed my house for sale, and made shipping arrangements for my household goods.

It was early July when I arrived in California, but my household goods never came. Nearly all of them were destroyed in a flood during the move. As I struggled in those first few months to find work and, at the same time, to salvage what remained of my property and to replace what had been destroyed, I learned how disconcerting it is to be unexpectedly stripped of one's possessions. Yet I also found that God still kept me in His Providence, as He has in every stage of my spiritual journey. When He takes away, He never fails to give back far more than He has taken. With my loss, He taught me a new compassion for the displaced and showed me that I don't need great possessions to live a happy and fruitful life.

Living close to my family again brought the unexpected joy of getting to know my sister, Alyssa, better than I had before. She often joins us for the weekend, full of laughter and love. With her patience, humility, and generosity, she has taught all of us valuable lessons in living.

A "fruitful life" for me still means Catholic activism, which has given me frequent occasion to recall Jesus' words about rejoicing when men speak evil against you for His sake. These days, for example, my primary activity is writing. A scurrilous morning radio show in San Diego features a weekly parody of the Sacrament of Penance, called "Lash Wednesday". One disc jockey pretends to be a priest in a "radio confessional", while listeners call in to compete for prizes by "confessing", on the air, their "worst" sins, usually sexual in nature. When my article condemning the show's sacrilegious anti-Catholicism was published, the disc jockeys mocked me on the air by reading it, with scornful hoots, to their audience of commuters.

Listening to their vicious insults stung, and I didn't feel any better when friends and family members criticized me for writing the story and "stirring up controversy". But I also found people who think as I do, and now I serve on the advisory board of the local Catholic League for Religious and Civil Rights.

In these times, when there is such grave disorder within the Church, I sometimes understand the emotions of those who do not stay. But the feeling never lasts long enough to become a temptation. Where else would I go? In my own life, these past ten years, I have seen more than enough evidence of God's loving Providence to keep me in the fold. Despite her current problems, I know with total conviction that the Church was founded by Jesus Christ Himself and she alone is heir to the deposit of faith given by our Lord to the Apostles and handed down in an unbroken line of apostolic succession from then to now. No institution could survive as she has if it were guided by mere human wisdom alone.

I know that our Lord is performing in me some work as yet unfinished, a work that I will not fully understand until I join Him in Heaven. He forgave me for leaving Him and reached out in tender mercy to bring me back. My hope is that I can show His face to someone else who is as lost as I once was. For I am home at last, and I will never leave again.

છે.

In addition to her day job as a technical writer for a major computer manufacturer, Allyson Smith is a free-lance writer for the Catholic alternative press. She lives in her native city of San Diego, after sojourns in San Francisco, Hawaii, and Chicago. A graduate of San Diego State University, she also holds a 1994 M.S. degree in management systems from Illinois Benedictine College. She serves on the advisory board of the San Diego chapter of the Catholic League for Religious and Civil Rights and is also active in the California Pro-Life Council and local pro-life activities, including abortuary protests. Her leisure activities tend to involve computers or cats.

I Was Robbed!

Leila Habra Miller

I was robbed.

I am a Catholic raised and catechized in the tumultuous aftermath of the Second Vatican Council. My peers and I were victims of "renewal" and experimentation gone awry. With immense regret and without exaggeration, I contend that the results have been catastrophic for my generation. The overwhelming majority of young Catholics don't have even a rudimentary understanding of their faith. As a direct result of their tragic ignorance, a steady stream of young Catholics has poured out of the Church.

It's not entirely accurate to say that I *left* the Catholic Church—though I seriously considered it—but it is clear to me now that during most of my young adulthood, I was not *in* the Catholic Church. Let me give you an overview of my upbringing, which will sound familiar to countless young Catholics. I was born in 1967 into a believing and practicing Catholic family. My sister and I were taught by our parents to love our faith. Barring illness, we attended Mass on Sundays and Holy Days of Obligation without exception. We attended public schools but were enrolled in weekly CCD classes at our parish every year.

Under the same title, a shorter version of this article appeared in *New Oxford Review*, September, 1996.

By the time I began CCD, memorizing the Baltimore Catechism was out and feeling the "experience of Christ" was in. My parish priest could not have known how the new, more "enlightened" pedagogy would affect the moral development of those in his charge. At the time, I believe, he was simply caught up in the so-called "spirit of Vatican II" and was implementing what were widely regarded as Council mandates. I have no doubt that my parents, and other parents, were confident that religious education classes would teach their children the faith, properly form their consciences, and launch their souls toward sanctification.

In general, the volunteer CCD teachers were well-meaning parishioners who tried their best with the vacuous materials they were given to use. Looking back, I see that a few teachers must have been alarmed at the new methods and wanted to teach us the fundamentals of our faith. One had us memorize the Ten Commandments; another, when I was in high school, used the word *transubstantiation* in my hearing for the first and last time. Aside from those rare moments, however, precious little substantive information was imparted to us.

I can tell you in three phrases the content of my catechesis over an entire decade: God is good; Jesus loves you; Love your neighbor. (All true and indispensable, but if you read your Bible you'll see that's only part of the gospel message. Sometimes a partial truth is more dangerous than an outright lie.) We saw a lot of cartoon slide shows depicting Jesus and His parables, so I have pleasant images of the multiplication of loaves, the Good Samaritan, and the empty tomb. I don't remember anything particularly *Catholic* about the presentations, though, aside from a cursory foray into the sacraments when it was time for First Communion or Confirmation. (If you had asked me to explain what a sacrament is, I couldn't have told you.)

We weren't taught Catholic prayers, although in my class we all knew the Our Father. I learned the Hail Mary along the way, too, but for many years I knew only the first half. We never discussed the lives of the saints or even mentioned their names. (Sitting at Mass, I wondered who this "Paul" fellow was who wrote so many letters.)

My parents' faith combined with the common themes of my religious education did instill some fundamental truths in my heart nonetheless: I never wavered in my belief in God Almighty and in the Incarnation, death, and Resurrection of His Son.

So I went through my school years believing I was a staunch Catholic—in fact, as I got older I would often identify myself as "devout"—and after my high school graduation I chose to attend a Jesuit university, in part to increase my chances of meeting and marrying a nice Catholic man and raising children in a steadfastly Catholic home. I made numerous Catholic friends during my years at Boston College, many of them products of Catholic elementary and high schools and most of them, like me, practicing Catholics when they arrived. But no one I know grew in his faith at BC. Indeed, many who entered Boston College as practicing Catholics were indifferent or hostile to Catholicism when they left it. I do not mean it metaphorically when I say that Satan is having a heyday at universities like BC.

To indicate what all those years of religious training and formation amounted to, allow me to list briefly some terms that had no meaning whatever to me for my first twenty-eight years:

Sanctifying Grace	Sacred Tradition
Pentecost	Apostolic Succession
Magisterium	Act of Contrition

Indulgences   The Four Last Things
Perpetual Adoration   The "Glory Be"
Sacramentals   Benediction
Mass Cards   Scapular
Corporal Works of Mercy
Spiritual Works of Mercy
Four Marks of the Church
Joyful/Sorrowful/Glorious Mysteries

Who the Holy Spirit was or what He did was anybody's guess, although I did recognize His name. I knew He was one of the Persons of the Trinity, but I didn't know what that term meant.

I challenge any reader to ask the "twenty-something" Catholics he knows to explain or even recognize the words above. Following are some terms that might sound familiar to some of my generation, but that are misunderstood and/or disbelieved:

Purgatory   Communion of Saints
Papal Infallibility   Transubstantiation
Mortal/Venial Sin   Immaculate Conception

Confession? "Sure, great—I'll get there one of these years (wink, wink)." No premarital sex? No contraception? "Yeah, right. Get real!" Evangelize? "Are you kidding? Why? After all, Buddhism, Islam, New Age, Christianity—they're all equal paths to God. Who are Catholics to say they have the truth? A mature spirituality requires the understanding that *everyone* can be right."

The attitudes of my Catholic peers are no mystery. Generation X Catholics don't feel that they actually *have to* do as the Church teaches. And I assure you they do not fear the

fires of Hell or the pains of Purgatory. But really, how could
they? They may have gone to Mass for decades and never
heard such topics mentioned, much less defended.

The culture we live in is merciless when it comes into contact with a poorly catechized Catholic. American society today is designed to destroy one's faith, as objective truth and
moral absolutes are rejected concepts. When contemporary,
"enlightened" catechesis echoes the messages of the culture,
and when those charged with informing the Catholic conscience and transmitting the faith take an "experiential" rather
than an instructional approach, what can we expect? We can
expect exactly what was taught. We can expect young Catholics who believe "conscience" means "opinion", and we can
expect subjective feelings and personal experience to supplant
objective truth. In fact, the prevailing philosophy of my generation is that there *is* no one "truth". Truth is whatever we
want it to be. You have your truth, I have mine. (Kind of puts
the lie to Christ's definitive statement, "I am the Way, and the
Truth, and the Life", doesn't it? It also doesn't sound like anything worth dying for, does it? Those foolish martyrs!)

We reap what we sow. When pop-psychology all but re-
places sound catechesis, the results should not surprise anyone. The practices and beliefs of my circle of Catholic friends
tell a sad story. Premarital sex? Yes, with a series of different
partners. Contraception? Of course—"it's a virtue." Living
together, a.k.a. living in sin? It's a non-issue. (One Catholic
friend did go so far as to find a "compassionate" priest who
consented to give her absolution *before* she moved in with a
man.) Active homosexuality? "A life-style choice." Abortion?
"Sad, and we don't like it, but it's a woman's private decision—too bad her partner didn't use a condom."

Most of my Catholic friends attend Mass sporadically or
not at all. Some get their spiritual guidance from gender femi-

nism (a fiercely anti-Catholic movement) and/or New Age philosophies. Overall, the Catholic call to holiness is an unfamiliar concept to them, and I do not for a moment exempt myself from this scrutiny. Confession is a sacrament that was *never* emphasized. I made my first confession at nine years of age, and, after my first couple of confessions during grade school, I never went back. I shudder when I think of how often I received Holy Communion unworthily.

So how is it that a Catholic who went to Mass every Sunday and went through all the sacramental preparation programs at her parish could receive Holy Communion unconcerned about the serious sins on her soul? My generation of Catholics grew up with a keen understanding of God's infinite love for us. We knew that His perfect mercy could not be exhausted, no matter how badly we behaved. But at the same time, we heard nothing about God's perfect *justice*. Maybe no one wanted to hurt our feelings with Church teaching—by telling us, for example, that by persisting in serious, unrepented sins, we could damn ourselves to an eternity in Hell.

Jesus Himself mentions Hell over a dozen times in the Gospels, but our teachers and priests presented us only with the Jesus of the Beatitudes, or the Jesus who continually forgave sinners. Jesus said, "Enter through the narrow gate. The gate that leads to damnation is wide, the road is clear, and many choose to travel it. But how narrow is the gate that leads to life, how rough the road, and how few there are who find it!" [1] We were never reminded that Jesus forgave *repentant* sinners, those with contrite hearts and the intention to sin no more.

The God presented to American Catholics today is the Rodney Dangerfield of gods: He gets no respect. He hardly

---

[1] Mt 7:13–14.

needs to be worshipped, since He's our buddy, our pal, our equal. No need to fear Him or stand in awe, no difficult obligations on our part—we need only enjoy the pleasant gifts He showers upon us until we die and He takes us to Heaven instantaneously.

Such was the image that my generation got of God our Father. But good parents don't reward bad behavior. They set boundaries that a child, for his own good, must not cross. Should that child choose to persist in disobedience and wrongdoing, good parents don't expand the boundaries to encompass his bad behavior; they hold firm and hope for his repentance. They do not cease to love him, even as they let him experience the consequences of his poor choices. So it is with God and sinful man. He loves us infinitely, but He will not force us to love and obey Him against our free will.

None of this was explained to post-Vatican II Catholics like me.

A year after I graduated from college, I married Dean Miller, a nice agnostic Jewish boy (so much for my plan to find a Catholic husband). My identity as a Catholic was strong enough so that I came to this relationship with certain non-negotiable positions: I would never get married outside the Church, and any children of mine would be baptized and raised Catholic. Dean, who had attended a Catholic high school, respectfully agreed to my conditions, and we were married in the Catholic Church by my childhood pastor.

Over the next four years, I gave birth to three beautiful babies, who provided me with any number of excuses to stay home from Mass often on Sundays and almost always on Holy Days. When one does not understand what happens in the Mass, it is easy to become lax about attending. When I did get to Mass, I felt as if I were putting in my time, mechanically fulfilling a duty. I did a bit of "church-hopping", looking for a parish I liked, but everywhere I met the same lame attempts to make the Mass "hip" and entertaining. I felt no awe, no reverence; there was nothing in these Masses to snap me to attention, to take me out of myself and focus my mind and heart on God in His Heaven. I wasn't "getting anything out of it", and so I often ducked out right after Communion. One of the things I didn't comprehend is that one doesn't go to Mass to "get something out of it" but to worship God.

Having been raised never to miss Mass, I felt guilty, as well I should have. My guilt was grave, and I blame no one but myself. But let me explain my state of mind. I had been exasperated to read the authorized words of Sacred Scripture in the missalette while a lector read an illicit "inclusive language" version of the same text from the pulpit. My intelligence had been insulted by liturgical thought police who excised words like "men" from liturgy and hymns, apparently sure that I was too stupid to understand that such words include me. At an Easter Mass, from a pew decorated with balloons, I watched a priest who had donned a bunny suit for his homily. I listened, mouth gaping, as another priest used another day's Gospel to condone homosexual activity.

The standard moral challenges issued from the pulpit were (and are) banal calls to help the poor and hackneyed admonitions against racism. Every humane atheist in society was saying the same obvious things. Why get out of bed for Mass on Sunday morning, then? Why bother being a Christian when any TV news program teaches the same message? Most young Catholics already understand it. What we don't understand is our faith! But I *never* heard about the need for repentance, for conversion, for personal morality, for holiness! After a while the American Church and the decadent world became almost indistinguishable in my eyes, and I could see little point to attending Mass.

Although many of my peers will leave the Church and Christianity altogether, many others will do as I did. I never once considered forsaking Christianity, nor did I question Christ's divinity; I felt strongly that to deny Him would be blasphemous. But I was guilty of dangerous presumption. I thought that because of my "deep faith" I could continue in one or another mortal sin, and God would forgive me or make an exception on my behalf. I was confident that He would respect my "conscience".

I never disagreed with the Church's stand on such contested matters as abortion and homosexuality. I had even heard, almost by accident, some of her arguments against contraception, and they made sense to me. Magnanimously, I thought the Church was probably right on this issue. But of course I could not be expected to actually follow this teaching. I did plan to learn Natural Family Planning someday, sure, but certainly not now, in my early married years. After all, God understands.

Though I presumed on God's mercy, I never went the way of moral relativism. In fact, another young mother and I spent a year and a half writing an editorial column for our state's largest newspaper, *The Arizona Republic*, in which we condemned moral relativism and defended the concepts of moral absolutes and objective truth. My friend, Kimberley Manning, had spent six years as a feminist and New Ager, but motherhood, reinforced by the reflection involved in writing our column, eventually led her back to Christianity and into a local Bible church.

Kim had been a lapsed Episcopalian, and I was an ebbing Catholic, so we had never had religious discussions until then, but because of my strong belief in objective right and wrong,

I was attracted to what she told me about the Bible church. Those evangelicals stood firm on moral issues and were not afraid of offending anyone by asserting Christian truth. I couldn't say as much for the Catholic parish I was sporadically attending, where moral courage seemed sadly lacking. A parish that sought to blend in with the culture was not the kind of religious community I needed. I was raising children in a scary society, and I needed support from others who believed as I did and who would help to make it a refuge from the "pagan world". In my dissatisfaction with what American Catholicism had become, I flirted with the idea of leaving it for Kim's nondenominational Bible church.

She told me about the powerful and courageous sermons she was hearing there. Week after week, her pastor spoke out against the immorality that surrounds Christians today. He talked about right and wrong and used Sacred Scripture to show his flock how a proper Christian should conduct himself. The evangelicals in his flock did not pretend to blend into the culture; they resisted it, in a loving, Christ-centered way, keeping their eyes on God. And they were actually being *instructed* in Christianity! Kim was attending Sunday services, weekly Bible study, a doctrine class, and a Christian parenting class. She loved it because her soul was being fed, and for the first time she understood what it meant to be a Christian. What I was experiencing in my Catholic parish was in painful contrast. No wonder a good portion of her church's congregation consisted of ex-Catholics—*young* ex-Catholics, like me, who were raising families.

We often hear from Catholic dissenters that young people are deserting Catholicism *en masse* because the Vatican refuses to change her "outdated teachings" to "conform to the times" by ordaining women, feminizing the language of liturgy, permitting remarriage after divorce, and approving the agenda of the sexual revolution. Feminists and New Agers lure Generation Xers out of the Church by tagging her with such derogatory labels as *patriarchal, oppressive, reactionary, judgmental, narrow, rigid,* and *outmoded.* Young Catholics who leave the Church with those reasons on their lips often mouth them to mask the real problem: that they have lost their faith. In such cases the need is not for accommodation but for conversion.

Meanwhile, at the other end of the spectrum, fundamentalist Christians have pulled millions of Catholics out of the Church just by quoting a few Bible verses out of context. A poorly catechized Catholic is virtually helpless against those tactics. For every young Catholic who leaves the Church in pursuit of the spirit of the age, at least one more—generally one raising a family—leaves for opposite reasons, because he sees the Church as too liberal, too morally lax, too reflective of the secular culture. These young adults are seeking an anchor in a world gone mad. Searching for Christ and for a standard of morality higher than they think they can find in the Catholic Church, they fill the pews of fundamentalist and evangelical churches whose leaders still preach the Ten Commandments. Tragically, in leaving Catholicism, these searchers in their ignorance abandon not only the faith that holds the highest of moral codes but Christ Himself, unrecognized but truly present in the Eucharist.

By February 1995, in my ignorance, I too wanted to get out. I leaned toward a Bible church infused with pride in Jesus Christ, because I knew I would find moral courage there and could expect to receive instruction in my faith, not excuses for it. I was ready to see how my mother would react to my trial balloon. I wouldn't approach my dad first, as I knew he would be heartbroken by it. But Mom had been raised a Protestant. She came into the Church when I was three, so I thought she would be easier to talk to.

"How would you feel if I left the Church for a Bible church?" I asked her.

My mom is a very composed and rational person, rightly noted for giving sound advice. When I popped that question, she gave me the answer that was to change not only my life but the lives of many others as well. "Before you leave," she said, "you should find out what it is that you're leaving."

Then she told me some of the reasons for her conversion to Catholicism. It had never made sense to her that Protestants place all their belief in the Bible alone, she said. The question for her became "which Bible?" There were many translations, and everyone had a different view on which version was authoritative. She was also wary of nondenominational churches in general, because of their tendency toward "the cult of personality", the phenomenon of a congregation gathering around a dynamic, popular pastor, often one with a dazzling new interpretation of Scripture. He would be the reason they came, and, if he left, they would leave, too.

Everything Mom said that evening made sense, and my thoughts of leaving the Church were at least neutralized. A short time later, she struck a deadlier blow against them when, in her matter-of-fact way, she presented me with a book of a kind I never knew existed. It was Karl Keating's *Catholicism and Fundamentalism*, a work of Catholic apologetics.

Some people find it hard to believe that I had never known apologetics existed. Even I can hardly believe it had never occurred to me that someone, at some time, might have found it useful, or necessary, or even noble to defend the faith. How could I have been ready to jump ship without even investigating the doctrinal issues involved? Why had it never crossed my mind that a Church two thousand years old might be able to present arguments on her own behalf? Maybe it was because in my entire lifetime as a Catholic I had never heard anyone defend the faith. No one had ever given me any reasons why Catholicism was right, why only the Church has the fullness of truth.

Once Keating's glorious book was placed in my hands, the contest was all over. I was impressed, excited, amazed, that someone had taken the trouble to spell out the differences between Protestants and Catholics, not with tepid neutrality, but in a passion of love for the Catholic faith. And Mr. Keating uses the Bible itself to illustrate the truth of Catholic doctrine. Reading only a few pages of this blessed book was all it took to keep me Catholic and to set me on a pursuit of knowledge that has led my soul to burn with love for the Faith. Sounds dramatic? It is! Thanks to God's grace, four years of study have shown me treasures that I never dreamed possible in this world—yet I understand that I have only dipped my little toe into the vast ocean of Catholicism.

Over the next several months, Kim and I engaged in a series of friendly but vehement theological debates. Back and forth we argued about papal authority, the Real Presence, the Blessed Virgin Mary, sanctification of the soul, and the meaning of the Inquisition. We gave special attention to the two doctrines that separate Protestants and Catholics: *sola scriptura* (the belief that the Bible is the Christian's only authority) and *sola fide* (the belief that we are saved by our faith alone). At times our exchanges resembled the blind leading the blind, but I used the best Catholic arguments I knew at the time, and Kim searched out the best apologetics Protestantism had to offer.

Our telephone calls lasted for hours and were so intense that they left us physically and emotionally drained. Then we hit what we called "the brick wall". Frustrated and apparently getting nowhere after six months of replaying the Reformation, we agreed that it was time to stop talking about theology for a while.

Meanwhile, Dean was being drawn into this "God talk" whether or not he wanted to be; I was so excited about what I was learning that I discussed it with him whenever he would let me. Together, Kim and I had discovered the Old Testament prophecies that so clearly point to Jesus as the long-awaited Messiah. Thrilled, I pointed out those passages to my Jewish husband. I'll never forget the look of near panic in Dean's eyes when he reluctantly conceded one night that it appeared Jesus *might actually be* the Son of God.

Both Dean and Kim followed one supreme principle in their journeys to the faith: they were searching for objective truth. Neither made any decision based on unsupported opinion or what "felt right"; they were not looking for what was comfortable but for what was true. And that, of course, is what God asks of each of us: to take up our crosses and follow in the footsteps of Truth Himself, even if it costs us our comfort, our security, or our very lives.

Kim's quest for truth at all costs kept her praying and studying even after we ended our debate. To give Catholics a last chance to make their case, she read Patrick Madrid's celebrated book *Surprised by Truth*, in which eleven converts— many of them former Protestant pastors—explain why they became Catholics. In three nights that she called the darkest of her life, she came to see the biblical and historical validity of Catholicism. Together we examined Scripture and the writings of the Fathers for evidence supporting the Church's doctrinal claims—and found it every time.[2] Six months

---

[2] The Catholic Church is the one Church *explicitly* founded by Jesus on the rock of Peter, the first pope: See Mt 16:18–19; Is 22:22; Jn 21:15–17; Lk 22:31–32; Tertullian, *Modesty*, 21, 9–10; St. Cyprian of Carthage, *The Unity of the Catholic Church*, 4; St. Augustine, *Various Questions to Simplician*, 31, 33.

later, at great cost but with immense joy, Kim received the sacraments of the Church and became a Catholic.[2] Despite his initial reluctance, within a year her husband announced his own intention to convert.

With great jubilance and enormous gratitude to God, I can also report that Dean, my agnostic Jewish husband, experienced a profound conversion and was baptized into the Church. So I got a Catholic husband after all, and a devout one, too.

Some other fruits of my "conversion"? I returned to confession after more than fifteen years away, and I now reap the graces of that wonderful, previously unknown sacrament. The

---

The Bible is a product of the Catholic Church: See Council of Hippo, 393, and subsequent Church confirmations in 397, 419, 1442, and 1546. St. Augustine, *Against the Letter of Mani*, 5, 6; see also *Where We Got the Bible*, by Henry G. Graham (Catholic Answers). (For a free catalogue from Catholic Answers, call 1-888-291-8000.)

As Christ promised, the Holy Spirit protects and guides the successors of Peter and the Apostles. See Mt 18:18; 28:16–20; Jn 16:13–15; 17:17–20; 2 Thess 2:15; St. Irenaeus, *Against Heresies*, 3, 3, 3; Tertullian, *The Demurrer against the Heretics*, 28, 1; St. Augustine, *Against the Letter of Mani*, 4, 5.

Submission to Church teaching is submission to Christ: See 1 Tim 3:15; Mt 18:17; St. Ignatius, *Letter to the Smyrnaeans*, 8, 1; St. Irenaeus, *Against Heresies*, 3, 4, 1.

The Eucharist is clearly evident in the New Testament: See Mt 14:13–21; 26:26–28; Jn 6:25–69; 1 Cor 10:16–17; 11:27–29.

The Eucharist is prefigured in the Old Testament: See Gen 14:18; Ps 110:4; Ex 16:15; 24:8; 1 Kings 19:4–8; Prov 9:1–5; Wis 16:20; Mal 2:11. See also *The Story of the Eucharist*, Inos Biffi (Ignatius Press).

All of the Church Fathers were firm believers in the Real Presence: See *Didache*, chap. 9:5, chap. 14; St. Clement of Rome, *Letter to the Corinthians*, 44, 4; St. Ignatius, *Letter to the Smyrnaeans*, 6, 2; St. Justin Martyr, *First Apology*, 66; St. Irenaeus, *Against Heresies*, 5, 2, 2; See also *The Faith of the Early Fathers*, ed. William A. Jurgens (Liturgical Press).

The sacraments of the Church were explicitly instituted by Christ: See Jn 3:1–5; 6:48–60; 20:19–23; Acts 8:14–17; 13:3; Mt 26:26–28; 28:18–20; Jas 5:13–15; Lk 22:19; Heb 5:1; Mk 10:2–12; Eph 5:22–33.

[3] See her story in *New Oxford Review*, September 1996.

Mass, which I used to avoid, is now a transcendent experience for me. Contraception? Gone, with great benefit to my marriage. I continue to uncover the treasures of Christ's Church, and Kim and I together have started to teach the faith to others. You could say that in Catholicism I have found the secret of the universe, and nothing can compare to its majesty.

Which brings me back to a sadness. How easily I could have lost it all! How easily my friends and contemporaries have lost or could lose a faith they have never really understood. Inoffensive, doctrine-free catechesis doesn't provide even a minimal foundation of faith, and faith built on so flimsy a foundation cannot withstand even the smallest challenge.

As I said when I began, I was robbed, and my peers were robbed. The loss is incalculable, for how do you count the cost of even a single lost soul? As for blame, there is enough to go around, and I am fully aware of my own culpability. I could have asked more questions, and I could have sought to do God's will as best I understood it, but in many cases I did not. My parents have willingly accepted their share of blame as well. But if I were giving prizes to those most responsible for the subversion of the faith, they would go to dissenting Catholics in positions of power in the Church, be they bishops, theologians, or catechetical directors. They have watched two generations of Catholics raised in complete ignorance of the faith as a result of catechetical bankruptcy; they see epidemic rebellion against Church authority; yet they continue to push more and more people out of the Light and into darkness.

I am not so naïve or despairing as to believe that even wide-scale apostasy among American Catholics at every level can destroy the Church. We know from Christ Himself that the gates of Hell will never prevail against His Bride. But if we needn't fear for the Church's survival, we should nevertheless be concerned for the accomplishment of her primary mission on earth: the salvation of souls. Too many souls have been allowed to slip out of the Church due to catechetical neglect or abuse, and it's time to stem the tide.

The first step in reversing this trend is to throw ourselves on the mercy of God, begging forgiveness for the mess we've made in His Church and His world. Second, we must pray for the conversion of those within the Church who seek to undermine the very faith they pretend to profess. Third, every Catholic must take it upon himself to learn the faith and commit himself to a lifetime of proclaiming the truth to others; this is the "new evangelization" by the laity advocated by His Holiness, Pope John Paul II.

Praise be to God that my joy at having found the faith is greater than my righteous anger at those who had a hand in keeping it from me for so long. I know that I cherish my faith even more dearly for having almost lost it. God chose this way to lead me back home, and I will be forever grateful. I only pray He will somehow lead the rest of my generation home, as well.

Leila Habra Miller grew up in Tucson, Arizona. After graduating *summa cum laude* from Boston College in 1989 with a degree in English, she worked in advertising until the birth of her children. Along with her friend Kim Manning, another stay-at-home mother, she wrote an opinion page column for *The Arizona Republic* for two years. She has also written for *New Oxford Review*. Currently, she teaches an RCIA program in a Phoenix parish. She and husband, Dean, have four children and hope to welcome more in the future.

An Eclipse of the Soul

Rachel Taylor Riley

Snuggled into my sleeping bag on a lawn chair, one crisp fall evening, I watched a total lunar eclipse for four hours. At the start, the full moon shone brilliantly in a dark blue sky. Almost imperceptibly, a shadow began to eat away at the bright circle, slowly expanding until the entire moon was blotted out and only a thin rim of reflected light remained visible. Then, just as slowly, the process reversed itself. The shadow began to move away, allowing more and more light to show, until the full white circle of the moon was bright again. Alone in the silence, I thought how much like a lunar eclipse my own life has been.

My mother was a Catholic, my father a Lutheran. I was the first-born of their eight children, all baptized as Catholics. When I was six, my parents moved their growing family from a cramped city apartment to five green acres in a lakeshore resort town north of Chicago.

Catholic education was a priority with Mom. I started first grade at St. Columban's, a parish school staffed by Sisters from the same Order as Mom's own teachers through grade and high school. The Sisters filled my soul with the warmth of God's love, and I learned to cherish the truths the faith embodies. On my First Holy Communion day, I went forward to receive my long-awaited Lord, dressed all in white and trembling with happiness. We sang "O Lord, I Am Not

Worthy", and I felt radiant with the pure white brilliance of Jesus' love.

A few weeks after First Communion, our parish church was packed every night for the stirring sermons of a week-long mission. At morning Mass, the First Communion class clustered conspicuously in the left front pews in our white dresses and suits. Walking back to my pew after Communion one day, I glanced up into the eyes of a sullen-looking teen-aged boy. Scandalized to realize that he didn't want to be there, I cried as I offered up my thanksgiving prayers for him.

As the elementary school years passed, my faith continued to grow, untroubled. During fourth grade, Jane, a classmate, confided that she had seen the statue of the Blessed Virgin move. We spent the next few lunch periods in church, staring at the statue and hoping to see this marvelous event, until Sr. Jude came to investigate and knelt with us for a time before ending our vigils.

In seventh grade, as we prepared to receive the Sacrament of Confirmation, choosing a new name was a privilege I did not take lightly. In searching through the "Lives of the Saints" section in the back of a huge family Bible for just the right one, I found the story of St. Catherine of Siena, who was clearly a woman of powerful faith and strong convictions. I wrote her name on the crumpled paper of the confirmation form, on the line headed "patron saint".

As an eighth grader, I was chosen to crown the statue of the Blessed Mother in our annual May Day ceremony. Thrilled to a quiver, I dressed in a white wedding dress bor-rowed from a classmate's sister. Although it was much too big for me, I was delighted to be able to walk down the main church aisle, dressed in white, to dedicate myself to my Lord a second time. As I prepared to leave St. Columban's for high school, my faith was strong, my devotion to Jesus and His

Blessed Mother fervent, and my soul still as white as those ceremonial dresses had been.

Fast-forward to the late 1960s and early 1970s, a time of experiment and change in the Church. At my Catholic girls' high school, taught by nuns from another Order, the shadows of doubt first began to creep across the brightness of my childhood faith. The shadows began when I was told in religion class that the Bible was "myth", a collection of entertaining stories with no basis in fact. That Adam and Eve were fictitious characters. That there was no flood. Even Jesus' Resurrection was called into question. This may not have been exactly what was intended, but it was the thinking I absorbed in my high school religion classes. Spiritually speaking, the rug was pulled out from under me, and everything I had believed through my childhood was now held to be false and rather ridiculous.

Outwardly, I still practiced my faith, but inside, its foundations were crumbling. One incident epitomizes this period in my religious education: a speaker from Zero Population Growth (ZPG) was invited to address the student body at an all-school assembly. A bright, intelligent, articulate young woman, apparently of college age, she was a very persuasive speaker. She left many of us convinced that we should have no more than two children in order to save the planet from a population explosion. My friend Rhonda refused to be taken in by her sales pitch. I remember being one of a group gathered around Rhonda, arguing with her, trying to change her mind. Thinking back on it, I am amazed both at her courage and at our gullibility.

Gradually, the shadow of doubt and disbelief eclipsed the light of God's truth in my soul. Sure that I was being open to new and exciting ideas, I lost sight of the eternal truths. With little comprehension but a sense of being *au courant*, I skimmed books by Teilhard de Chardin, Andrew Greeley, Gregory Baum, and Paul Erlich, and I concluded that the world was where the creative answers were. Evolution, contraception, and population control became the tenets of my new creed. The moral bottom line became, "Everyone is free to decide in his own conscience what is right and what is wrong." With these distortions firmly planted in my mind, I prepared to move away from home and its safety net into the world of Catholic higher education.

In the fall of 1971, I started college at St. Brigid's, a small Catholic women's college nestled in the hills of a Midwest river town. The quaint old brick dormitories were charming and the surrounding bluffs beautiful. But I was primed less for learning than for freedom from constricting rules and regulations. I meant to keep to a minimum my association with such Church activities as Sunday Mass. Feminism sounded good to me. I believed I could make my own decisions, set my own standards, make my own rules. Over Christmas break, I even announced to my mother that I planned to start my own religion.

As we cleaned a classroom one day, my friend Anna and I were discussing sexual morality. On the blackboard, I drew a diagram of a moral spectrum ranging from married sexual lovemaking, at one extreme, to sex for pay, at the other extreme. The notion that I could determine right and wrong for myself had born its fruit. I remember explaining that my own behavior fell about midrange on that spectrum and was therefore morally acceptable.

Inevitably, my so-called philosophy led to suffering. By the time I was a sophomore, I was pregnant. It was 1973, and abortion on demand had just been ruled legal by the Supreme

Court. The baby's father, when he learned of my condition, had blurted, "I don't want to get married! I'll pay for the abortion." I was alienated from my parents, my Church, and my God.

So, alone and frightened, I began three tormented months of decision making: Would I give birth to the child growing within me, or would I have an abortion?

Every day I woke up with a cold knot in the pit of my stomach, wondering, "What am I going to do?" Some days I thought, "Yes, I can do it. I can have the baby and go back to school." Ironically, my career goal at that time was to become a doctor. I even made an appointment with a physician to have a pregnancy exam and see if everything was all right. He was very understanding, and my talk with him was like an oasis in a desert of pain and indecision. But I continued to waver.

All my friends at school accepted the idea that each of us invents his own moral code; whatever I decided would be the right thing for me to do. No one said abortion was wrong. When I saw pictures of an unborn child in a display in the college library, I turned away and tried to block the images out of my mind. I was considering aborting my baby.

Finally one day, I woke up and said to myself, "This is it. Today I decide." One classmate had a sister who lived in the state capitol, near the Planned Parenthood abortion clinic. She offered to pick me up after the procedure and help me get to the train station. The call was made, the appointment set.

The deed done, I prepared to go home for Easter vacation.

The time that followed was the darkest, most sordid period of my life. The life of God's grace in my soul was entirely eclipsed by sin. I had thought aborting my child would solve my problems, but my problems remained. Even now I cannot find words to describe the sense of anguish and abandonment

I experienced. Feeling totally alone, unloved and unworthy of love, I continued to slide ever deeper into a spiritual morass. To numb the painful voice of conscience, I turned to drinking and drugs. I told myself that I was a sophisticate, the kind of self-sufficient person who had reckless affairs and, if pregnancy resulted, solved the problem by abortion. To cover my yearning loneliness, I started hanging out at singles bars, striking up casual one-night affairs with men I cared nothing for and usually never saw again. In the undifferentiated dark blur that constituted my life, I don't know how I managed to stay in school, but somehow I did.

As I hit bottom emotionally, an interior image came to me, as if from the heart of Heaven. I could see myself clearly, standing on the brink of a deep, dark, rock-strewn canyon. I knew that continuing on my present path would take me down into the darkness, where I would become as hard as the canyon rocks. In an agonized moment of grace, I was able to look up to God and cry out, "Are you there?"

With that feeble gesture, the shadow of sin ceased advancing. Just as the shadow of the earth moves so slowly away from the face of the moon that its motion is almost imperceptible, so did God slowly, patiently lead my soul back to life. I did not immediately reform my life, but I stopped the most degrading of my activities. And the circumstance that eventually brought me to real reform began very soon, when the man I would marry walked into my life.

Sean was fresh out of the Marine Corps and returning to college. We met when a group of mutual friends gathered in a dorm room to sing to his guitar. He told me he had been looking for a blonde who could sing and asked me out the following night. Thus began our three year on-again off-again romance.

On our first dates, I was uncharacteristically shy and quiet. My self-confident assertiveness had evaporated, now that I had shame to hide. Sean kept probing, trying to find out what was behind the silence I carefully maintained.

Neither of us was attending Mass, except when I went home on vacations. Sean was reading the Bible, and we talked about God occasionally; but that was the extent of our faith practices. Asked whether we were Catholics, both of us would have said Yes, but asked what "Catholic" meant, we could not have told you. It was a tenuous lifeline that bound us to the Church.

The rest of our personal relationship was far from moral. Soon we were having sexual relations on a regular basis and justifying our behavior on the grounds that we were in love. But when I discovered that my period was late, I was unwilling to face another three months of grueling decision making. On my own, I found a place that would do an immediate abortion procedure on condition that my period was less than ten days late. Afterward, the doctor called to tell me that I had indeed been pregnant. When I broke the news to Sean, he was distraught. When he said he would have wanted the baby, my grief was too much for me to handle. I stormed from the apartment in blind confusion, rage, and guilt. Shortly after that, we broke up.

With that second abortion, my life seemed to lose all purpose. I drifted in and out of various relationships, always hoping that Sean and I would somehow get back together. After a time, we began to talk again, as "just friends". Then, some three months after our break-up, we started seeing each other again. This time our relationship seemed more serious, and we even talked about marriage. But I was still pursuing medical school, so marriage was something for the far distant future.

After finishing my undergraduate work, I got a job in a research laboratory at a prestigious Midwest clinic, moved into a house with two other single women, and began to live on my own. Sean and I continued our affair by long distance and spent most weekends together.

Being in love with Sean had awakened a spiritual hunger in me. I desired to know God, but as I wasn't yet ready to go where I knew He could be found, my spiritual hunger led me to search in some strange circles. I signed up with an ex-nun who was teaching a yoga class, and, at first, doing the yoga exercises gave me a feeling of physical well-being. Then I began to want more. Sr. Beverly had told us about yoga meditation. She taught us how to empty our minds, focus on our breathing, and let ourselves unite with the power within. Fascinated by this Eastern philosophy, I soaked it up like a dry sponge. I went to the city to meet a guru and hear speakers talk about yoga; I became a vegetarian and arranged a meditation area in my bedroom where I would begin every day with a half hour of exercises and a half hour of meditation. I was hooked.

Although it wasn't presented in religious terminology, the final step in becoming a yoga disciple was to participate in a mantra-receiving ceremony. Using a mantra was supposed to lead to a deeper degree of movement toward nirvana. I was eager to participate. There was only one problem. Sean didn't want me to do it. In fact, he was insistent that I not go through with the mantra-receiving ceremony. The thin line binding him to the Catholic faith was stronger than it looked. He knew the ceremony involved offering token worship to a false god and sensed that to commit such an act of idolatry was to place myself in danger.

My reaction was anger. I remember stamping out of my apartment in the middle of our argument, filled with a rage that amazed me and scared me at the same time. After I had cooled down, standing at the river's edge, I wondered, "Why am I so angry?"

The anger seemed to have a life of its own, as though it came from somewhere other than me. I decided maybe it wasn't a good idea to get a mantra after all. With that decision, the light grew a little stronger in my life. God had used Sean, imperfect as he was, as an instrument to keep me from plunging deeper into the occult darkness.

At the same time that I was delving into Eastern mysticism, I became acquainted with a young priest at the downtown parish. On lunch breaks, I would walk over to the rectory, and Fr. John would graciously spend an hour or so talking to me about all the ideas and philosophies I was encountering. It was the first time I had talked to a priest as an adult, and I found great comfort in our friendship. I was trying to find out where I stood, who I was, and what I believed. Our conversations ranged from Heaven to Hell and back again. Being able to bounce ideas off Fr. John was a great blessing. Fascinated with the idea of reincarnation, I asked him what he thought about it. Somehow, he was able to lead my thinking in the right direction without making me feel guilty for having asked the question. I trusted his word. I sensed an integrity about him that was attractive. He would talk about his family, his call to the priesthood, his interior life.

Once, I recall, Father talked about his annoyance with an associate pastor who never cleaned up the bathroom after himself. I began to see Fr. John as a human being subject to all the weaknesses and frailties that I was. His report of struggling with everyday realities made life seem safe and concrete. Contrasted to the fact that I was trying to detach myself from the material world in order to achieve oneness with the power within me, it suggested that holiness is to be found not in abstraction but in real life—even amid dirty bathrooms and the irritating quirks of roommates. It was a wholesome antidote to the excessive spiritualism I had been trying to cultivate.

There was one part of my life in which I had made no attempt to detach myself from the material world. Besides dabbling in false religions, I was also wallowing in sexual sin. I kept telling myself that my relationship with Sean was a moral one because "we loved each other". We had even begun going to Mass on most Sundays. One Sunday, the pastor of the parish where Fr. John served gave a strong sermon on fornication and adultery. Without qualification, he said that it was a mortal sin for unmarried people to have sexual relations. It had been a long, long time since I had heard the truth proclaimed so boldly and authoritatively. Shaken to the core of my somnolent conscience, I thought, "What if it's true? How can I ever change my life? What would Sean say about it?"

Upset, I stopped to see Fr. John and asked him if he agreed with the pastor. "I think you had better talk to Fr. Mountain about that", he replied.

"But we love each other. Doesn't that make it right?" I asked.

"Fr. Mountain preached the truth. It would be a good idea for you to tell him how his sermon affected you."

There was one insurmountable problem: I was afraid of Fr. Mountain. Like his name, he was a mountain of a man. I'd never have the courage to challenge him. On some deep level I recognized that he was right and I was wrong. The suggested conversation with him never took place, yet his sermon shocked me out of my moral complacency and compelled me to examine my whole life.

After hearing this disturbing sermon, I started going to Mass regularly and decided to return to the Sacrament of Pen-

ance. I had never experienced face-to-face reconciliation before, and I found it to be a healing experience. As I stood in
line, filled with fear, the thought occurred to me: "What am I
afraid of? God wants to forgive me!"

Yet on a Saturday afternoon not long afterward, I ap-
proached the confessional with a renewed sense of fear. I had
committed a sin I was particularly ashamed of, and I decided
on confession behind the screen so Father wouldn't know it
was me. I told him what I had done and his response as-
tounded me.

"Why don't you get married?" he asked. "What are you
waiting for?"

I was flabbergasted. No one had ever suggested that to me.
I wasn't ready. I wasn't mature enough. I wasn't the starry-
eyed innocent kind of girl who married. Marriage seemed
like too great a commitment for me to make, or for anyone to
make to me. A stream of excuses rushed through my brain.
Yet here was this good man telling me the simple answer to
my predicament. In the meantime, he added, we must stop
living in sin. No more weekends together.

Six months later, Sean and I were married in the Catholic
Church, with Fr. John officiating. I was attending Mass regularly by then and rediscovering the joy of being in an honest
relationship with God. Sean was not quite there yet, but he
did consent to go to Mass on Sundays to please his new wife.
Easily forgiving ourselves for our past transgressions, we
were as cheerful as carnal children, delighting in God's love
without fully realizing what an extraordinary blessing His
mercy is.

Meanwhile, Father John kept feeding us good books.
Sexual Suicide by George Gilder was one that touched both
of us. I loved C. S. Lewis' *Chronicles of Narnia*. Yoga was no
longer a part of my life. Soon we began teaching Sunday

School to tots and getting involved in the parish community. Sean was finishing his degree at the university, and life was on the upswing.

While we were preparing to move north to the small town where Sean would take his first post-college job, Fr. John was becoming interested in the charismatic renewal. He gave us some information about it, and it sounded wonderful to me. On television we watched a documentary about a priest with a noted healing ministry. But lacking the opportunity then to act on it, I pushed the interest to the back of my mind.

Brady Lake, a small farming community in the northwest corner of the state, was a whole new experience for me. Having grown up in the Chicago area, and coming now from the cosmopolitan city where I worked, I saw it as a foreign country and spent the first month of our stay in a state of culture shock. The Catholic community was small, and the pastor a crusty older man. I felt as if I had been snatched back into pre-Vatican II days, and I was not happy about it. But God was watching.

After living in Brady Lake a few months, we got involved with a Christian youth group called "The Good News Singers". Ted and Nancy, the group leaders, were another newly married couple, friendly and outgoing. They had grown up in the Lutheran Church, attended a "Life in the Spirit" seminar in a Catholic church, and were now in a nondenominational church. They began telling us about their dramatic experience of Baptism in the Spirit.[1]

One night, after we had played volleyball with the youth group, the teenagers sat around and prayed—aloud—for each

---

[1] Baptism in the Spirit is not the same as, nor does it replace, sacramental Baptism and Confirmation. It is a moment of deeper conversion to the reality of the Holy Spirit that opens the individual to the graces and gifts received in the sacraments—ED.

other and even for us. This spontaneous kind of prayer from the heart was so new to me that at first I was rather offended. "I'm a good person," I thought, "I don't need their prayers." But I was also attracted to the intimacy and freedom I saw in their relationship with God. I wanted to know more.

Ted and Nancy gave us many books about the charismatic renewal. We were thrilled to read of all the miracles God was pouring out on His people. Sean and I had established a custom of reading a chapter of the Gospel aloud to each other before we went to sleep. One night I read the last few lines of Mark's Gospel: "And these signs will accompany those who have believed: in My name they will cast out demons, they will speak with new tongues; they will pick up serpents, and if they drink any deadly poison, it shall not hurt them; they will lay hands on the sick, and they will recover" (Mk 16:1–7, 18).

We looked at each other. "We believe, but those things don't happen to us", my husband said. "Why not?"

It seemed to us that the Holy Spirit needed no more prompting than that question. Within a week, Sean had agreed to be the musical director of the Good News Singers. To handle that responsibility, he wanted all the spiritual strength he could get his hands on. So we asked Ted and Nancy to come over to our house and pray over us for Baptism in the Spirit.

The restoration of God's light in my soul took a giant step forward that night. I felt a closeness to God and His love that I had never felt before in my adult life; I wanted to read the Bible during every spare minute; prayer became an absolute joy. I received the gift of tongues, which seemed to add a new depth and richness to my blossoming prayer life. I was in love with God as I had never been in love before.

Our close friendship with Ted and Nancy brought another

change to our faith life. They began to ask us about teachings of the Catholic Church that they didn't understand. I had few answers for them, having never studied the Church's teachings as an adult. Challenged by their questions, I began to read catechisms, and as I gained greater understanding of the incredible richness and beauty of my faith, my love came to embrace the Church in all of her glory.

At that time, I was still irritated by our pastor, traditional Fr. Keefe. Through the reading and the praying I was doing, I came to believe the Lord was showing me that I needed Fr. Keefe for my spiritual life. A thought came to me, "Consider your toenail. How would it be if it wasn't there?"

"Pretty sore and tender", I thought.

"Fr. Keefe is like your toenail", the thought continued. "Kind of tough, but very necessary. You need his protection and guidance."

Beginning then, Fr. Keefe and I became great friends.

After about a year we said a fond farewell to Brady Lake and started a new chapter in our married life. Sean took a job in St. Placid, an old Catholic community, where the charismatic renewal was going full steam ahead. When we moved to town, we started attending about three prayer groups a week and loving every minute of it. We were on-fire, Bible-banging, Praise-the-Lord charismatics, eager to take part in all the spiritual opportunities that we could. We settled into the music ministry for a large prayer group at Assumption Church and eventually assumed various leadership posts. We attended daily Mass and became involved in our parish, teaching CCD, hosting a study group, and praying with our neighbors. God's light was again at full radiance in my soul, and I felt that the words of Psalm 103 had special significance for me:

Bless the Lord, O my soul;
  And all that is within me, bless his holy name.
Bless the Lord, O my soul,
  And forget not his benefits;
He pardons all your iniquities;
  He heals all your ills;
He redeems your life from destruction;
  He crowns you with kindness and compassion.
He fills your life with good things,
  And your youth is renewed like the eagle's.

When I thought back on all the experiences I had gone through, it seemed these words could have been written just for me. "He pardons all your iniquities; He heals all your ills." With God's divine light shining on my soul, I could see there were many areas that needed healing. The guilt, pain, and loss I experienced after my abortions were wounds that did not quickly heal. For many years I prayed for healing. God was faithful to His word; with His gentle touch He gradually eased the sharpness of the pain, but the wounds were there. It was as if the surface of my soul was pocked and pitted like the surface of the moon and still swollen and tender as with infection. Only after years of counseling and prayer, offering up the pain to God, was I able to accept God's forgiveness and to forgive myself. In fact, the scar tissue is still there.

As the process of conversion continued, the restored light of God's love grew brighter in my soul. As in one scene in C. S. Lewis' Narnian Chronicles, where the characters are invited to come "further up and further in", our Lord has continued to invite me to a deeper realization of His love for me. His invitation has led me to many unexpected and distant places, including a little village in Bosnia-Herzegovina named Medjugorje.[2] Twice—once in 1990 and again in 1992, during the war—Sean and I traveled to that place where we felt that the veil between heaven and earth is thin. Our Lady's presence in the village seemed unmistakable to us. And it was in Medjugorje that I experienced an extraordinary inner healing.

Each Saturday, the eucharistic chapel in Medjugorje remains open all night for adoration. During our trip in 1992, I awoke from a deep sleep at 2:00 A.M. to hear an interior voice saying, "Come to my heart." I lay a while deciding whether I would respond or not. Finally I prayed, "Lord, I'll come to the chapel on condition that I don't wake Sean while I'm getting dressed." (He is a very light sleeper.)

Quietly I dressed, finding everything easily by touch in the unrelieved blackness. As I walked the road from our guest house to the chapel, I prayed ceaselessly, "Jesus, Mary, and Joseph, please guide me." As I got closer to the church, I passed a bar with lights still on. Inside a soldier dressed in uniform was standing up with arms outstretched, wailing in a long, loud, drawn-out sound. My hair stood on end. At any moment, I expected that the doors of the tavern would fly open and soldiers with loaded guns would pour out. I ran as fast as I could past the door and didn't stop until I reached the safety of the chapel, where all was peaceful. (Later, I learned that the man had merely been singing a Croatian folk song.)

When my heart stopped thundering, I knelt to pray. Then I felt moved to lie prostrate before the Lord in the Blessed

[2] The reported apparitions of the Blessed Mother in Medjugorje have not been authenticated by proper Church authorities, and visits to the site are not to be encouraged before an official declaration is made. The caution exercised by the Vatican is necessary for evaluating the phenomena that have occurred there, but it does not negate the personal consolations, conversions, and healings that have resulted from God's grace.—ED.

Sacrament. He seemed to show me all the wounds of my heart, those others had caused and those I had inflicted myself. It seemed as though Jesus were lancing my heart, and I was seeing all the sorrow and shame and anguish drain away. As I continued to pray, it was as if I could now see my wounded heart resting on Jesus' wounded heart, and I rejoiced in my wound. Filled with joy, I walked to Cross Mountain just as dawn was breaking over the village.

That night was the culmination of many years of counseling, prayer, and crying out for healing. Since then, the agonizing pain has been gone. I can't stop thanking God for His wonderful gift of mercy, for all the gifts He has poured out on me since that moment long ago when I looked up from the pit of Hell and asked Him, "Are you there?" He was there. He is here now; He always will be here.

Our trips to Medjugorje bore much fruit in our faith lives. One of those fruits was active participation in the Marian Movement. We have attended Marian conferences from North Dakota to Oklahoma and points between. I have found a renewed love for the traditions of my faith, such as Eucharistic Adoration, litanies, fasting, and the Rosary. All of these are a regular part of my faith life now. Each renewal experience has brought me closer to the heart of the Church, which is Jesus' Sacred Heart. I desire to continue to draw closer to the center of the Church and to be in obedience to all her teachings.

I came back to the Church through the charismatic movement, and I love its spontaneous prayerfulness. But today I think we need to emphasize the sacred in our worship. Converts to Catholicism from Protestant religions have told me again and again that what attracted them was a sense of holiness in the Mass, as expressed by our genuflections before the tabernacle, our kneeling at the Consecration, and every reverent gesture demonstrating belief in the dogma that the bread and wine offered at Mass becomes the real Body and Blood of our Lord. As Catholics, we ought to practice our faith in all its sacred solemnity, not water it down in hope of making it bland enough for those who do not understand or believe.

Many factors played a part in the eclipse of my soul. It began in my own sinful inclinations and rebelliousness. The compromised teaching I received in high school was another cause, as the errors transmitted by dissenting teachers fueled my own mutiny. Another factor was the attitude prevalent in society at the time I was growing up and my eagerness to espouse the spirit of that age. As I remember my high school and college friends, I see that the experience of leaving the Church was extremely common. I am unutterably thankful to God that, in His mercy, He did not abandon me as I deserved but drew me back to the faith I knew as a child, but which I now embrace as an adult.

"The heavens declare the glory of God and earth proclaims his handiwork" (Ps 19:1). As I watched the lunar eclipse on that glorious fall evening, I was reminded of my life. As a child, I was radiant with the light of God's love, innocent, pure, and very much in love with Jesus. Just as the full moon reflects the light of the sun, my soul was bright with the light of God's grace. But slowly, steadily, the shadow of my sins began to diminish His light, until my soul was totally eclipsed in it. God's light was still shining on me as before, but I could no longer reflect it. Then, by God's grace, I turned around, not in an instant, but very slowly. Little by little the shadow of sin moved away, and more and more of God's light could be reflected again. This process is still continuing. I praise Him for His incomprehensible love that never gave up on me but kept shining on my soul. I hope one day to stand before His throne with no shadow of sin left on my soul at all, radiant before my Lord and King.

%

Rachel Taylor Riley lives in the Midwest with her husband, Sean, and their two children. She is active in a Catholic home-school association and participates in doctrinal study groups and in parish music ministry.

The Faith Knit into My Bones

Diane Yelenosky Spinelli

Growing up in my family was wonderful. I was born in Mount Carmel, Pennsylvania, in 1955, exactly in the middle of the "baby boom" decades. In my own family the boom had just begun: I was the first of six Yelenosky children. My earliest recollections are of a secure and loving Catholic home, lots of lively siblings, and all of us worshipping reverently together at Mass.

We moved at least every three years, as Conoco Oil Company transferred my father around the country, but our closeness as a family preserved my sense of stability. Debbie and Stephen were born in Ardmore, Oklahoma; Mary and Mike in Columbus, Ohio. Joseph, the fourth baby, was stillborn. We moved on to Kansas, then back to Oklahoma, before coming to rest in Houston.

I remember Mother's pregnancies and the delight we all took in encouraging the baby to creep to us across the carpet. Sometimes we acted out a solemn "Mass", with the girls all wearing veils, while a brother, coerced into service as the priest, placed "communion hosts" of squashed Wonder Bread on our tongues. We communicants were very careful not to chew "Christ's body". Wherever we lived, we attended Sunday Mass faithfully, received the sacraments, and practiced virtues taught both explicitly and by example. We were nurtured in an atmosphere of love and respect for the things of God.

St. Thérèse of Lisieux was my mother's favorite saint, and during ferocious Kansas thunderstorms we little ones would cling together at the window, gazing in awe at the turmoil outside, praying, "Little Flower, in this hour, show your power."

Until fourth grade, I attended a parochial school taught by nuns in full habit. The bus ride seemed interminable, but the education was excellent in every way. I remember kneeling at morning Mass with my class, all in uniforms and navy blue beanies, with hands folded and bodies quietly attentive. Both my sister and I had nun dolls, and for a time I wondered whether I might have a vocation to religious life.

I always preferred the companionship of my siblings to that of other children because I could be my spontaneous, dramatic self with them. I loved coming home from school to be with them and to enjoy my mother's busy company. We played in our yard, sometimes dressed up as visitors from exotic countries, sometimes imagining fairy paths through the bushes around our house. The high winds and sweeping wheat fields of Kansas stirred my imagination. Always attracted to the beautiful, I read fairy tales avidly, collected postcards by favorite illustrators like Cicely Mary Barker and Arthur Rackham, loved paintings, classical music, and the performing arts.

Though Mom was in perpetual motion with the duties of raising her family, she was always so warmly available that I could never feel deprived. When I was five, she took my friends and me to a play, all of us in fancy, ruffled 1960s party dresses. I was greatly taken with the theater and longed to be onstage and always to be the star, even of Christmas home movies. Mother, who had an eye for classical ballet, investigated classes and enrolled me in an outstanding ballet school when I was seven. Later I tried other dance forms, but the esthetic grace of ballet seemed perfect to me. I loved it so much that I never stopped dancing, and eventually I became a professional ballet dancer.

My devoted father was the disciplinarian who set the standard of obedience and order in our home. Sincere, responsible, and deeply humorous, he is a first-generation American, born to Slovakian immigrants in a Pennsylvania coal-mining town. When he came home from World War II, he used the GI Bill to attend the University of Pittsburgh, where he majored in geology and graduated *magna cum laude*. He and Mother met when he started working in Mount Carmel. Raised in the Russian Orthodox Church, he converted to Catholicism when they married. Mother was of Tyrolean descent. The last of seven children, she was only eight when her father died. Afterward, she and her mother lived with her married sister. Mom is kind and engaging. Together she and my father created the happy atmosphere in which we grew up.

Each summer, Mom would mastermind great family vacations. We traveled all over the United States in our tightly packed car, sleeping like sardines in the station wagon or at campgrounds, with occasional motel stops. That was how we visited relatives in the Northeast and how we saw the great natural wonders of the Southwest. Once we took a Christmas trip to New Mexico, where we recklessly tried skiing without any lessons.

As I entered adolescence in 1967, we moved to Texas, and things started to change. Vivid in my memory is our first Mass in the prosaic new rite, face-to-face with the priest in our auditorium mission church. The symbolic drama of meaning and mystery had been pruned from the Mass, and culturally adapted banality replaced it. Its rich, dramatic beauty gone, the Mass seemed to lose its power to inspire me.

One Sunday during Mass my little brother pulled "the Pill" out of Mother's purse, and I saw her embarrassment as she hastily took it away. When I inquired about it, she explained that the Church didn't approve its use. Now she had something to hide. Later I learned that she had started using it after consulting a priest.

My father had always been the head of the family, with Mom as his counselor. But now Mom's role changed into something different in nature, but not better. She began reciting slogans like "A woman's place is in the House—and Senate." Her youngest child was then nine years old, so she decided to take a secretarial refresher course and enter the paid work force.

Our parents insisted that we attend CCD classes through junior high school, but the classes, like the homilies I heard on Sunday, were watered down to a thin soup with the fullness of the faith strained out. I remember, for example, listening to the Simon and Garfunkel song "Bridge Over Troubled Waters" and trying to discuss what it meant. Devotion to the Blessed Virgin was treated as out of date. Instead of doctrinal truth, I was getting the same humanitarianism and simplistic political liberalism from CCD as I was getting at school.

In my high school, long hair and rebellion prevailed. "Love" and "Peace" symbols abounded. An ad in a favorite magazine for "Zero Population Growth" really captured my attention. It seemed like a noble cause to embrace for the sake of our planet.

By then I was crazy about ballet, so totally immersed in the rigorous daily discipline of it that I never entered the world of drugs, smoking, and sex. I was also busy with drama after

school. These preoccupations kept me out of the popular social circles where peer pressure was high, but even in my own
group I was regarded as different because I would not drink
or use drugs.

Yet I lived an entirely self-centered teenaged life, absorbed
in my own interests, completely uninvolved in my family. The
kind of faith being presented in church and CCD class left
me alienated and disillusioned. An emotional idealist, I craved
knowledge of my ultimate purpose, a stronghold of convictions on which to base my life choices. I was ready to respond
to heroic demands, but there were none in the diluted, spine-
less, "feel good" religion being offered to me. When I started
college, I tried attending Mass at the campus Catholic chapel.
What I was searching for was truth with a capital T. I was
searching for God, but I was repelled by culturally adapted
Catholicism.

I already knew that I wanted to dance professionally, so at
the University of Texas in Austin, I concentrated on dance
and drama. Vicki, my roommate there, was a student of art
and architecture and a lively Christian, who introduced me to
a compelling personal relationship with Jesus Christ. She read
the Bible, and I fell in love with Scripture. Here was meat at
last, and I was hungry! I attended Bible study groups and met
generous, zealous Christians. With the help of Campus Cru-
sade for Christ, I embraced the fundamentalist evangelical
movement, eager to share my faith. Accepting the claim that
nothing of my Catholic faith was valid, I submitted to baptism by submersion in a pool. For the next twelve years I kept
my back firmly turned on Catholicism, even to the point of
agreeing that the Pope was the antichrist.

After a single year of college, my parents indulged my eager
love for dance by sending me to London, to finish ballet
studies at the Royal Ballet School. I made the most of this

tremendous opportunity by working conscientiously in my dance classes, exploring London with my international friends from the school, and finding a Pentecostal church where I could continue my growth as a Christian. Touring historic Catholic cathedrals in Europe, I was relieved to think that I belonged to a living faith rather than the dead and barren one in which I had been raised.

While in London, I auditioned for and won a position with the National Ballet of Iran, in Teheran. In a spontaneous decision, I signed the contract and then called my parents to tell them I was going to work in the Middle East. I spent my twentieth year there, performing at the palace and at the theater for the Shah and his guests, touring Iran, and learning ballet repertoire. It was an exotic, enthralling year, even for my faith. Daily reading of God's word sustained my faith. Friday is the Islamic holy day, so that was our free day. I participated in Friday worship at an American Bible church, where longtime church members who spoke Farsi were in the process of translating the Bible into Iranian dialects. Missionaries came through with inspiring reports of their experiences.

When the ballet board hired a new director, I decided to move back to London. I had permission to use the Royal Ballet School for daily classes while auditioning with European ballet companies. But after six months without any desirable offers, I decided to move home to Houston, where, my teachers advised me, a British ballet director had just signed a contract with the Houston Ballet Company. Since I had been trained in British style, it seemed likely the move might prove fruitful.

Settled back at home, I was allowed use of one of the cars to get to and from the studio, much to the chagrin of younger family members. I studied at the Houston Ballet

School for another year, until I was accepted into the company. During those months, neighbors took me along to their evangelical church on Sundays. Later I transferred to a Bible church closer to home. It was in those Protestant communities that I first met homeschoolers. Taken with the notion of passing on the faith while providing the best possible education, I decided I would homeschool if I ever married and had children.

Once again I was absorbed in my own world, oblivious and even indifferent to the problems of my youngest brother, Mike, and to the painful confusion gripping my parents as they tried to deal with them. At fifteen, Mike was beginning to exhibit symptoms of schizophrenia and his debilitating mental illness inflicted great anguish on my mother and father. At the same time, my father had taken over care of his mother, who had lived with a daughter for many years. He installed her in an apartment near our home, where he visited her daily, planted a garden for her, and tended fondly to her every need. I loved spending time with my grandmother, too, because she was so quaintly "old world" in her crisp aprons, praying from her exquisitely decorated Russian prayer book. Her patient attention to Mike during his visits was wonderfully consoling to my parents.

At last I was offered ballet employment and no longer had to impose on my family's generosity. Allured by the glamour of the theatrical life-style, I shortly discarded my faith and began a regrettable relationship with a male dancer. After a year of unsettling guilt, I came to my senses, repented, and promised God that I would henceforth put Him first in my life. Further, I pledged to share my faith, no matter how scornfully that offer might be received; I would not be a respecter of persons, timid before those with position and power in the ballet world.

That new attitude bore me unexpectedly generous fruit. Those of us in the ballet organization who were believers formed a "God Squad". We spent part of our daily lunch breaks studying His word together. The group attracted luke-warm Christians as well as lost dancers seeking God. We all joined an independent Presbyterian Bible church that was thought to have a rather intellectual following. Soon we were meeting after dance hours with other single friends from the congregation, to support each other in our faith. We became a close-knit company of friends. But in the end, Donald Spinelli and I were the only ones to marry within the group.

Our acquaintance developed slowly from a rather conten-tious start, and for much of seven years I remained skeptical and cautious. He was one of only four of us in the Bible group who were cradle Catholics, and the only one who was a musician from the ballet orchestra. From our first meeting, he made it clear that he was attracted to me. But I took him for a Don Juan whose intent to reform might be sincere but who had a long way to go before he achieved it. Sometimes I warned other women from the ballet company against him, while they prayed for me to love him as my brother in Christ. Since I openly acknowledged my distrust, I never dated him, but we had so many mutual friends that we were often to-gether in group situations. His family did not live in Hous-ton, and to my annoyance he virtually adopted mine. He spent a great deal of time at our home and especially pleased my parents by befriending my afflicted young brother.

Through those seven years, I loved being single. I was happy dancing and traveling with the Houston Ballet and felt it un-likely that I would ever marry. Gradually, however, God soft-ened my heart toward Don, and I realized that I wanted more than his brotherly friendship. Ironically, I had fallen in love with him just as he concluded that our marriage must not be

God's will, since his years of prayer and courtship had not overcome my indifference. Consequently he was puzzled, doubtful, and cautious when I began making overtures toward him. But finally we admitted that we loved each other.

Already he was nearly a part of our family, and although my parents had never even hinted that they thought of us as a couple, I knew they would approve. Like Mom, Don was Italian and, like me, he had been raised as a Catholic, so our backgrounds were similar. He had the dominant personality and humor of my father. His light-hearted manner fitted well with my more serious one; he was good with children; and, most important of all, he was a Bible-loving Christian.

During our year-long engagement, I began working at a Protestant-sponsored crisis pregnancy center. Soon I noticed that much of the pro-life movement's support, its material resources and volunteer help, came from Catholic sources, and it was Catholics who provided the homes for unwed mothers. Next door to our center was a Catholic-run pro-life center, where I would chat with staff workers when I went in to obtain information. One of the women offered me a copy of the encyclical *Humanae Vitae*, and I was struck with the truth of what I read. Brochures on Natural Family Planning (NFP) were available at our own center, and I first found them appealing because what they proposed was natural. Eager to learn the method before our marriage, I applied for training as a certified teacher of Dr. Thomas W. Hilger's Creighton Model of the Ovulation Method.

When we began planning our wedding, I was startled to find myself reacting defensively to a friend who assumed we would be married in our starkly plain Bible church. At my wedding, I wanted to be surrounded by glorious liturgical music and magnificent sacred art, and I proposed that we find a beautiful cathedral in which to marry. As a musician,

Don had connections to a variety of churches, so he scheduled a wedding date for us at an ornate Episcopal cathedral. As a gesture of cooperation, I felt obliged to go to a few services, which were sparsely attended, and we were required to join the pastor for a counseling session. We went to an Engaged Encounter weekend that happened to be Catholic-sponsored, but its exposition of a Catholic vision of marriage was insipid. The one thing we did learn during the weekend was distasteful; these young adult Catholics were frankly scornful of the virtue of chastity and casually open about their current sexual activity. Once again I was grateful to be a Protestant.

As Protestants, we helped each other to practice the virtue of chastity and, with God's grace, first gave ourselves completely to each other on our wedding night. That beginning continues to strengthen our marriage even today.

Nevertheless, despite our encounter with 1985 Catholic morality, an attraction to my childhood faith was awakening. Catholicism was more than laxity, I knew, because I had experienced it as a child. And somehow I did not feel that my Protestant faith was knit into my bones. It was more a cerebral system to which I could assent than a living culture infusing my whole being. I consciously worked at virtue but did not wholly surrender my will to God or practice awareness of His presence. Reading about saints helped me to understand that God works in all kinds of people, in all their circumstances, and that He could work in me all the time if I were willing for Him to do so.

I was thirty years old and had been dancing professionally for ten satisfying years. Now it was time for me to retire. We wanted to begin a family right away and to be a traditional family. I would work at home, caring for and eventually homeschooling the children God would send us.

During my NFP training in Omaha and my later work at St. Joseph's Hospital in Houston, I was surrounded by authentic Catholics of a kind I had not met before as an adult. The Holy Spirit used them to humble me and soften my heart by speaking the truth, kindly but forthrightly, even if it was only in a single encounter. Once, while we were praying with a group in front of an abortuary, a Catholic woman who knew I was not practicing the faith advised me quietly that my husband and I really should sanctify our marriage by receiving the Sacrament of Matrimony. Another time, when I telephoned a vital Catholic pro-lifer, she asked me outright if I had been reared a Catholic. She suspected so because, she said, so many dynamic evangelicals whom she met were lapsed Catholics.

My NFP mentors, Chuck and Margaret Howard, accepted me lovingly. They were luminous exemplars of their Catholic faith, uncompromising in their practice, who invited me to attend daily Mass as they did.

In their unwavering acceptance, my parents, too, gave me reason to consider the nature of unconditional love. Though I contemptuously rejected the Church, they never rejected me. They clung to their own faith while bearing the cross of their son's mental illness.

Then, at the crisis pregnancy center, I met Margie Harper, a young woman from a vibrant evangelical family. She, her five vivacious siblings, and their parents all practiced their faith wholeheartedly and exemplified the virtue of charity. The Harper home was a "Grand Central Station" for Christians from all faiths, including Catholic priests and seminarians. One day, I said to Margie in passing that the Catholic Church was "off-base" about something.

"Do you really know what the Catholic Church teaches?" Margie asked.

Her challenge took me by surprise. I had not realized it, but she was exploring possible conversion to Catholicism. She had been a student at Grove City College in Pennsylvania, she explained, when Scott Hahn was a Protestant professor of theology there, wrestling with the decision to enter the Church Jesus founded. Dr. Hahn went on to become a noted Catholic convert, and his reasoning had strongly influenced Margie.

Her reasoning strongly influenced us. Shaken, Don and I counseled with a priest, prayed together earnestly, and decided it was possible that we were wrong.

Our first daughter was born eleven months after our wedding. Her birth impelled us to plan the future, reassess our lives and our faith. How were we going to raise our children? Undoubtedly it would be in the fear of the Lord, loving Jesus Christ, and knowing the Bible. But exactly how were we to live it out each day?

The Catholic Church could offer us concrete help, using the tangible things of the world to glorify God and lead us toward Him. Her sacraments incorporate natural substances as outward signs of what they accomplish. Her statues and paintings and Stations of the Cross would inspire us to practice the presence of Christ. The physical action of saying the Rosary would help us to focus on the episodes of Jesus' life. The liturgical year, too, would keep Christ at the center of our lives, recalling the events of His life while encouraging family traditions and building family unity. The sacraments would give us the assistance we needed at every point in our lives, from the supernatural life of grace received in Baptism, through forgiveness of sin, supernatural food, the strength of the Holy Spirit, healing and final pardon, priests to offer sacrifice, and the grace of marital union in Christ.

Fearing that the Church might contradict the Bible he

loved and trusted, Don moved more reluctantly than I did along the path homeward. But the divisions in Protestantism were becoming ever more disturbing to him. A Protestant who disapproves of his pastor or a church policy can simply begin a new church, with himself at the head, and start competing for followers. In scriptural interpretation, one opinion is as good as another. Don began to appreciate how the Magisterium and the Pope's infallibility protect the Church's teaching on faith and morals.

Once I understood that Sacred Tradition preceded formal establishment of the New Testament canon by hundreds of years, I realized that the Church herself had given us the Bible. When Protestants proclaim it to be the inspired Word of God, they effectively admit that the Holy Spirit truly has been present in the Catholic Church since Christ founded her with St. Peter as her visible head. Loving the Bible even more in the knowledge that it is really a Catholic book, I felt buoyantly confident that re-conversion would take us home to the remembered faith of childhood and the fullness of truth.

At last we decided that we must rear our children where we were reared ourselves, in the Catholic Church. We received the Sacrament of Matrimony on the day of our daughter's Baptism, in October 1986. The Blessed Mother became our loving guide and intercessor. We began to receive the sacraments and attend Sunday Mass faithfully.

We love the Church more ardently every day. Over time we have come to realize more clearly what a tremendous gift Christ has given us in the Holy Sacrifice of the Mass. It so penetrates the temporal world with the glory of Heaven that we can never appreciate it enough. Our eyes are too weak to comprehend its light fully in this world, but we believe we will one day see Him face to face. Protestants who love Jesus would never leave the Catholic Church if they knew that we are in His very presence, Body and Blood, Soul and Divinity, when we kneel before the Blessed Sacrament.

For some years we have been privileged to live in the healthy Diocese of Arlington, Virginia, where our parish teaches the faith without trying to adapt it to the world's tastes. Because young people are attracted to the truth when they hear it and eager to meet its heroic challenge, this diocese ordains more than a dozen new priests each year, while most American dioceses suffer from a vocational drought.

Don is a percussionist and frequent soloist with the United States Marine Band. We have four girls and one boy, two of them still under school age. For eight years we have been educating our older children with a Catholic homeschool curriculum. As I realized long ago when I first met Protestant homeschoolers, it allows us to provide them with an excellent general education while transmitting the faith to them in all its richness. We do not want them to lose their way as so many of our own generation did.

As children grow into teen years and young adulthood, they need more searching explanations of Catholic doctrines, presented with the conviction that tells them this is momentous information. They are ready for apologetics—rational explication of the meaning of Catholic doctrines and practices and a sound understanding of Church history. The words of apologists like Scott Hahn, Peter Kreeft, and Karl Keating are welcomed by young Catholics like water in the desert. Once the faith is understood, we can hope that it ceases to be an imposed duty and becomes their own deepest conviction, for which they would give their lives.

The freedom of the human will means we cannot guarantee that our children will remain true to the faith, but if they are properly educated and fortified by the grace of the sacraments and the practice of virtue, they will not make their choices in ignorance.

I believe without a whisper of doubt that the gates of Hell cannot prevail against the Church God established. But my heart is sad for all those still lost in the world and those who have settled for Christianity without the sacramental Presence of Christ. I pray for them that they too may be given the grace to come home.

⁓

Born in 1955 in Mount Carmel, Pennsylvania, Diane Yelenosky Spinelli trained at the Royal Ballet School in London and danced professionally with the National Ballet of Iran and the Houston Ballet. She now lives in Springfield, Virginia, with her five children, ages two through 12, and her husband, Don, a percussionist with the U.S. Marine Band in Washington, D.C. They are a homeschooling family of nine years and members of T.O.R.C.H. (Traditions of Roman Catholic Homes), a Catholic homeschool support group.

My Flight from Vatican II

Mary Epcke Kaiser

"What is it like to grow up in such a large family?" a judge asked the Miss America finalist, who was one of five children.

"Five? Such a large family?" We hooted with laughter, elbowing one another and mimicking the questioner. There were nine of us altogether, five girls and four boys, not counting two who had died at birth. Yet we never thought of ourselves as "such a large family". Families of twelve or more children were not extraordinary in our small Catholic farming community.

Most of my childhood memories are cheerful. Like many children, I accepted my experience as normal. It is only when we see it reflected in the eyes of others that we recognize our reality as not entirely conventional. At the time, the troubled parts did not seem to be the most important, and where reality was harsh, my imagination made up the difference.

To be sure, we were very poor. We worked hard, especially after we moved to the farm. My father, a convert from the Lutheran faith—the only other church in town—was an alcoholic; for anyone who knows an alcoholic, no more need be said.

After eight pregnancies in as many years, Mother had a breakdown while pregnant with my youngest brother. Her doctors had counseled her to abort him, warning that she could not carry the baby to term, that they would both die. She spent a great deal of time during those months gently preparing my older sister and me to take charge of the family afterward. But neither of them died. And the following year, my youngest sister was born.

Yet I remember even the distresses of those years with a survivor's pride. I was a headstrong tomboy with a healthy body and a gritty determination to "be tough". At the same time, I was a dreamer. My imagination transformed everyday drudgeries into thrilling adventures, as I pretended to be a pilgrim or a prisoner of war. A walk through the snow, carrying a little sister whose wet feet were frostbitten, became a heroic trek to save a wounded woman from marauding Indians. Doing the dishes was often a test of endurance against the heat of the water. I was Cinderella when I scrubbed the floor and Paul Bunyan when I chopped wood. If I had no companion to play with, I flew solo. Trucks and toy animals in the sandbox consumed much of my playtime. But I never played with dolls; I never wanted to be a girl.

In the wonder world we lived in, I investigated every turn in the creek, every spray of green leaves. And how I loved the living animals! The ugliest stray dog became a personal friend. Still, like a good settler, I found it another adventure to butcher the chickens or dress out the rabbits when the time came. It was awesome to inspect the inner design of God's creatures too, and being practical meant using God's gifts as He intended.

As a matter of course, we attended the parish school through eighth grade. Sr. Mary Louis was my beloved first-grade teacher, and she too expected us to work hard and strive always to be the best we could be, thus reinforcing the lessons learned at home. Even when she disciplined me, I loved her intensely, because it was clear that she wanted me to learn from my mistakes.

Often she read to us from the lives of the saints, encouraging us to imitate their example. The first real book I ever read was the life of St Thérèse of the Child Jesus. After that, it seemed natural to pretend to be that lovely saint or others who lives I read. Along with the guidance of Sr. Mary Louis, my mother's example, strength, and love led me to an awareness of the spiritual realm. I remembered that my Guardian Angel was my companion wherever I went. Often I saved a spot beside me for him to sit or commented under my breath to this unseen companion.

The height of my joy came with my First Communion. The nuns had prepared us with meticulous thoroughness to understand and long for this great sacrament. I told everyone I encountered about the event. Imagine! Jesus Christ Himself wanted to be with me in this most intimate way.

In my quest to become a saint, I sometimes crawled into the darkest parts of my closet to pray, so that only my Heavenly Father would see. Other times I slipped pebbles into my shoes or knelt on the roughest available surface during morning or night prayers, and more than once I crawled into the thorn bushes to share the pain of our Lord's Passion. Occasionally, trying to overcome my tendency toward sloth, I would do a kind deed unseen, like making Mother's bed or picking up litter. The hardest sacrifice came when I tried to keep quiet while someone else received the credit. Still, the harder I worked for others, the more at peace I was with myself. Striving to imitate the saints made me immensely happy.

By the time I entered seventh grade, we had taken over my grandparents' dairy farm. Here we found hard work, new experiences, and a new world to explore. We rode a bus to school, and once, when I missed it, I had to walk the whole five miles home, an unforgettable lesson about punctuality. Lunch hours I spent cleaning the sacristy and the sanctuary; being allowed to do it was so great an honor that forgoing lunch meant little. Dusting the statues on the altars was a thrill because I could kiss a hand or foot of those plaster models of heavenly friends.

Milking, baling hay, or even pitching manure seemed preferable to any household chore, but boys were of little interest to me. Often my chief concern about one of the opposite sex was whether I could beat him in some contest of physical or mental prowess.

As I look back, now, on my early life, I am anguished that I abandoned all this for the secular world and its empty promises of excitement and experience. I had no substantial excuse for my stupidity: no tragic accident, no abuse, indeed, no particular bad experience at all. One defect of fallen human nature is a tendency to turn away from those whose love is selflessly benevolent and instead follow others more exciting but less interested in our good. No rational explanation can be found for such an irrational choice. My only excuse is that of Eve: the devil tempted me, and I listened. I succumbed to the rebellion and hormonal turmoil of those years, in the world and in myself.

Thus, when a young assistant pastor told us that cursing was no sin at all, as long as one didn't mean it, those words became part of my vocabulary. Beginning in my junior and senior high school years, traditional notions of authority were systematically eroded, as certain teachers at first implied that our parents didn't know everything (why, some of them hadn't even gone to high school and were not as well informed as we were). Gradually, these subversives raised the pitch, until it was no longer implied but stated as fact that our parents had no right to "live our lives for us", because we were smarter than they were ("the best-educated generation in history!"). We were subtly led to pursue our own whims, serve our own appetites and ambitions, and invent our own "values". Objective truth was either irrelevant or unknowable. Freedom became synonymous with license. These were the 1960s, and everything was in transition from old "outdated" ways to freer new ways.

By the time I started college, I was no longer interested in my Guardian Angel, the saints, the Church, or the Ten Commandments. During my freshman year, the drinking age dropped to eighteen, and I plunged into a highball glass. For two weeks I went to classes giggly, weepy, or angry, never completely sober. Studying became intolerable, and life in general seemed a burden. Each new quest for self-fulfillment only brought greater disappointment. With mixed disgust and amusement, I listened to the calls for emancipation: What, exactly, were we freeing ourselves from? The rhetoric was of liberty and love, but what I saw was rage and rebellion. Told that I wore my virginity like a badge, I tossed it away for liberty and love. Afterward I felt no freer and less loved. When the school year ended, I entered the Air Force.

A feminist mentality had invaded the military, and I was pushed into a traditionally masculine career field. Though still determined to find fulfillment the world's way, I knew on some deep level even then that my path was self-destructive. Before the end of Technical Training School, I was standing before a Justice of the Peace, one month pregnant. Allen had been married before, in the Catholic Church. To this day, however, I am not sure whether he himself was ever a Catholic. After the ceremony, my new husband asked why I had hesitated so long before saying "I do." It was because I knew I was making the wrong choice. Nevertheless, I made it.

On our wedding night, I wept openly. The adage that women marry men like their fathers seemed to be coming true in my life. Whatever my doubts about Allen, however, there was never any doubt that, with all his heart, he loved Jason, the son I bore him.

During some of the very difficult times in our marriage, I made feeble gestures at turning back to God, but it seemed that the churches were always locked at the moments when I longed to pour out my sorrows and emptiness before the Blessed Sacrament. Half-believing that it was true, I told myself I had gone too far away from God to expect Him to take me back.

Two months after Jason's birth, unsure whether or not I meant to raise him as a Catholic, I nevertheless arranged for his Baptism. For a year and a half, ambivalently, I took contraceptive pills, fully conscious that the Church condemns mechanical and chemical birth control. Uncertain whether it mattered to me, I still absolved myself of guilt, as Allen had issued an ultimatum: either I would take the pill or he would have a vasectomy. But remembering to take the pill on schedule every day was a nuisance, and the steroids in it made me feel bloated. Besides, I did not want my baby to be an only child.

Easter weekend during my second pregnancy, my mother gave me a brown scapular of Mount Carmel. She disapproved of my life-style and my invalid marriage, but she also loved me, prayed for me daily, fasted for me, and offered God her own trials in my behalf. Throughout my life she has always loved me and been ready to help, to listen, to give of herself. It shames me to admit how I took her for granted. Her prayers were my insurance policy, just in case Hell truly did exist. In that attitude, I put the scapular around my neck like a talisman.

Almost at once I became aware of outside influences edging me back toward God. People came briefly into my life, saying the right words. At work or among friends, discussions seemed, suddenly, to turn to religious matters. As I leafed through magazines or newspapers, the words that caught my eye provoked memories of my religious upbringing. Probably the external events of my life changed little, but the scapular lay over my heart. My sins had locked it shut, but I believe our Blessed Mother began to pry it open.

More and more I felt the absence of any substantial purpose or meaning in my life. I began to feel the weight of my sins, though I didn't call them by their proper name. One quiet day, I suddenly found myself facing a frontal assault of self-inflicted misery. Too blinded to see what I had become, I argued with myself that I was no different from most others and not so bad as some. There had been a time, I vaguely remembered, when I hadn't been miserable. What could explain the metamorphosis I had undergone since my childhood? One after another I proposed and discarded possible reasons. What had been so different then? With a bizarre mingling of relief and shock, one single word tumbled from my lips: "God".

Yes. That, or rather He, was the difference. I had tried what the world had to offer, embraced its promised emancipation from the rigors of religion and outmoded moral codes, and in consequence found myself reduced to less dignity than a barnyard animal, and far less contentment.

Within the month, my daughter was born and baptized. I wanted true peace and happiness for my children, but I knew I could not give them what I did not have myself. The following few months I struggled with indecision in an on-again off-again search to recover what I had discarded. My desultory attempts at prayer were more an annoyance than a joy.

Easter came again; it was a year since I had put on the scapu-lar. I resolved to go to Mass.

How vividly I remember that Mass! So much had changed in the seven years I had been away that I had to look around to be sure I was really in a Catholic church. The Mass was not greatly different from any Protestant service I had attended, and I was horrified. Still, I determined not to miss Sunday Mass again and also to recite the Rosary daily. If I made such a good-will effort, I reasoned, if I could show Him that I was willing to try, then maybe God would accept me back into His Providence.

Realizing, too, that I was living in sin, not married in the eyes of the Church and therefore not in the eyes of God, I began praying in earnest that God would somehow rectify the mess I had made of my life. I knew He could. Slowly a measure of peace returned to my life, and a smile returned to my heart.

Though I was no longer in the Air Force, my husband, Allen, was going for the full twenty years of service. Daily, I prayed that he would be able to get his first marriage annulled so we could be married in the Church. I was pregnant for a third time, and this time I consecrated the child in my womb to the Blessed Virgin, who always makes our offerings pleas-ing to the Father through her Son. I consecrated the two older children as well and asked for their protection and salvation.

Married life seemed better now, too, and I was beginning to feel renewed affection for the father of my children when, in my sixth month of pregnancy, Allen filed for divorce. I was stunned.

"What are You doing?" I demanded of God. "This is not how it's supposed to go. I turned to You, and now You're supposed to fix everything. It's simple for You! You can do it!" Disappointed and bewildered, I assured Him that I would keep my end of the bargain, nonetheless. Because I had nowhere else to go and no alternative but to trust Him, He was stuck with me.

With my two children, I moved into my mother's home. Mother herself had recently become a single parent. The Church bureaucracy was handing out annulments like Halloween treats, it seemed, and my father was among the recipients. A marriage tribunal had ruled that, after eleven children and nearly thirty years, my parents' marriage had never been valid. Though my father soon remarried—in the Church—my mother has remained faithful to her wedding vows.

Transition to life as an extended family was not difficult, since the advantages outweighed any discomforts of change. Two adults to raise six children—with a seventh on the way—made better sense than two single mothers each struggling on her own. As always, my mother's faith and trust in God were extraordinary. Even in times of need, when she was concerned about unpaid bills, she would write a check to some charity for the amount of her bank balance. Always, the bills got paid: someone would give her money or groceries, or she would get extra hours at work. Other times, money simply turned up inside her purse or tucked into the Bible.

Since a third-trimester pregnancy did not attract prospective employers, I tried to take over the household duties. Besides, I needed time to pray, to read, to atone, and especially to return to full communion with the Church. Our pastor was a holy priest, gentle but firm, who had served on the marriage tribunal for ten years, so I turned to him for help. The process seemed to take forever. Once I remarked to Father that my dad had popped in and out of the court and been granted an annulment with little delay. Why was my case taking so long, when it concerned a simple and obvious nonmarriage? The pastor replied that my father would account for his sins; I would account for mine. Through my attempted marriage, I had publicly repudiated the Church, and I must make restitution. So I waited, yearning to receive our Blessed Lord. When the Decree of Nullity came through at last, I wept for joy.

My new son was born on the Feast of the Epiphany. His father was with me during the difficult delivery. As I faded in and out of consciousness, hemorrhaging, I remember thinking, "If this is what death is like, it's not so bad."

Afterward, the final divorce decree was postponed, rescheduled, postponed, rescheduled, and postponed again. When my baby son was one year old, I buckled under pressure from his father to reconcile with him. My mother in particular tried to warn me that I was making a grave mistake. I insisted that we could build a home for our children and live as brother and sister until his annulment was granted. Then we would be married in the Church. What followed was the worst year of my life.

The enormity of my blunder soon revealed itself, but I felt trapped and incapable of asserting myself. Somehow I kept my pledge of a daily Rosary and Sunday Mass, and my confessions were frequent. The glaring disparity between my desire for God and the life into which I had plunged myself drove me nearly to despair. Life with this man had become unbearable, yet I had allowed myself to become totally dominated by him. Numb to everything around me, I simply tried to hang on for one moment at a time. With no means of transportation, no income or friends or even acquaintances, I smiled for the sake of my children and begged God to rescue me again. Acutely aware of my duties as a mother, I no longer asked to be married in the Church, only to escape with my little ones.

Then, one evening, the doorbell rang. The woman who

stood there apologized, saying she was in the wrong place. A few minutes later she returned. She was the same woman whose name had appeared with my husband's on the apartment lease. During the long months while our divorce was pending, she had become involved with him, under the impression that he was already divorced. They had made wedding plans, she said, but Allen wanted to gain custody of my eldest son. She had come because she wanted to know for herself who I was.

Secretly, I began to see more and more of her. She helped me to file for divorce and bolstered my strength to leave. She herself returned to her home state, and I returned to my mother's home.

The night I departed with my children and our possessions was an ordeal. Mother, my sister's husband, and his brother had come to move us. Terrified, I kept praying, "Please, God, please. My children. Your children. Protect them, oh, please!" Miraculously, they slept through it all.

In the next few days, I slept very little, feeling as if I had escaped from prison and fearful of being recaptured. "You were always so strong-willed and independent", my sister told me. "It makes me sad to see you reduced to such a little mouse!"

Within a month of the final divorce decree, my ex-husband, Allen, had a new wife to introduce to the children. Two weeks later, he was granted an annulment of his first marriage. How merciful God is! He knew how weak I had become; if the annulment had come first, I would have married the father of my children in the Church. Now I began daily prayers to St. Joseph, asking that he find a "St. Joseph" for me and my children.

Meanwhile, my distress continued to mount over the changes in the Church. Most of them had come while I was away, so

I had neither become gradually accustomed to legitimate change nor been indoctrinated to tolerate abuses. Ignorant about which were which, I wrote to priests, bishops, even to our cardinal. In several instances I enclosed self-addressed, stamped envelopes, but not once did I receive a reply.

When I tried to talk to local priests, I was brushed off, sometimes quite rudely. Usually I was told that the Second Vatican Council had changed or abolished or replaced the "old way". Yes, they insisted, Vatican II had called for the gutting of beautiful churches, the removal of statues, crucifixes, and in many cases even the tabernacle. Vatican II had rejected organ music in favor of guitars, flutes, or anything else that would give the liturgy a livelier atmosphere. Vatican II had transformed the priestly vocation, so that the priest could enjoy the same nine-to-five schedule everyone else did. Vatican II had dismissed certain saints, along with indulgences and frequent confessions. (Only frequent Communions were encouraged now.) Vatican II had forbidden kneeling to receive our Lord and, in fact, permitted zealous pastors to refuse Communion to worshippers who declined to stand. Vatican II had wanted to make the Mass acceptable to Protestant tastes, so that we could meet them in the middle as "one fold". Vatican II had allowed priests to make up the prayers as they went along. Vatican II had insisted that the meal aspect of the Mass be its focus, and therefore women were to bustle into the Sanctuary because women are the traditional servers of family meals. (This seemed not entirely consistent with the parallel explanation that women must be elevated above their traditional condition of servitude.) The distressing list went on and on, and I began to suspect that Vatican II had come straight out of Hell. Oddly, I did not read the Council documents myself, nor was I encouraged to do so.

It was my great-aunt, Matilda, who told me about the Society of St. Pius X. At the same time, I read several articles in our local Catholic newspaper about Archbishop Marcel Lefebvre, the founder of the Society of St. Pius X (SSPX). I still have the articles and still wince when rereading them. In his statement, our archbishop referred to Archbishop Lefebvre and the Society as "poor man, poor deluded followers". Another author claimed that Archbishop Lefebvre had come "slithering out of the tall grass", and prayed, "may the angels lift Lefebvre by the hair and transport him back to the tall grass in which he hides."

"At this delicate moment when the pudding is beginning to jell," the column continued, "Archbishop Lefebvre decides to spit his venom all over Cardinal Dearden." His reference was to Lefebvre's stated opinion that the cardinal was moving toward heresy. I was shocked at the spiteful tone and the lack of well-reasoned arguments to justify his opinion.

Determined to learn why this foreign archbishop was being so harshly maligned, I wrote to one of the SSPX priests in the area and received a prompt and eloquent reply. He welcomed me back into the Church and commiserated with me in my confusion. Before long we attended an SSPX Mass, offered in the traditional rite. This was the Mass I knew from my childhood. I was hooked.

Within a few weeks we began attending that Mass exclusively. Mother and I, with the six children, would rise at 4:00 on Sunday mornings to drive to Mass. If we couldn't go to the Tridentine Rite, we missed Mass. My youngest brother, who had been serving the New Mass, learned to serve the ancient Latin Mass. My eldest son made his First Confession and then his First Holy Communion with all the reverence these august sacraments deserved. Here was the dignified beauty due the Sacrifice of the Mass. Here, the mystery of the Eucharist was recognized and adored. These priests never indicated that sin didn't matter; they spent long hours in the confessional. In their sermons, the SSPX priests told us not only of God's love but also of our duties as His creatures. I was home at last.

During this period I had gone back to college on the GI Bill, graduated, and earned teaching certification. I applied and was accepted to teach in one of the SSPX schools. My children and I packed our few possessions and set off across the country to our new home, a two-bedroom apartment across the road from the church and school in St. Mary's, Kansas. My daughter, Vera, and I shared one bedroom, while the two boys shared the other one. My younger son, Jeremy, was still in kindergarten, so a parishioner watched him after his half-day of school.

An average day began about 6 A.M. We dressed, attended Mass, then set off to school. After school came supper, cleaning, and time with the children, followed by the Rosary. As soon as my little ones were in bed, I began lesson plans, class preparations, and grading papers. In between, I did laundry, dragging it across the road to a laundromat, load by load, because we had no car. Then I carried it back to hang in our yard. Between 2 and 4 A.M. I crawled into bed myself. It was a schedule no one could maintain for long.

"Dear St. Joseph," I would pray, "where is that good man, like you, to be my husband and the father of my children? I can't do this by myself much longer!"

Soon God sent my sister and her five children to join us. She was running from her husband. I hated him momentarily in the shock of seeing her distress, yet she was a godsend to me. Living in the apartment below mine, she took over my household duties. From what little income I had, I paid the bills for both families and took care of discipline. In short, I became the "father figure", while my sister was the "mother."

God was in the center, and He took care of us: meagerly, to be sure, but sufficiently. Once when I was $350 short for our impending rent payment, I asked her if she ever worried about finances.

"No, I leave that to you", she said.

Her answer held such childlike confidence that I hadn't the heart to tell her I was failing. That night I begged God not to allow me to let my sister down, reminding Him of His promises, and pointing out that we certainly were like the birds of the air. Three days later, just as the rent was due, a check arrived from my oldest brother, in the amount of $350.

Eventually, my sister and her husband reconciled and took up residence in St. Mary's, only a few blocks from us. Six months after that, Mother, too, moved to St. Mary's, with my two youngest siblings, who were in high school by then. When Mother bought a house, we moved in and were a family again.

My world was limited by necessity to home, church, classroom, and teacher's lounge. Within this circumscribed community, I sensed an attitude of male superiority. While I understood that the husband must be the head of the family, it did not seem emphasized enough that the heart—a woman—is equally important. More than once, I observed that, if anything could have made me a feminist, it would have been the SSPX.

Externals seemed to take on an exaggerated importance to those in the society; often a woman's orthodoxy was judged by whether she wore a chapel veil or slacks, or whether she displayed outward acts of piety. Woe to any Catholic of either sex who received Communion in the hand. Clearly, the ordinary flaws of human nature had not been left behind, outside the society. So, there were some extremists in the parish, I told myself, but then, one finds all kinds of people in any parish.

Except for my family, my best friends have always been male. The school principal, Kenneth Kaiser, the most reasonable and intelligent of all the faculty, was a gem whose feet were planted squarely on the ground. Without conspicuous show, he had great love for God. For the good of the students and the school, he put in tremendously long hours, often unnoticed and unappreciated. His only imperfection, as far as I could judge, was that he didn't seem to take enough time for his wife and children. My respect for him grew even greater when I heard the affection with which he would refer to his wife as his "home".

We worked together a good deal as he was preparing to leave the school. Ostensibly his reason was to finish his doctoral dissertation, but as we became closer friends, I learned that the problem went deeper. He was seriously beginning to question the SSPX. Our priests discouraged us from attending any but a Tridentine Rite Mass, for fear of contagion with a false spirit of Catholicism. Most of us in the SSPX, I believe, gave little thought to the whole notion of union with the Church and to the conflicting claims of the Pope and Archbishop Lefebvre. We had all come from parishes that were in tumult, where our pastors had been less than orthodox. The SSPX priests, like the Novus Ordo priests I had argued with back east, agreed that Vatican II was responsible for all the shocking changes in the Church. Only the SSPX resisted Vatican II, they told us, in a spirit of "obedience to God rather than to man". The society seemed like a sanctuary, where we did not have to fight religious authority figures or fear that our children would be lost to a secular society whose corruption clerical leaders now seemed to endorse. It was commonly said that anyone would lose his soul if he went back to the Novus Ordo.

But the problem of union with Rome was profoundly distressing to those like Mr. Kaiser, who gave it serious thought, for the archbishop seemed, increasingly, to be more at odds with the Pope than in union with him. His questions planted in my mind the first doubts about the SSPX.

At the school there were a few single male teachers near my age. I confided to Mr. Kaiser that I hoped to find a husband, and he asked whether I had ever considered his younger brother, David. In several conversations with David, I had come to appreciate his frank and logical mind, but I had not imagined that so eligible a man would be interested in a woman with my history and the "baggage" of three children.

When Kenneth Kaiser left the school, he passed on to David the unfinished remodeling job he had begun on our house. David and I, both very straightforward, found it refreshingly easy to communicate. Several months later, having overcome a few stumbling blocks, we were married by a SSPX priest. I have not the slightest doubt that David is the good husband for whom I had asked St. Joseph every single day for seven years. Once when I told David how amazed and grateful I was that he had never thrown my past in my face, he seemed surprised that I could have expected such behavior.

"The past is the past", he said. "You made mistakes. So what? Besides," he smiled, "you're a good woman."

Nine months and two days after our wedding, I gave birth to our first son, Nathaniel. Three more healthy sons have been born to us since then. Gregory, the second, arrived two years after the first, shortly before Archbishop Lefebvre consecrated bishops illicitly.

I had continued teaching part time in the SSPX school. The new principal was a priest I had always respected, partly because his sermons centered on ideas and the means for improving our spiritual lives, rather than carping about the New

Ordo. But gradually they changed, until he too was denouncing the New Mass and "Novus Ordo Catholics" from the pulpit.

Only six months before the unlawful consecrations, many people we knew agreed that such an action would be more than they could accept. As sermons took on a new intensity, however, the community was exhorted to "maintain the faith". We were assured that we could never be condemned for maintaining tradition and adhering to the Mass protected by *Quo Primum*, the four-hundred-year-old Apostolic Constitution of Pope Saint Pius V, permanently establishing the Tridentine Mass.

Ultimately, very few left the SSPX or even asked David and me why we did. Both of us had been respected members of our parish, yet when my husband tried to discuss the matter with several of the SSPX priests, including one who later was made bishop, they answered his questions about legitimate papal authority and union with Rome by listing ostensible papal abuses. The Pope's transgressions numbered nearly two hundred, one of them told us, with the ecumenical prayer service in Assisi near the top of the list. More and more, the attitude prevailing within the SSPX seemed like garment-rending over the tragic descent of Pope John Paul II into purported Modernism. The quality of one's faith seemed to be measured by the degree to which one was scandalized by those abuses.

David could see the course on which the SSPX was headed, but I could not. I would not. When negotiations began between Rome and Archbishop Lefebvre, David hoped an agreement would be reached but did not think it likely. I, however, refused to consider any alternative to success. The archbishop simply had to submit to papal authority and accept Vatican II "as interpreted in the light of tradition". Then we would have it all! Not only could we continue to worship in the beautiful old Latin Rite, but also would we be in full communion with the Church, with her doors open to all other Catholics who tired of the circus atmosphere in their local parishes.

David and I argued for a year. David was consistently gentle but persistent, with his characteristic ability to cut through rhetoric to the core of an issue. First he asked me to read *The Ratzinger Report*. I read every word, searching eagerly for minor faults to which I could object, because I could find no general fault with the book. But when I raised them, I had no rebuttal for David's calm explanations.

My husband is no novel-reader, but he enjoys philosophical, political, and religious works. One Sunday, as I was bustling around the kitchen preparing dinner, he appeared with a book. "Honey, who does this sound like?" he asked. "Whatever I do will be done . . . by the counsel of God. If the work be of God, who shall stop it? If it be not, who can forward it? Not my will, nor ours, but Thy Will, O holy Father, which art in Heaven . . ."[1]

"Marcel Lefebvre", I announced triumphantly.

"No. Martin Luther", came David's matter-of-fact response. "How about this one: 'It was never my intention to revolt from the Roman Apostolic chair.'"[2]

"Marcel Lefebvre?"

"No. Martin Luther. Try this one: 'These things are clearer than the light to all men: the Church of Rome, formerly the most holy of all churches, has become . . . the very kingdom of sin, death, and hell; so that not even Antichrist, if

[1] J. H. Merle D'Aubigne, *History of the Reformation in Europe in the Time of Calvin* (London: Longman, 1878), bk. 3, chap. 6.
[2] *Catholic Encyclopedia* (Encyclopedic Press, 1913), 9:457, article from DeWette and Seidmann, *Luthers Briefe).*

he were to come, could desire any addition to its wickedness.' "[3]

"Martin Luther, of course", I answered.

"Right", David smiled. "Try just one more: 'The See of Peter and posts of authority in Rome being occupied by Antichrists, the destruction of the Kingdom of Our Lord is being rapidly carried out even within His Mystical Body here below . . .' "[4]

"Martin Luther said that one too. What's your point?" By now I was irritated.

"Archbishop Lefebvre said that one. What could he mean, that the See of Peter is occupied by an Antichrist? Do you suppose he thinks Christ lied when He said the gates of Hell would not prevail? Maybe Christ didn't know what He was doing, when He set up His Church the way He did, to be managed by mere men? Wouldn't it seem logical that if this Pope or this Council is in error, then the Protestants are free to say that some previous Pope or Council erred? If they could ever err, what guarantee have we that they never did before?"

I was livid! How dare he attack the Archbishop and the SSPX? Yet he hadn't been gloating; he hadn't been scornful. I was angry with the messenger because I didn't like the message.

And so it went; my husband's persuasive tactics consisted chiefly of questions designed to make me think. He read me passages from the documents of Vatican I, stating explicitly that the Pope must be obeyed in all matters pertaining to faith, morals, and discipline. That Council—accepted as valid by the SSPX—also held that only the Pope is guaranteed not to lose his faith. Sometimes David read explanations from the

[3] Martin Luther, *Concerning Christian Liberty* (Harvard Classics), p. 338.
[4] Marcel Lefebvre, "Letter to Future Bishops", August 29, 1987, reprinted in the *Angelus,* vol. 9, no. 7 (July 1988) pp. 1, 29.

Catechism. How could it have struck me as at all odd that Catholicism requires unity of belief, sacrifice, and sacraments, with and under the Pope?

Negotiations between Rome and the SSPX were severed by Lefebvre, who then set the date for his episcopal consecrations.

"Well, dear?" My husband asked, warily.

"I will not go back to that Novus Ordo Mass!" I said. My vehemence shocked even me.

"Oh. You mean, Thy will be done." David said. He walked away, leaving me to reconsider.

Though calm and gentle as always, his words pierced me with the realization of exactly what I had said and implied: "*My* will be done! *Non serviam!* I will not serve." I don't like it; I don't want to comply. I would have to humble myself and return to what I had willfully left. Acutely ashamed, I realized that it was akin to that first sin of Lucifer: not a matter of intellect but a matter of will. "Dear Jesus, forgive me again—and again, and again." The next few days were extremely difficult, as I faced the full impact of the only choice left open to me.

On the Sunday before Archbishop Lefebvre's consecrations, in June of 1988, my brother and his family were visiting. They went to the local parish Mass; we went to the SSPX Mass. I still hoped that, at the last minute, negotiations would reopen, and all would be resolved in the manner I wanted. At Mass, Father began justifying Lefebvre's position: the archbishop, he said, was insisting that the Church return to tradition—as if the Pope did not understand tradition.

David rose, motioned with his thumb toward the door, and we filed out, grateful that our seats were near the back of the church. It was a rare gesture from a man who normally tries to avoid drawing attention to himself.

We never returned. On learning that the parish priest was going to offer Wednesday's Mass for the SSPX and the avoidance of schism, I decided that was a good reason to test the waters, so I attended that Mass. It wasn't as bad as those I remembered.

In the years since then, I have found that weekday Masses are usually tolerable, and, depending on the parish and priest, some are even beautiful. Sunday Masses, however, for a long time plunged me into an agony of anger, resentment, and depression. I marveled that anyone present could raise mind and heart to worship our Creator. More than once I begged David to return to the SSPX. I knew we couldn't, but I needed to hear the explanation again.

At first, I tried comparing the old Mass as "fine cuisine" with the new Mass as "bread and water". When David asked how Jesus could be more truly present in one valid Consecration than in another, I changed my analogy. The old Mass was fine cuisine in a palace; the new was fine cuisine in a barnyard. About then, I met an elderly woman who came to be a good friend. She invited me to join the Legion of Mary and explained that she always placed herself at the foot of the Cross with Mary, who neither condoned nor took part in the spectacle of the Crucifixion. That was how she had endured the liturgical experimentation that plagued so many parishes. The thought has been a great help to me as well.

There had never been much social contact between the SSPX parish and the local Catholic parish. Once we had begun attending the latter, we found it a growing struggle to remain on friendly terms with our SSPX neighbors and relatives, and no doubt they struggled on account of us, too. Predictably, there were heated arguments with family and friends who remained in the SSPX. One colleague from the SSPX school—a close friend who was a weekly guest at our home—was warned by a priest that he would lose his job if he continued to see us socially. Before the school year began, he left the state.

Within a year of the Lefebvre consecrations, we were allowed an Indult Mass. When it began, I was surprised that so few of the SSPX members attended, since the Tridentine Mass had always been at the heart of their movement. We heard that SSPX priests were forbidding their followers to attend the Indult Mass, explaining that a priest who would offer both the New Mass and the Old could not be very orthodox and so must be a hazard to the faith.

At last we moved away to another part of Kansas. Now we live on a little farm with our five youngest children, as well as a dog, a varying number of rabbits, and some amiable goats. Memories of my own destructive first college year make me unwilling to send our children to any public school or even to most Catholic schools, so we have been homeschooling them for the past eight years.

The Priestly Fraternity of St. Peter is active in our diocese, making the traditional Latin Mass available to us, but I sometimes attend the New Mass as well. Every day, from my heart, I pray for the SSPX, especially for our family and friends. Any fallen-away Catholics I encounter are also remembered in my daily barrage of petitions to God. It is not because I am holy that I pray so urgently, but precisely because I am a wretched sinner. Where else should a sinner like me be but in the arms of her Heavenly Father and her Holy Mother, the Church?

જી

Mary Epcke Kaiser spent her first two decades in rural Michigan. From 1973 to 1977, she served in the U.S. Air Force.

Afterward she returned to college on the GI Bill and earned a B.A. and a teaching certificate from Michigan State University. In the mid-1980s, she moved with her three children to St. Mary's, Kansas, where she taught at the Academy of St. Pius X. Today she lives in Topeka with her husband, David, homeschools the younger five of her seven children, and, for recreation, raises goats and rabbits.

Ransomed from the Darkness

Moira Noonan
as told to Donna Steichen

The three classic sources of temptation are the world, the flesh, and the devil. In my case, the flesh was less significant than the world—I was highly susceptible to the *Zeitgeist*—but the chief reason I fell away from the faith was fascination with the devil's tricks. I was born into a Catholic family, yet for more than twenty years I pursued the works of darkness, and during the last ten of them, I was a professional New Age therapist, as deep in the movement as one can go.

My introduction to the inner life of the New Age came after I was seriously injured in an auto accident in Hawaii in 1980. Two years later, I was still in too much pain to raise my own coffee cup to my lips. My sister, a California attorney, called me to recommend a pioneer pain clinic in the Midwest that was showing impressive results in getting patients off pain-killers and back to work. My insurance company quickly agreed to refer me there and pay the tab for my treatment. At the pain clinic, I was launched into a dangerous way of life that led me ever deeper into the occult.

The Church, of course, has always warned the faithful against meddling in the occult, but, like many of my generation, I didn't listen to her.

New Age practices are variations of the sorcery condemned in the Old Testament (Deut 13). They violate the first Commandment by putting a creature in the place of the Creator. Yet most New Agers are not deliberately foisting demonic paganism on society; they are looking for something they see as good, something they think is scientifically explainable or at least experientially demonstrable. People outside that milieu may find it hard to believe, but there can be perceptible power in esoteric techniques, and that is what lures adepts ever deeper into the occult world. That power is not of God, however, so it does not lead to good but down to its source in the Prince of Darkness.

He tempts recruits with the same bait he offered to our first parents—the promise that they can be gods. Once they swallow it, the idol they serve is actually the self. Only gradually do followers learn what it means to say that the self is divine: it means we are each an autonomous consciousness, alone in the universe, with no one to save us, no one to help us. Everything depends on that lonely, isolated self. The New Age "holy trinity" is "Me, Myself and I."

After ten years, with unsolicited, unforeseen, and unmerited love, God rescued me from that life of darkness. For His astonishing mercy, I owe him my gratitude for all eternity.

How could I have turned my back on my Catholic faith to walk without hesitation into the world of esoteric phenomena? It was possible because I had already rejected Catholicism ten years before my auto accident, for a weaker dosage of the same spiritual illusion, received at second hand from a favorite high school teacher.

My earliest Catholic memory is of my mother saying that she would send her children to Catholic Schools because the nuns could raise us better than she could. My first school experience was a kindergarten at a Sacred Heart convent in Detroit, run by the Religious Sisters of the Coeur Jesu, the prestigious teaching order founded in nineteenth-century France by St. Madeleine Sophie Barat. By the eighth grade, I was at Eden Hall, then a fine R.S.C.J. convent boarding school in Philadelphia. But when I was in tenth grade, Eden Hall burned down. In the wake of the fire, a guidance counselor suggested that my parents send me to a secular college-prep boarding school, MacDuffie School for Girls, in Massachusetts, and so they did. In that entirely secular environment, students were on their own about attending religious services. The girls who became my best friends were neither Catholics nor churchgoers, and I quickly adapted to prevailing custom.

One of my teachers, an engaging young woman in her twenties, was also my housemistress. As she lavished time and interest on us after school, she made a strong impression, and I soon took her as a role model. She had studied in India, was a practicing Hindu, and was engaged to a Hindu professor from Princeton University. He often came to visit her at school, exotically attractive in his turban. Captivated by the mysterious Indian culture, we went with her to Ravi Shankar concerts, and listened respectfully to everything she said about Indian religion: karma, nirvana, chakras, and reincarnation. Dismissing Catholicism as a relic of the outgrown past, I buried all thought of the Sacrament of Penance and went to Mass only on major holidays at home, when family practice made it impossible to avoid. But incongruously, I still believed in the Blessed Mother.

By the time I graduated from high school, the seed of this exotic new belief system had rooted solidly in me and was germinating as a longing for enlightenment. Many New Agers follow gurus, in a common belief that only a living teacher can show them the way home to God. I was convinced that I, too, must go to India to find my own guru.

Instead, after graduation in 1970, I went to college, first at the University of Denver and afterward at the University of Colorado. But in the back of my mind I still intended to go to India eventually. For my junior year, I went to college in Avignon, France, through a University of Washington transfer program. When the year ended, I traveled to Greece and Turkey, thinking I would take the train right on to India. I didn't feel I needed to finish college, but I knew I needed to get enlightened.

My devout and resolute grandmother undid that plan. She tracked me down in Europe by telephone and told me to come home and finish college or be cut off financially. So I came back to the University of Washington in 1974, when virtually everything our parents valued was being questioned on college campuses: their beliefs, their culture, their way of life, the entire American system. Hindu influence was still strong. The Beatles and other popular musicians were frequently pictured in the media visiting their Indian gurus. At UW, as at many colleges, meditation classes sprang up, and groups of devotees promoted one or another guru.[1] The cult of the late Bhagwan Shree Rajneesh, for example, caught on so strongly that, as some readers may remember, he eventually moved from India to Antelope, Oregon, where he drew flocks of young followers until the federal government at last deported him.

By the time I finished college, however, worldly ambition had diverted me from spiritual searching. Having internalized the feminist dogma that an American woman is nothing

[1] By the 1990s, Eastern religions, with their meditations, chants, and gurus, were rampant on the campuses of Catholic colleges as well. For example, in 1996, at Jesuit Xavier University in Cincinnati, Ohio, one of the oldest Catholic universities in America, a visiting Catholic priest who claimed to be a Zen master was teaching Zen Buddhism.

without a career, I set India on a mental back shelf and aimed toward success in a publishing career. That journey went smoothly for a half dozen years. Through most of my twenties, I was working so hard that I never thought about anything spiritual. At age twenty-eight, I was a publisher with Visitor Publications in Hawaii; I had my own house, and the future looked limitless.

That changed abruptly the day I crashed in the company car. I was left seriously disabled. Month after month I endured constant pain; I could not work or even drive. Pain pushed me back toward a spiritual search mode that made me receptive to the ideas I encountered at the model pain clinic in Wisconsin.

One of the first such clinics in the country; it had already won a good deal of media attention and has since achieved international prominence in its field. But even as dimly as I remembered Christianity, I soon noticed that its perspective was not Christian. The treatment offered was based entirely on "New Thought".

"New Thought" is a metaphysical theory holding that reality is immaterial. It describes God as the abstract, impersonal "Divine Mind" expressed in each human being as "the Christ". The more fully we are attuned to our "Christ consciousness"—our awareness of the universal, "cosmic Christ" existing in us—the more effectively we can use its power to achieve such desirable goods as healing, happiness, love, or wealth. This power is accessible to those who understand that reality is an illusion projected by the self.

While this theory has elements in common with older gnostic belief systems like alchemy, transcendentalism, theosophy,[2] and Hinduism, it was articulated and labeled in

---

[2] Helena Blavatsky was the grandmother of nineteenth-century theosophy and hence largely responsible for the New Age movement. Theosophy is a

mid-nineteenth-century America under the "New Thought" label by Phineas P. Quimby, a faith healer and medium who made a disciple of Mary Baker Eddy when he treated her for back pain. After Quimby died, Mrs. Eddy amplified the ideas she had absorbed from him and like-minded others[3] and expressed them in her own writings as Christian Science. International Religious Science, another outgrowth of the same movement, was founded in the early twentieth century by Ernest Holmes, author of *The Science of Mind*. Currently the Unity School of Christianity is the New Thought denomination most widely known and most clearly identified as New Age.[4] Divine Science is another, as are the Church of Divine Man, the Church Universal and Triumphant, and Self-Realization Fellowship. In all of them, the only reality is the universal Mind. God is seen as supreme creative intelligence, a "Life-Force" of which we are all inseparably part. Since matter is an illusion, the essential human self is in fact part of the same divine spirit, and its ruling principle is that of New Age pantheism: "All is One, all is God, I am God."

Obviously, these are not Christian churches, though they may be listed under that heading in telephone directory yellow pages. As New Thought has subdivided, its message

---

gnostic belief system, e.g., one claiming to offer "secret knowledge", that claims there is in human beings a latent psychic power which, if he can develop it, will give man godlike power over matter and events. Christians who don't know their faith are easily misled by such claims.

[3] Another influence was Pir Vilayat, a Sufi teacher who introduced the ideas of that Islamic mystical sect into the United States early in the twentieth century. He married Mary Baker Eddy's cousin, Ora Ray Baker.

[4] Among organizations incorporating New Thought are the Church of Mental Physics, the I AM movement, the Church of Divine Man, Rosicrucianism, Self-Realization Fellowship, L. Ron Hubbard's Dianetics, and, to some extent, the Unitarian-Universalist church. The same ideas are found in witchcraft, now called the religion of Wicca.

about the need for transformation through changing consciousness has more explicitly separated the person of Jesus from the identity "Christ". We are not saved by Jesus, the unique God–Man who atoned for original sin, but by "Christ consciousness", that is, knowledge that we are expressions of the one Divine Mind. Jesus is not our atoning Savior—because we were never separated from God or in need of forgiveness. Instead, Jesus is an example of one who so fully attained "Christ consciousness" that he manifested power over matter, sin, and death. All men and women can do the same if they too become "self-actualized" through "Christ consciousness". When we become self-actualized enough, we will realize that we ourselves are the divine "I Am".

This system of thought reawakened the interest I had developed in "enlightenment" when I was in high school. It never gave me the answers I sought, but the expectation of fulfillment, never satisfied but always promised, impelled me on to ten more years pursuing the New Age.

People involved in Science of Mind or similar New Thought groups seemed to be over-represented on the staff of the model clinic. All New Age systems first require followers to set aside their basic beliefs, so their minds can be reprogrammed. The field of pain control uses brainwashing techniques to implant a mind-over-matter attitude. They took away our pain pills, and we spent eight hours a day being indoctrinated with "autogenics", a system combining self-hypnosis and "New Thought", from tapes intended to alter our brain waves. In this "subliminal mode", our minds would open to absorb the new belief system that would free us of pain.

The completely non-Christian perspective of New Thought was evident in videos we were shown of psychic surgery, in the talks on shamanism, and in the endless repetition of messages condemning any acceptance of suffering. There can *never* be virtue in suffering, we heard repeatedly; no suffering can be from God or be redemptive. Suffering is a result of our errors in thinking and our self-punishing guilt. They warned us against hope, telling us that to wait for a Savior was as pointless as "rocking in a rocking chair, going nowhere". If we wanted ever to be pain free, we would have to do it ourselves. To remind ourselves of that focus, we wore red lapel buttons reading, "ME FIRST". This drumbeat of suggestions went on hourly, daily, for the duration.

Some patients stayed at the pain clinic for months, and many came back regularly to have the hypnotic effect reinforced. But I was so highly suggestible that after a single month, I no longer felt unmanageable pain, and I didn't need pain pills anymore. This was the effect of hypnosis, not a physical healing.[5] To stay well, I would have to keep doing self-hypnosis daily and constantly reassuring my ego that I could do it.

Clients were sent home with autogenic tapes and mind-control programming for continuing self-hypnosis. For help in keeping those New Thoughts vivid in my mind, I was also advised to seek spiritual support. As the clinic staffers displayed common spiritual attitudes, I asked them what churches they went to. They urged me to try Science of Mind churches, preferably the Church of Religious Science or a Unity church, which can be found in most American towns today.

Back home in Hawaii, I obediently started attending a Unity church, and I found it very interesting. It is seductive to hear that you are the ultimate power and the absolute moral

---

[5] After my conversion, when I repudiated self-hypnosis, I had to return to conventional medical treatment because the condition had not been cured, only masked by the self-hypnosis.

authority. It was also less trouble than going all the way to India to search for a guru.

I also sampled the Human Potential Movement, by way of Werner Erhard's est (later renamed the Forum, and still later called Transformational Technologies, Inc.). Next I tried Silva Mind Control. Then came *A Course in Miracles*, a program that synchronized perfectly with New Thought. Not only is it still going today, it has become an international business phenomenon. Many Christian churches offer it to members, and it is even sold in some Catholic bookstores. That fact should astonish anyone who knows where it came from.

Between 1965 and 1973, an inner voice dictated the twelve-hundred page *Course* to the late Helen Shucman, an atheist research psychologist at Columbia University Medical School, whose mother had been a Christian Science practitioner. Bewildered by the phenomenon, Dr Shucman simply transcribed, in shorthand, what the inner voice told her, without clearly understanding its significance or even its literal meaning. Ironically, though she wrote in the *Course* that suffering does not exist, she spent her last two years in the blackest of psychotic depressions.

A Course in Miracles uses a redefined Christian vocabulary to indicate that its spirit-author is Jesus, bringing a new revelation to "purify" the teachings of Christianity. His old revelation, it declares, was "not the lesson I intended to offer you" and for that reason has only added to human suffering a crushing burden of guilt. The "miracles" referred to in the title are not supernatural interventions in the natural order, but products of corrected thinking, just as in other New Thought systems.

The *Course* was published in 1976, and study groups began using it in New Age churches around the United States. Its later wildfire success owes a good deal to the promotional

talents of Marianne Williamson, who discovered it at the West
Hollywood Church of Religious Science, a New Thought
center famous for the many movie personalities in its congregation. *A Return to Love*, Williamson's 1992 blockbuster
(thirty-nine weeks on the *New York Times* best-seller list) was
an interpretation of the *Course* as a "program of spiritual psy-
chotherapy", aimed at those who found the original too complex. Her 1993 book, *A Woman's Worth*, spent nineteen weeks
on the *NYT* best-seller list. By 1997, *Mother Jones* magazine
was profiling her as the *Course*'s "public face". In that capacity, she has built an avid audience for her lectures and tapes,
and her psychic counseling practice has involved such clients
as Hillary Clinton, Shirley MacLaine, and Elizabeth Taylor.

Nothing is ever enough in the New Age way of life; there
is always pressure to do more, learn more, be more, get more.
Its goal is "progressive spiritual evolution" to accrue enough
good "karma" to escape from the "wheel of reincarnation"
and at last become one with the Universal Mind. So I studied
the "Ascended Masters", the hierarchy of fully self-realized
spiritual leaders purported to rule the planet, having advanced
beyond the cycle of reincarnation, yet somehow retaining
their individuality, instead of being assimilated into the Universal Mind. In standard theosophical theory and in the
variant interpretations of Elizabeth Clare Prophet (Church
Universal and Triumphant), Alice Bailey (New Group of
World Servers), and similar sects, Jesus is considered one of
the Ascended Masters—but not superior to such others as
Buddha, St. Germain, Kuthumi, or Maitreya.

Next I studied Native American Shamanism and Native
American Medicine Cards, which are tarot cards displaying
Indian symbols instead of the traditional tarot symbols,
though they are nevertheless read in the standard way.

In 1983, I was married in an Episcopal church in Seattle, in a ceremony compatible with my spiritual condition: the officiating clergyman was a former Catholic priest who had defected to marry a nun. Contracted without the graces of the Sacrament of Matrimony and lived without the support of the true faith, our marriage did not survive the clash of our conflicting personalities. The New Age, focused only on the self, had neither grace nor practical advice to offer us. But by the time we separated in 1991, Roger and I had our lovely daughter, Malia.

While I was pregnant with her, I went to Europe on a holiday with my mother. In Paris, Mother said, "Please come to Mass with me."

As we entered the magnificent Basilica of Sacré Coeur, I saw, behind a bank of votive candles, a beautiful statue of our Lady. The Holy Spirit must have moved me to do what I did next, because I didn't even know a prayer of consecration. Leaving my mother behind in the pew, I went over to the shrine, lit a candle, and consecrated my unborn baby to the Virgin Mary. "Blessed Mother, this is your child," I whispered. "I give this child to you."

When our daughter was born, I called her Malia, the Hawaiian form of "Mary".

My fascination with the New Age did not fade, however. We were living in Southern California when I enrolled in a ministry training program at the North County Church of Religious Science in Encinitas. For a text, the program used Holmes' book, *The Science of Mind*. I spent the next four years learning about ministry from the pastor, who like me was a former Catholic.

My preparation for ministry was the same kind of mental reprogramming I had first encountered at the pain clinic, but now promoted in greater depth, with more sophisticated brainwashing techniques, until I truly did have a new belief system. It was based on denial of original sin and offered the same deceptive promise Satan offered Eve in the Garden of Eden. With my "I Am presence" thus "activated", my self-image inflated from self-confidence to self-idolatry.

In my first venture as a New Age professional, I became a "prayer practitioner" at the Seaside Church of Religious Science in Del Mar, where my stipends came from client donations to the church. My work had nothing to do with God or prayer as Catholics use those terms. Prayer practitioners use their "Christ consciousness" to help people "manifest" (obtain) what they want by commanding the Universal Mind as a magician would command a genie, rather than by beseeching God's help, in the way a creature addresses his Creator. My role in the "prayer" sessions—called "treatments"—was to lead clients to get what they wanted by using the right techniques.

Prayer practitioner work led me into healing and counseling. Having suffered pain for so long, I was drawn to the New Age healing arts. These are various kinds of psychic alternative or "holistic healing" therapies, including Reiki, Aruvedic healing, trance healing by mediums (like the late Edgar Cayce), psychic healing, yoga, and chakra treatment.

First I became a certified Reiki Master healer and teacher. Reiki is a system that calls on spirit guides to transmit healing energy through touch or simply by directed thought, even from a great distance. Next I took training classes from Barbara Brennan, founder and director of the Hands of Light School of Healing. Hands of Light healing is similar to Reiki, but focuses on diagnosing and treating the "aura" or energy field that is believed to surround and flow through all living things and is visible to clairvoyants. Soft-spoken and gentle,

Barbara Brennan is sometimes called to consult with legitimate medical personnel, but, like Reiki, her method calls on
spirit guides.

My experience with Reiki made me want to learn more
about the psychic world. So I went for psychic training classes
at the Teachings of the Inner Christ church in Lemon Grove,
to get more closely connected to my spirit guides, and to learn
to see, feel, and hear beyond the normal physical range of the
senses. And I did become clairvoyant. When I told people I
saw something, like their childhood experiences, I really did
see them. I could sit down beside a stranger and see his past
life unreel like a movie. Sometimes I could even converse with
the people I was seeing. But eventually, like other clairvoyant
channelers, I couldn't sleep at night because the sheer volume
of "messages" demanding attention in my mind became a tor-
ment, and I could not turn them off.

My daughter Malia instinctively hated the Inner Christ
church and adamantly refused to be present at any services,
even though I was "in ministry" there.

Next, I trained in Neuro-Linguistic Programming (NLP)
under Anthony Robbins, at his noted Research Institute in
San Diego. NLP is a system of hypnotic verbal techniques
used in communication and persuasion.

From NLP, I moved into more intense study of Ericksonian
Hypnotherapy as a private student. Many people assume
Ericksonian Hypnotherapy to be a scientific system of psy-
chotherapy. Actually, it is a complex of techniques for
manipulating people who don't know they are being sub-
jected to hypnotic techniques.

The emphasis in my own training was on past-life regres-
sion therapy—and even "future-life progression" therapy.
Those therapies of course presuppose belief in reincarnation, the doctrine that we have many lifetimes to reach

enlightenment and self-actualization—which is central to New Age theory. If New Agers really had no savior but themselves, as they insist, not even all those lifetimes would be enough. None of us can save himself.

I used this training professionally, with private clients acquired through the Del Mar and Lemon Grove churches. I helped them draw "mind maps", to unblock places where I thought past life influences were trapping them in unproductive behaviors that kept them from manifesting as successfully as they might. In the hope of gaining greater effectiveness, I went back to Hawaii in 1990 for a more advanced program and became a certified Ericksonian Hypnotherapist. There I was immersed still more deeply in the practice of hypnosis. It led to an ever deeper "reprogramming" of my own mind, an enslaving dependence on self-hypnosis, and a progressive weakening of personal will power.

While waiting in the lounge between classes one day, I came on an article in *New Age Journal* that started changing my life in ways that might have surprised the editor. It was an account, by New Age leader Sondra Ray, of a trip to visit the site of recent apparitions of someone she called "Mother Mary". Sondra wrote that she was in London, preparing for a visit to her guru, when she first heard reports that the Blessed Mother was appearing in Yugoslavia.[6] She decided to stop on her way to India so she could see for herself.

At St. James Church in Medjugorje, the priest invited her to come into the upper room with the visionaries during an apparition. She said she felt our Lady's presence but did not see her. Ray did not have a conversion, but she was moved to write the dramatic article I was reading. While traveling on through India and back home to America, she decided that

[6] See p. 280, n. 2.

"Mother Mary" was a goddess from heaven, come down to meet the earth goddess, "Gaia". In light of that conclusion, she felt she was meant to promote the goddess movement, a growing strain in the New Age movement.

Reading the article, I was stirred with strong but ambivalent emotions. Up to that time, I had heard no claims that Our Lady was visiting anyone in the contemporary world. I was thrilled that Sondra Ray, who was not a Catholic or even a Christian, would go to such an out-of-the-way place to look into a reported vision of the Blessed Mother. But some residual shred of the truth I had learned in childhood assured me that Our Lady is not a goddess.

When I got back to San Diego, I stopped in Long's drugstore, and there I found a new issue of *Life* magazine with a statue of Our Lady pictured on the cover, above the title "Do You Believe in Miracles?" Hastily, I bought a copy and read every word, comparing it to the one in *New Age* magazine. To my relief, I found that the *Life* version did not portray Mary as a visiting goddess. I decided that I needed to go to Yugoslavia, too. That would entail substantial expense, for travel as well as child care, and I still believed I had to manifest what I needed.

When I first started ministry training, I used to take Malia to Sunday school at the Church of Religious Science. But before she was six, she refused to go anymore. "Mom, this isn't right", she said. "I don't like what they're teaching me."

I didn't know what to do, because I had to be there every Sunday. It didn't occur to me to send her to a Catholic church; I was sure they would never accept the child of a fallen-away Catholic New Ager like me. But I believe the Blessed Mother took a hand in what happened next to her little protégée. Just before the beginning of the school year, at the neighborhood swimming pool, a woman I barely knew walked up and asked, "Do you have your daughter in Sunday School?"

She was a Lutheran, and she said she made it part of her Christian mission to invite children to Sunday School. I didn't know much about Lutheranism, except that it is Christian, but it seemed possible to my divided mind that God might prefer to have her there rather than at the New Age church. So I said, "Oh, yes, she can go. It is kind of you to ask."

"If you can have her completely dressed and ready to go by 8:30 every Sunday morning, I'll take her to church with us", she said. So for the next five years, Malia went with our generous neighbors to the Lutheran church.

She even went to First Communion there. I was still in the New Age ministry at the Religious Science church in Del Mar, but by then I had started reading about our Lady visiting at Medjugorje, and I knew something was missing from the Sunday School books she brought home to prepare for the Lutheran First Communion.

"Malia, I don't want to offend our good neighbors," I said, "but I know that what you were taught is different from what I learned when I had First Communion. So would you be willing to go to First Communion at the Catholic church, too?"

I called a nearby Catholic parish and told the secretary honestly about our tangled situation. I said I was a New Age minister at the Church of Religious Science, but I really wanted my daughter to make her First Communion in the Catholic Church. With great kindness, the secretary took Malia under her wing and enrolled her in the Monday night CCD program. Meanwhile, she continued to go to the Lutheran Sunday service.

About that time, my grandmother died, and among the things she left me was her Miraculous Medal, on a chain. I began to wear it, and I also started saying the "Memorare" prayer of St. Bernard that was printed on a card that came with it. That was the real beginning of my conversion, though it took me several years to come all the way out of the New Age world.

Later, when I had come back to the Catholic faith, Malia said, "I really owe a lot of thanks to our neighbors, because they saved my soul from all that New Age stuff."

Ciéra, a friend with whom I had discussed the Medjugorje apparitions, called one day and told me excitedly to watch Joan Rivers' television show, because her guests were two priests and a woman who was receiving messages from Mary. I watched the program, and my interest rose even higher. Afterward, Ciéra and I looked in the telephone book for a Catholic bookstore where we might be able to learn more about it. We found the address of a "Catholic Charismatic Center" in La Jolla. When we called and asked whether any-one there could tell us about the apparitions, and the possi-bility of visiting Medjugorje as tourists, we were told, "Come right over. A speaker is going to talk about it this very day."

We listened eagerly to what the speakers said about the ap-paritions and bought a beautiful Medjugorje poster. But when the talks ended, and they invited us to stay on for a Bible study, we said, "No, thank you." For years, we had been study-ing the Bible "metaphysically", and we thought we knew more about it than they did. So we decided to go off by our-selves and do some crystal work instead. (Most confirmed New Agers carry their crystal pendulums with them, just as most good Catholics carry their Rosaries.)

As we came out of the Charismatic Center and headed for the beach, we met Beverly Nelson, a lay coworker with

Mother Teresa's Missionaries of Charity. Beverly proved to
be an important guide in my journey back to the faith. That
day, she asked whether the meeting was over. We said it was
over for us; we had found what we were looking for. We
showed her our Medjugorje poster and told her that we were
trying to figure out how we could go where Mother Mary
was appearing.

"You don't have to go all the way to Yugoslavia to get to an
apparition site", she said. "There are Marian apparitions being reported right now from Scottsdale, Arizona, just six hours
from here." [7]

That was exciting news, because we could drive to Scottsdale anytime. We went on to the beach, and as we settled
onto our towels, Ciéra took out her crystal pendulum, to
channel her spirit guide. But when she asked it a question,
she couldn't get it to respond; it hung motionless in the air.
At last she held it out toward me and said, "You try it; you're
always good at this."

I reached for it, but I could not touch it. It was as though
there were a glass wall between me and the crystal pendulum.
I was still clairvoyant then, and I looked down and saw a beautiful crystal Rosary lying across my hands. At the same time,
in my head, I heard a voice saying, "Pray the Rosary. Through
prayer all is answered."

"I need to pray the Rosary", I said.

The next morning, Ciéra called to tell me that she had
already gone out to buy a Rosary. I still had to get one of
my own. Then we learned that a group of New Age friends
were arranging to drive to Sedona, just north of Scottsdale,

[7] St. Maria Goretti Church in Scottsdale is only one of many sites where
apparitions have been reported in recent years. Like most such phenomena,
these are not approved by the Church, and all reports rest on the word of
those making the claims.

to sit in the vortexes and watch for UFOs.[8] That was how it happened that I found myself not long afterward in St. Maria Goretti Church in Scottsdale. We learned that the evening service was not going to include an apparition but a fifteen-decade Rosary and a healing service, followed by Mass.

After being away from the sacraments for twenty years, I stayed in church for more than four hours that night. At Communion time, I had the audacity to go forward and receive our Lord unworthily. Instantly, with scalding conviction, I recognized my sinfulness and my desperate need for the Sacrament of Penance.

When the Mass ended, I rushed to the sacristy and asked to speak to a priest. "Father has already left", an altar boy said. "You might be able to catch him in the parking lot if you hurry." So I dashed out the door and searched the parking lot for the priest. When I found him, he was getting ready to leave.

"Father, I've got to make a confession really fast!" I said to him. So right there, standing in the lot beside his car, he heard my twenty-year confession.

Meanwhile, some of my New Age friends, unfamiliar with Catholicism, had decided they would be uncomfortable in church, so they chose to wait through the long hours of the services in the Eucharist Adoration Chapel. They were so entranced with the peace and grace they experienced there that they were all reluctant to leave for Sedona.

The next night, UFOs forgotten, we all came back to the Scottsdale church, where a charismatic prayer meeting was being held. We were completely unfamiliar with charismatic

[8] Vortexes are special sites that New Agers and American Indians think have healing energy.

prayer and bewildered when people began praying in tongues, but the charismatics were so hospitable that they prayed over us with true Christian love. One of our group, Gary, dates his conversion to that night. He is now a devout Catholic and works as the cook at a Benedictine Abbey in Southern California. Another New Age friend, our driver for the weekend, had been separated from his wife. Both were lapsed Catholics. He went home from Scottsdale, told his wife that the Blessed Mother wanted them to stay married, and persuaded her to reconcile. They are now happily married.

Once back in the Church, I had much to learn or to re-learn. During more than twenty years away, I had forgotten a great deal about the faith, and I had been oblivious to what was happening within Catholicism. All that time, I had been absorbing false notions from New Age gnosticism mixed with westernized Hinduism. It was a difficult adjustment, on coming out of the New Age movement, to hear and try to assimilate the news that I am not a co-creator, but a mere creature of the Creator. It also required a disconcerting mental shift to stop believing in "the wheel of reincarnation". Ironically, that belief is one of the hardest for converts from the New Age to overcome, despite the fact that it makes them feel trapped and isolated in a bondage from which not even suicide offers escape.

The "ancient wisdom" of which the New Age Movement boasts consists entirely of occult practices. Now I know that God has explicitly condemned all these practices in Scripture, as He told Moses: "Let there not be found among you anyone who immolates his son or daughter in the fire, nor fortune teller, soothsayer, charmer, diviner, or caster of spells, nor one who consults ghosts and spirits or seeks oracles from the dead. Anyone who does such things is an abomination to the Lord" (Deut 18:10–12).

Back home in San Diego, I began saying the Rosary daily and visiting all the parishes in the area, looking for a Mass and a homilist that seemed right. At last I settled at St. Francis parish in Vista and enrolled in their RCIA program. People kept advising me to get a spiritual director, so I went to Prince of Peace Abbey, a Benedictine Abbey in Oceanside where everyone I met seemed to go for spiritual direction. The first time I went there, I was strongly attracted by the name of the abbey.

"Who is 'The Prince of Peace'?" I asked my friend Gary.

"That's a name for Jesus", he said. "You surely must have learned that in Sunday School or somewhere!"

But I hadn't, or if I had I could not remember it. I went into the chapel and prayed without moving for two hours. "Oh, Jesus," I said, "If you are the Prince of Peace, I really need you, because no one has been able to give me peace." My head was like a metro train station at rush hour because the clairvoyant visions would not leave me alone.

God in His infinite mercy had guided me to exactly the right place. The spiritual director I found is a priest who grew up in India, and his familiarity with Eastern religions gives him penetrating insight into the spiritual errors I had lived by for so long. He has advised me what to read, taught me how to pray, introduced me to St. Thérèse's Little Way, and led me through my personal history step by step in an ongoing healing of my memories. With the help of friends, I spent days clearing my house of thousands of dollars' worth of New Age books, tapes, videos, tarot cards, crystals, pictures of gurus, and other artifacts.

Finally, in the Sacrament of Penance, I had to renounce by name, one at a time, each of the occult practices I had used. That deliverance took a cumulative sixteen hours, with one single session lasting eight hours. Healed by this minor exorcism, I lost my psychic skills and abilities. I was no longer clairvoyant. The voices in my head fell silent. It was a tremendous gift of peace.

God has poured His graces on me with unimaginable mercy. I am certain it was the maternal intercession of our Lady that guided me home to her Son, Jesus. She is reaching out with the same love to all the foolish children lost in the New Age. Many of them are afraid of Jesus and His justice, but they are strongly drawn to His Blessed Mother. To all those who long to escape from the despairing darkness of the New Age, I urgently recommend her Rosary. Take one step toward Mary and she will come to where you are, and lead you to her Son.

❀

A native of San Francisco, Moira Noonan now lives in the San Diego area. After her return to the Church in 1992, she was horrified to discover New Age practices being introduced to Catholics through some retreat centers and church-related organizations. Because of her history, she is often called upon to explain the dangers of the New Age, as a guest on Catholic radio and television and in lectures and press interviews. An ardent Catholic evangelist, she has also helped to lead seven friends out of the New Age and into the Church.

CONCLUSION

What Makes a Prodigal Turn Homeward?

This book was not intended to be a generational study, but it has become something of the sort: a portrait of a unique generation of Catholic women. All the authors were born in or soon after the "baby boom" era, the post-Depression, post-war decades when births increased because babies were symbols of life and hope. These wanted babies were endowed to a degree unprecedented in history with wealth, peace, freedom, and easy access to a technology their dazzled ancestors would have taken for magic. Yet finally they were a tragic generation, for reasons these chronicles help to illustrate.

Their first misfortune was growing up during a convulsion in Western society initiated by worldwide cultural revolution. Even greater misfortune made them victims of "the Spirit of Vatican II", a misinterpretation of the Second Vatican Council so egregious and sweeping as to seem demented.

One professional religious educator admitted in a 1998 address that the "instruction" he and his colleagues provided during the 1960s and 1970s swung abruptly from the Baltimore Catechism "to Simon and Garfunkel theology with scissors and paste and making collages. I mean, it's amazing that *anyone* has any faith, after what we've gone through in the last thirty-three years. It's unbelievable, when you think about it!"

Yet, when asked whether he now sees that wholesale revisionism as error, he replied, "I don't think we did any harm."[1]

To others who might harbor similar illusions, the narratives in this book offer harrowing evidence of how much harm was done. Many of these women grew up without learning that they were created by God for an eternal destiny. It was not only the disappearance of doctrine from their catechisms that deprived them of that essential knowledge. Even graver harm resulted from the deliberate deconstruction of Catholic culture engineered by the same Church professionals responsible for catechetical deconstruction. Because the chaos in the Church and in society seemed to negate traditional doctrine, everyone was adversely affected by the collapse of Catholic culture, even the fortunate minority who were taught the doctrinal formulas of the faith.

Through God's mercy, the stories included here end happily. The authors have returned to various points on the Catholic spectrum—from garden-variety Catholic practice to Tridentine Indult communities, homeschool motherhood, the pro-life apostolate, Medjugorje discipleship, and the charismatic movement—but all are firmly at home in Holy Mother Church, who actually does encompass a good deal of diversity within her strong walls.

Tens of thousands of their generational peers, however, have not yet found similar happy endings. Parents, siblings, relatives or friends, guilt-haunted pastors or religion teachers, any readers yearning for the return of particular lost lambs, may read this book in hope of finding conversion strategies suited to their own prodigals. What can they learn about their own obligations from these conversion stories?

[1] Fr. Terry Odien, quoted in "Can Reform Come?" by Donna Steichen, *Catholic World Report*, May 1998, 45–53.

CONCLUSION 347

The authors' conversions seem mysterious. Why were they guided back to their Father's house, when others in virtually the same circumstances were not? What makes a prodigal turn homeward?

The short and absolute answer is God's grace. We know that everything depends on it. God acts as He wills, and His will remains a mystery to us. Faith is a pure gift, unmerited. We cannot demand it or will it into being or earn it by study or good works.

As faith is pure gift, surely the apostate is the most wretched of sinners, the recipient who throws the gift back in the Giver's face? How can one who scorned it, or traded it for the world's acceptance, dare to expect, or even dare to hope, that it will be offered a second time? A third time? Knowing the deadliness of sin, we could not hope for such magnanimity if Jesus Christ had not given us permission to do so, with His story of the Prodigal Son. From that parable we learn that God is the chief actor in conversion, and tender mercy is His greatest gift.

Attraction to God's beauty and goodness, hunger for truth, contrition for sin, a longing for forgiveness and restored integrity, and the soaring elation experienced at absolution are all graces from God's hand. But His graces do not always come as joys. Everything that moves the prodigal toward God is His grace: shame at seeing oneself deformed by the ugliness of sin, the pain of alienation from family and community, the sufferings that come with sin's natural consequences, and the misery of the apostate are also movements of grace in the soul. It was misery, we recall, that drove the original prodigal homeward. Christ, the Divine Physician, thus impels sinners to seek healing.

Knowing our shameful failures, we find hope and solace in the knowledge that He came to heal. When carping Scribes and Pharisees complained that He ate with sinners, He told them, "Those who are healthy need no physician, but those who are sick. I have not come to call the just, but to call sinners" (Mt 9:11–13).

Christ attracted eager crowds in Galilee by healing the blind, the deaf, lepers, and the paralyzed. He showed that He could heal even the dead, like the son of the widow in Nain and Lazarus in Bethany. He can also heal the spiritually dead, those guilty of mortal sins. By healing physical illnesses, He demonstrated His power so that the multitudes following Him could believe His claim that He could forgive sins. This is clear in one incident Matthew, Mark, and Luke describe. When crowds in Capernaum prevented his friends from bringing a paralyzed man to Jesus, they lowered him through the roof on a pallet.

Touched by their faith, Jesus said to the man, "Son, your sins are forgiven."

The Scribes and Pharisees muttered to themselves, "He blasphemes. Who can forgive sins but God alone?"

Jesus, who knew their thoughts, said to them, "Which is easier to say, 'Your sins are forgiven' or to say, 'Arise and walk'?"

Then He turned to the paralytic and said, "So you may know that the Son of Man has power on earth to forgive sins, I say to you, 'Arise, take up your bed and go home'." And the man stood up and walked home.[2]

Lacerating details in the stories in this book make it easy to see sin as sickness and the sinner as one in need of healing. In the normal course of events Christ heals the spiritually dead through the sacraments of His Church, by giving them the grace of repentance. But if He chooses, He can act directly

[2] Mt 9:1–8; Mk 2:10; Lk 5:24.

on the soul, restoring it to life in an instant. He did it when
Mary Lou Pease opened the Bible and, for the first time, read
it in His light. He also did it the brilliant Easter Sunday when
He set Constance Buck on a new road. Even in cases of direct divine intervention, however, the one healed is required
to resort to the sacraments in the ordinary way, as evidence
that her repentance is genuine, that she is willing to submit
obediently to the authority of the Church Christ established
to protect the faith and administer the sacraments.

Christ assured us that it is not we who choose Him, but He
who chooses us. We cannot presume to say whom He will
choose. We can only pray, steadfastly, that He will give that
gift to those we love and that, in their free will, they will
accept it, for against their will they cannot be saved. We believe that every prayer is heard and somehow answered.

This does not mean, however, that there is nothing concrete we are obliged to do to reclaim the apostates we love.
Faith is a gift from God, but in a subsidiary way it is also a gift
from our parents, who, in the ordinary course of Catholic
life, will have presented their child for Baptism, where he re-
ceives that gift. God uses secondary agents, so the means that
were effective in these lives may suggest something that can
help others to reach their beloved renegades.

What made these cases different from so many others like
them? From their conversion accounts, we can sift major
pieces of evidence:

Apostasy may be caused by simple ignorance rather than by
changed convictions. Most of these writers had never learned
enough about the Catholic faith to have formed Catholic
convictions. You cannot love and defend what you do not
know.

Some apostles of our time have changed the direction of
many lives by helping to repair that religious illiteracy. Dr.

Scott Hahn has done enormous good among such people. In explaining his conversion to Catholicism from evangelical Protestantism, he has introduced multitudes of miseducated young Catholics to their own unknown heritage. His work is especially important in rebutting Protestant arguments against the Catholic faith. Among the women represented here, Julie Maguire, Rosemary Fielding, Kathleen Robbins, Zoe Romanowsky, and Diane Spinelli were all influenced by him.

Eager to illumine the faith of housewives, philosophy professor Ronda Chervin organized an informal neighborhood class that changed the life of Marcella Melendez forever. Reconciled with the faith, Marcella went on to become a leader of Hispanic pro-life activism in the Los Angeles Archdiocese.

When her mother gave her a copy of Karl Keating's book *Catholicism and Fundamentalism*, Leila Miller read it and discovered in one galvanizing evening the meaning of basic doctrines that no one had ever explained to her in sixteen years of "Catholic" education. She turned back from the verge of apostasy to become a fervent Catholic evangelist.

After swiveling between incompatible beliefs like a weather vane in a whirlwind, Rosemary Fielding learned from author Richard Weaver that everything is *not* relative, that in fact truth is unchanging. That principle, unknown or denied in secular society, transformed her life.

A striking number of these women were led to conversion by the men they married. Husbands and fiancés swayed some of the authors to a degree that seems surprising in women who had renounced their traditions. Rachel Riley embraced her faith when her future husband did so, as if his conversion somehow affirmed and enabled her to accept her own.

Though she returned to the Church before he became a Catholic, Maureen Quackenbush too was led there by the man she married. Kathleen Robbins was influenced by her husband's progress toward conversion, though she did not fully surrender to God's grace until she was facing death. Mary Kaiser's respect for her husband's judgement enabled her to overcome her own uncertainties and reject schism.

The Blessed Mother can guide back to her Son even souls lost in sin. "Take one step toward Mary, and she will come to where you are, and lead you to her Son", promises Moira Noonan. Moira's own astonishing experience of being delivered from the New Age movement began with just such a step. An introduction to the Rosary might be the start of a spiritual journey home for those with enough humility to try it.

Affection for the prayer "Hail, Holy Queen" helped Allyson Smith to rediscover her childhood faith. After coming home, Allyson learned (from *The Wanderer* and *HLI Reports*) of the enemies besetting the Church in today's society. Confirmed into adult faith, she became a soldier of Christ in Catholic activist movements.

The Church's countercultural insistence on the sacredness of life shines like a beacon in a culture of death and darkness. That beacon led Juli Wiley out of a community that was moving in an opposite direction. She made her way from the fallacies of feminist dissent back to traditional Catholicism and heroic witness in Operation Rescue.

Diane Spinelli was contented with Protestantism until, seeing the constancy of Catholic witness and support in the pro-life movement, she was moved to investigate Catholic teaching, and then to return home, with her husband and, eventually, their five children.

Some responded to an appeal to the intellect. Debby Harvey's path to conversion was primarily an intellectual one, as she conscientiously but reluctantly followed the truth out of a Protestant church and back to the Catholic faith of her

ILDILDCHILD

childhood. Leila Miller, Rosemary Fielding, and Marcella Melendez were also converted primarily by intellectual evidence of truth.

Personal example is a powerful force. Constance Buck knew she was not satisfied with the life she and her feminist peers were living. God intervened in an extraordinary way to remind her of His reality. But it was amazement at the self-assured joy of a Catholic colleague that gave her hope of learning how to live as a Catholic again. The shining examples Diane Spinelli saw in her NFP mentors, Chuck and Margaret Howard, and her pro-life friend Margie Harper were powerful enough to overcome the scandal of bad example she encountered elsewhere and draw her back to the Church.

Parents have a sacred obligation to their apostate children. The Old Testament tells how God condemned and deposed Eli, mentor of the prophet Samuel, because "though he knew his sons were blaspheming God, he did not reprove them" (1 Sam 3:13).

In this present troubled era, all too many parents accept their children's immoral lives with a silence that implies consent, and some indeed decide that these cherished children could not be wrong in their choices. By contrast, Mary Kaiser's mother reminded her, lovingly, that she was living in sin and needed to repent. Mary accepted a brown scapular from her mostly as a conciliatory gesture, but when she started wearing it, her long journey back to the Church had begun.

Paternal prayer in combination with Mother Angelica's television show was instrumental in two of these re-conversions. Kathleen Howley's father prayed regularly before the Blessed Sacrament for her return to the faith. Finally, one night, Kathleen watched "Mother Angelica Live" intending to laugh at her and instead was so stirred in conscience that she went back to confession after years away from the sacraments. For twenty years, Kathleen Robbins' father made novenas for her return to the Church. Eventually, admiration for Mother Angelica's wisdom and integrity reminded Kathleen of her abandoned faith, and prepared her heart to accept the painful grace of conversion.

Similarly, Moira Noonan's grandmother prayed for her throughout her long, dangerous years of infidelity. When she died, she left Moira a Miraculous Medal and a copy of the Memorare. Moira wore the medal out of love for her grandmother and an abiding love for the Blessed Mother quite inconsistent with her New Age practice. The dramatic results in Moira's life suggest that she had a powerful intercessor.

In almost every Catholic family today, parents and grandparents are praying and worrying over their lost sheep. Like other faithful Catholics, they often do not realize what a difference their prayers and witness can make to someone's eternal salvation. It takes courage to raise the subject of apostasy with the family infidel, to offer a scapular, a Rosary, a book of apologetics, or a Scott Hahn tape, knowing that it may be rejected with a sneer, fearing that the only result may be a deeper rift. Earnest prayer and the example of one's own lived faith are of primary importance. But offered at an appropriate time, in love, with at least as much conviction as would be involved in recommending a good medical doctor to a beloved child with a fatal disease, such practical means may prove to be the first step homeward. Like the welcoming embrace of the Prodigal Father, they may be essential in restoring to others of this generation the birthright of which so many were tragically deprived, the eternal treasure of life in Christ.

Donna Steichen